INTRODUCTION TO
SOCIAL WORK PRACTICE

For Mom and Dad

INTRODUCTION TO
SOCIAL WORK PRACTICE
A Practical Workbook

Herschel Knapp

Mental Health Clinician and Health Science Researcher

Los Angeles • London • New Delhi • Singapore • Washington DC

For information:

SAGE Publications, Inc.
2455 Teller Road
Thousand Oaks, California 91320
E-mail: order@sagepub.com

SAGE Publications Ltd.
1 Oliver's Yard
55 City Road
London EC1Y 1SP
United Kingdom

SAGE Publications India Pvt. Ltd.
B 1/I 1 Mohan Cooperative Industrial Area
Mathura Road, New Delhi 110 044
India

SAGE Publications Asia-Pacific Pte. Ltd.
33 Pekin Street #02-01
Far East Square
Singapore 048763

Printed in the United States of America.

ISBN: 978-1-4129-5654-3

This book is printed on acid-free paper.

09   10   11   12   13   10   9   8   7   6   5   4   3   2   1

Acquisitions Editor:	Kassie Graves
Editorial Assistant:	Veronica Novak
Production Editor:	Tracy Buyan
Copy Editor:	Melinda Masson
Typesetter:	C&M Digitals (P) Ltd.
Proofreader:	Gail Fay
Indexer:	Sheila Bodell
Cover Designer:	Bryan Fishman
Marketing Manager:	Carmel Schrire

Contents

Preface

Tell me, and I'll forget.
Show me, and I may remember.
Involve me, and I'll understand.

—Anonymous

Welcome to this workbook. The purpose of this text is to orient you to the field of social work practice. In a nutshell, one might think of the social work profession as an opportunity to help improve the quality of people's lives. One of the privileges of being a social worker is the diversity of opportunities that are available in the workforce. Depending on your talents, training, interests, and opportunities, you may find yourself working in a variety of capacities ranging from adoption to hospice care. While some members of the social work profession dedicate themselves to the administrative, planning, or policy development services, others will have more direct contact with clients. Regardless of your long-run goals, your proficiency with the skills detailed in this text will provide you with an essential foundation for advancing your social work career.

This book presents an introduction to the practice principles and ethics of the social work profession, an essential set of communication skills that can be used to work effectively with clients and peers in a variety of settings, and an intuitive five-step problem-solving template to help focus your collaborative efforts with clients. The text is organized into three sections:

Part I, Defining the Professional Relationship (Chapter 1), delineates key differences between your role as a *social helper,* informally providing supportive guidance to family, friends, and acquaintances, and your evolving role and responsibilities in your professional capacity as a *social work practitioner.*

Part II, Mutual Understanding (Chapter 2), provides a variety of communication skills and principles used for working proficiently with clients and colleagues.

Part III, The Process (Chapters 3–7), presents a five-step problem-solving model—Assessment, Goal, Objectives, Activation, and Termination (acronym: **A GOAT**)—as a vehicle for collaboratively advancing the client through the change process:

Step I	Assessment	*Where is the client now?*
Step II	Goal	*Where does the client want to be?*
Step III	Objectives	*How does the client get from here to there?*
Step IV	Activation	*Moving from intention to implementation*
Step V	Termination	*Continuing the mission independently*

You have likely used something akin to this intuitive problem-solving model, perhaps without articulating each discrete step, in your efforts to achieve a variety of goals, as in this tangible example:

Step I	Assessment	*I have a car, and I'm currently in Southville.*
Step II	Goal	*I want to get to Northland.*
Step III	Objectives	*I need a map, directions, fuel, food, and drink.*
Step IV	Activation	*Starting tomorrow, I'll drive from 8:00 a.m. to 4:00 p.m.*
Step V	Termination	*When I arrive in Northland, I'll get my bearings* [next Assessment], *and then here's what I'll do...* [next Goal] *...*

The above example demonstrates how you can apply this model in a successive fashion wherein the accomplishment of one goal logically leads to the identification and pursuit of the next step in a progressive mission. Alternatively, the accomplishment of one goal may lead to the pursuit of an entirely different project.

The five-step process demonstrated in Chapters 3–7 should be considered as a suggested framework for conceptualizing and executing the path through a case. As with many other stepwise models, it is recognized that real life does not necessarily happen in a linear order. For example, the first topic that a client may wish to discuss may be his or her goal (Step II in the model). Alternatively, a client who is allotted a limited number of sessions may feel driven to discuss concerns regarding termination (Step V) early in the process. Additionally, expect that throughout the natural course of working with clients, there may be a bit of justifiable jumping around from step to step. Consider a case in which the client is at the activation phase (Step IV), during which a critical figure in his or her life becomes no longer able to provide support, whether in the form of emotional encouragement, financial aid, accommodations, or other assistance. This may require revisiting other steps, which might involve reassessing the client's condition (Step I), reevaluating the goal (Step II), identifying alternate objectives (Step III), and so on. In short, consider thinking of the proposed model as a guide, not a straitjacket. Also, keep in mind that in most stepwise models, the advancement from one step to another may take the form of discrete, identifiable breaks; other times, advancement through the steps can be more of a seamless progression. As you gain experience, consider adapting the model proposed in this text in a fashion that accommodates your own personality, approach to social work, theoretical orientation, setting, and each client's distinctive characteristics and needs.

For sake of brevity and clarity, the examples and exercises contained in this workbook focus primarily on interventions with individuals; however, this problem-solving model is relatively portable. It is compatible with a variety of theoretical orientations and settings (e.g., couple, family, group, community).

In simplistic terms, you might think of the social work process as an intertwined two-part mission: Part 1 involves gaining an understanding of the client and the client's system/living environment. Part 2 entails using your comprehension of the client's realm to collaboratively work toward helping him or her evolve into the next higher version of him- or herself. This is accomplished via setting and executing meaningful goals based on the client's talents, resources, and preferred life direction.

Some acronyms are used to present systematic models throughout the text. It is not the author's intent to have you merely memorize and reproduce these models verbatim on demand—that kind of learning has little real-world value and is typically forgotten promptly after finals. Rather, the mnemonic devices and proposed models are presented as tools to organize concepts in order to help you build a cohesive image in your mind. Naturally, you will need to be flexible when applying these tools and techniques in order to accommodate the unique characteristics of each client, his or her situations, and your own style.

Throughout the text, there are dialogue examples consisting of two streams of text: (1) Italicized text represents the script of the spoken words between the social worker and the client. (2) Roman (nonitalicized) text provides a running commentary detailing the social worker's thought process, progressive impressions, intentions, and rationale.

Throughout this text, there are multiple references to the *Code of Ethics of the National Association of Social Workers* (NASW). It is recommended that you familiarize yourself with the most recent version, which can be found online at the NASW public Web site: http://www.social workers.org. It will be helpful to have access to the NASW *Code of Ethics* as you proceed through this text.

Through your desire to help, your natural curiosity, and the application of social work theories, ethics, and principles, you will have the opportunity to come to know the unique world that is each client. Embrace the privilege to help advance the quality of life of those you serve.

Overview of Exercises

This text is presented as an interactive workbook, enabling you to apply and reinforce your understanding of the materials as you advance through the text. Exercises in the form of concept reviews, discussion points, and role-plays are presented at the conclusion of each chapter.

Concept Reviews

Concept reviews provide a means for consolidating key ideas presented in each chapter. In addition to the meaning that you derive from the text, your personal perspective, experiences in your field settings, and peer consultations will undoubtedly influence your unique interpretation and implementation of each concept in your actual social work practice settings. Hence, make an effort to use your own ideas and experiences when responding to concept review questions as shown in Figure A.

1.1   Selection (p. 2)

What are some of the criteria that may be used in determining a client's eligibility or ineligibility for care at a social service agency?

It's wrong to discriminate—client selection should be free of bias based on the client's personal characteristics; however, agencies usually have admission criteria, such as age, diagnosis, or need— never promise services to a client until a thorough assessment is done. Most agencies have a specific range of services. There's no such thing as a one-stop-shopping facility. It would be wrong to accept a client who is a poor match to the services offered as he or she would not get the quality of care that he or she deserves. If a client isn't eligible for service at this facility, the social worker should explain why and respectfully offer appropriate referrals to the organization(s) best suited to the client's characteristics and needs.

Figure A   Sample Concept Review

Discussion Points

Discussion points offer you and your colleagues the opportunity to exchange ideas and opinions on a diverse array of social work issues. The purpose of such discussion points is to provide a forum to help you integrate the discrete points raised in the text with your personal experience and perspective.

The goal of these discussion points is not necessarily to identify *the* right answer and to arrive at a generally acceptable consensus, though in some cases this may occur. Rather, consider these discussion points as a means for exploring the diversity of clinical issues, alternatives, dilemmas, and ethics from multiple subjective vantage points. Such open discussions can provide you with alternate ways of conceptualizing a case or suggest additional frameworks within which to approach a problem.

Write down the ideas that emerge. You may use "+" and "−" signs to flag ideas that you *do* and *do not* agree with, as shown in Figure B. Your instructor may have you complete these exercises as class discussions, small groups, pairs, or solo (without the + / − indicators).

1.1 Were we meant for each other?

Upon completing your initial assessment, you determine that the client is eligible for services at your facility. The client, who is of a cultural/ethnic background that is unfamiliar to you, asks if you will be his or her social worker.

+ *Ask my supervisor re: agency policy.*

+ *Confer w/ peers.*

+ *Do some research on the client's background, cultural beliefs, and so on.*

− *Attempt to find a social worker who's a better match.*

+ *Ask the client if he or she has any preference.*

− *Insist on working with this client since social workers should be unbiased.*

+ *Discuss the issue with the client; find out how he or she would like to proceed.*

Figure B   Sample Discussion Points

Role-Plays

The role-play exercises enable you to practice implementing the principles and skills presented in a safe, simulated, real-life setting. Each role-play specifies the client's characteristics and circumstances and suggested performance parameters for the client and the social worker. The role-plays are meant to approximate an actual encounter with a client. As such, try to avoid the temptation to script or rehearse the role-plays in advance, as this can stiffen or constrain the spontaneity and natural flow of the experience.

Before or during the role-plays, feel free to enhance or modify the existing scenario, within reason. As you gain more experience, you may choose to invent additional role-play scenarios of your own. This can help bring a sense of realism to these practice situations.

The clients in the role-plays have been assigned unisex names and gender-free circumstances. This means that either a female or a male can plausibly play the part of the client.

The person playing the part of the client should adjust his or her performance to the approximate skill level of the person acting as the social worker. For example, if you are finding that a role-play is too easy for the social worker, consider incrementally stepping up the situation by adding some complicating factor(s). Conversely, if the social worker seems to be struggling with the role-play, consider reducing the complexity of the client's problem or adjusting the client's attitude accordingly.

The person playing the social worker may use the skills suggested but need not necessarily constrain him- or herself to that brief list. As your skill base builds, you will likely become more comfortable in the role-play process. Consider saying, within reason, whatever seems necessary in order to effectively implement the role-plays.

You may wish to specify supplemental client characteristics that are not stated in the text. Briefly negotiate this with your partner prior to embarking on the role-play. For instance, as you gain more experience and comfort in performing the role-plays, you may want to consider portraying the client as coming from a cultural or an ethnic background that is different from your own. To facilitate authenticity, you may wish to consider aptly renaming the client. This can offer the person playing the social worker the opportunity to implement the communication skills in a fashion that is conducive to the client's unique social attributes.

During a role-play, you may find yourself stuck or having an unexpected adverse emotional reaction. Occasionally, engaging in or even observing a role-play can conjure up strong feelings, thoughts, or memories. If this happens, raise your hand and say, "Wait" or "Stop," indicating that you need to suspend the role-play. Take some time to confer with your partner, classmates, or instructor to address your questions or feelings. Also, if you notice that your role-play partner or someone else present is having an adverse reaction to the role-play, consider halting the role-play to tend to his or her reaction. Remember: Real life takes precedence over role-plays. After the issues are settled, the participants should mutually decide if a role-play should be resumed from where you left off, restarted from the beginning, or abandoned.

Role-Play Debriefing

Role-plays should run about 5 to 10 minutes. Consider using a stopwatch or a countdown timer. To end a role-play, say something like, "OK, let's stop here" or "Cut." This explicit statement marks the end of the role-play, at which time both participants are to halt their portrayal of the fictitious characters.

After each role-play, participants should take some time to informally talk about their emotional experience as it pertains to their portrayals in the role-play. Next, the person who played the social worker should discuss the role-play from an evaluative standpoint:

- What skills did you feel most comfortable with?
- What skills do you feel you need to improve?
- What were the most challenging parts of the role-play?
- What do you wish you would have said or done differently?
- What goal did you have in mind?
- Did something surprise you?

Providing Role-Play Feedback

The purpose of the role-plays is to offer you the opportunity to take the skills from the printed page and "test-drive" them in a safe, near-to-real-life environment where nobody can get hurt. The ultimate goal of role-playing is to recognize points of proficiency and, most essentially, to identify opportunities for improvement.

Constructive criticism can be challenging to assemble and tactfully deliver; however, politely withholding negative feedback essentially defeats the purpose of the role-play experience. Failing to point out areas that can be improved is a disservice to the individual, as well as to the multitude of clients that he or she will encounter who may benefit from more effective communication.

After each participant has processed his or her initial feelings, the person who played the client should provide some feedback to the individual who portrayed the social worker. The person who played the social worker should take detailed notes as he or she is receiving the feedback.

The person who played the client should start by offering some genuine positive feedback. Describe the skill(s) that the person demonstrated most proficiently. Next, it is time for some constructive criticism. While it is important to provide an honest appraisal of your peer's performance, it is equally essential not to overwhelm him or her. Focus on offering feedback on *one or two* skills that you feel need the most improvement.

People are more receptive when feedback is phrased in a *positive* and *specific* fashion.

In terms of speaking *positively,* instead of saying, "You had a very cold attitude," consider saying something like, "I can see that you were trying to be efficient, but I think I would have felt more relaxed if you were a little more personable and less officious."

With respect to *specificity,* it is OK to begin with some general feedback (e.g., "You seemed to have a judgmental attitude with this client."), but to the extent possible, provide specific examples supporting your general evaluation. Wherever possible, use actual quotes or paraphrase specific instances in the interview that support your claims (e.g., "When you said, 'I can't believe that you'd even think of doing XYZ,' it felt like you were judging me. From that point on, I really didn't want to tell you much more about anything."). Consider taking some notes during these exercises. These notes can be useful in providing specific feedback after the role-play.

Next, the person who portrayed the social worker may respond to the person who played the client.

If observers are present, they may offer their impressions of the social worker's performance one at a time. Observers are welcome to briefly reiterate positive feedback that has already been given, but each observer should restrict negative feedback to one recommendation. Avoid repeating negative feedback that has already been mentioned.

Finally, the person who is being reviewed should take some time to verbalize his or her peers' positive remarks, along with the recommendations that were given and his or her related feelings. The ultimate goal of the role-play process is for the person playing the social worker to compose a customized "to-do" list (e.g., "It seems like I'm fairly solid with skills A and B—those come pretty naturally—but it looks like I need to work on applying X and Y. Those still felt a little bit awkward to me.") and build a plan for improving those skills.

After each role-play wherein you play the social worker, complete the corresponding self-evaluation worksheets. As objectively as possible, rate your proficiency with each skill used according to the numbered scale (1 = needs further work, 5 = excellent), and write a brief note as shown in Figure C. Notice that in Figure C, two additional blank rows are provided for you to list and evaluate your use of supplemental skills (e.g., Clarification) that were not specifically included in the role-play parameters. The purpose of this self-evaluation is to focus your skill development efforts by identifying proficiencies and specific areas to improve.

(1 = needs further work, 5 = excellent)

1	②	3	4	5	Empathy	*Inappropriately used sympathy instead of empathy.*
1	2	3	④	5	Reflection	*Paraphrased client's messages to check for proper understanding. Once or twice repeated the client's words verbatim.*
①	2	3	4	5	Summarizing	*Missed the opportunity to summarize the client's story.*
1	2	3	4	⑤	*Clarification*	*I wasn't sure exactly what the client meant when referring to a supervisor as a "yutz," so I asked and the client explained it to me.*
1	2	3	4	5	_____	

Figure C   Sample Role-Play Evaluation Form

Role-Play Case Notes

Document your brief encounter in case note style, as if you were making an actual entry in the client's chart as shown in Figure D. This will enable you to practice your documentation skills while considering the nature of the exchange that you had with the client.

Role-Play 1.1 Case Notes

Cl. presented as relatively guarded, with moderate eye contact, but cooperative and responsive to questions. Cl. reported problems getting to sleep due to multiple recent stressors, including an overload at work, financial issues, and concerns regarding a family member who's developed some potentially serious health problems. Cl. has discussed disturbing nightmare/dream images and now tends to wake up two to three times per night, including weekends. This leaves Cl. tired and unable to concentrate during the day. Cl. reports feeling increasingly depressed and frustrated.

Figure D   Sample Role-Play Case Notes

Role-plays, though simulated situations, can be exhilarating. These exchanges can be emotionally and cognitively intense for participants and observers. After completing a role-play, debriefing, and documentation, consider taking a moment to clear your head. After a brief break, you and your partner may choose to exchange roles and rerun the exercise for additional practice. As your skills evolve, you may wish to consider revisiting some of the role-plays, taking note of improvements in your performance over time.

As you embark on the role-play exercises, try not to be too hard on yourself or your peers. As with any skill that demands real-time implementation, this sort of communication can take some time to achieve proficiency. Even the most capable social workers occasionally misspeak or misunderstand. With practice, you will find yourself intuitively employing these skills, enabling you to focus less on the names and parameters of each skill and more on the client's issues. Enjoy the process.

PART I

Defining the Professional Relationship

1

What Does a Social Worker Do . . . and *Not* Do?

The role of the social worker is in many ways different from the role as the helpful friend, offering aid in a well-meaning, informal manner. This chapter details key differences between being a good friend and being a competent social worker in three domains: (1) social/emotional factors, (2) professionalism, and (3) self-disclosure.

Social Work Diversity

Social work may concisely be defined as "efforts to understand and improve the quality of people's lives." This broad definition aptly entails the rich diversity of social work capacities, such as child welfare caseworker, family counselor, social service caseworker, eligibility worker, casework supervisor, social service administrator/director, psychiatric social worker, clinical social worker, private practitioner, medical/hospital social worker, school social worker, instructor/trainer, and industrial social worker (Wittenberg, 2002). This is by no means a comprehensive list. Your personality, interests, education, goals, and opportunities will naturally guide you toward a setting and field of service that uniquely suits you.

Social/Emotional Factors

Selection

In your personal life, you are free to select who will and will not be your friends, with whom you will and will not associate, and in what fashion you will relate to them. In your private life, your personal tastes, desires, and motives are among the many factors that can draw you to an individual. Any number of attributes may compel you toward another person: similar interests, common history, appearance (e.g., clothing, grooming, physique), talents, ethnicity, culture, attitude, sense of humor, common friends, and so on.

In the professional realm, you typically do not have the privilege to select clients based on these criteria. In your capacity as a social worker, you are obligated to set aside your personal preferences and provide appropriate and quality care without bias regarding the client's age, ethnicity, culture, race, disability, gender, religion, sexual orientation, or socioeconomic status (National Association of Social Workers, 1996).

Whereas in personal contacts you appropriately make decisions as to whom you choose to associate with, in the professional realm it is often the clinical supervisor who designates client assignments to social workers. Supervisors may base such decisions on any number of variables, including workload distribution, gender, age, ethnicity, or expertise. In some cases, for example, gender may be the deciding factor: A client who is a rape survivor would most likely be paired with a clinician of a gender different from that of the rapist. In other cases, experience level may be critical: A client who is dealing with end-of-life issues would typically be assigned to a staff member with specific training in this area as opposed to a less experienced social worker.

Whereas casual relationships can begin any number of ways, ranging from incidentally chatting in a random public encounter to an arranged date, the selection process in a social work setting involves some deliberate and specific information exchanges. Potential clients are usually required to complete a thorough screening process involving scheduling (and keeping) an appointment, filling out forms, and partaking in an assessment interview in order to determine the client's characteristics, needs, level of care, and the type of services that would best suit that individual. Upon review, the client may be eligible for services at your agency, a different facility, or some combination thereof (Neukrug, 2002).

Determining who will or will not be your client is also contingent on the mission (statement) of the agency. Social service agencies are typically set up to provide a specific set of services to clients; hence, the nature of the client's problem and characteristics of the client must be compatible with the kind of services that an agency is configured to offer. Some examples of the diversity of agency types include centers specializing in care for substance abusers, homeless people, runaways, single mothers, military veterans, and senior citizens.

Personal Contact

Your personal relationships can vary significantly among those in your life. The variety of individuals with whom you associate in your personal sphere can vary (e.g., casual friends, close friends, significant other, family, other loved ones). Additionally, each individual may fulfill one or more roles (e.g., travel companion, teammate, sex partner, study buddy, confidant). Such relationships and roles may be stable or flexible—waxing and waning in terms of the type and amount of contact over time.

Though your roles as a social worker may inherently be laced with variety, it is inappropriate to extend your client contact beyond the professional realm. Legal and ethical principles appropriately prohibit social workers from having dual or multiple relationships with clients. A dual relationship would involve serving as a social worker to a client, plus having another type of relationship with that person. For example, you would be involved in a *dual* relationship with John if he was (1) your client *and* (2) your friend (outside of the social work setting). A *multiple* relationship would involve serving a client with whom you have two or more other relationships: Jane is (1) your client, (2) your friend (outside of the social work setting), *and* (3) your business partner.

The principle of avoiding dual or multiple relationships means that you are to have only *one* relationship with your clients—in the capacity as a social worker. Other forms of contact with clients that occur outside of your professional duties, such as socializing, (outside) friendships, recreational activities, or lunches, are contraindicated.

The principle and practice of having only a *single* professional relationship with clients are designed to protect the client's interest. Engaging with clients in a social setting could likely carry the air of authority that is (implicitly) established in the professional setting. This could lead to a potential power imbalance in the social setting, thereby risking the establishment of a possibly manipulative relationship. Additionally, events occurring in the personal relationship, such as a personal conflict, could adversely affect the functionality of the professional relationship.

The principle of avoiding dual relationships is a two-way street: Just as your clients are not to become your personal friends, those with whom you have an existing relationship (e.g., friends, family, coworkers) should not become your clients. Functioning effectively as a social worker requires a level of professional objectivity. As such, it is not plausible to assert that it is possible to simply switch off your (appropriate) preexisting feelings and thoughts regarding those with whom you are close. Also, if you are personally involved with a client, that client may constrain the issues raised in the professional setting based on concerns of how such topics may adversely affect your personal relationship with him or her. In summary, the principle of avoiding dual or multiple relationships designates that your clients cannot become your friends and your friends cannot become your clients (National Association of Social Workers, 1996).

Admittedly, social friends have some substantial advantages over the professional social worker: As a social friend, one has the advantage of knowing the person via interacting with him or her with a variety of people in a variety of settings; hence, a friend may have the privilege to construct a more comprehensive image of that individual.

In the role of a social worker, you have the advantage of a social science education and access to the agency's resources. Lacking access to firsthand observations of the client's life, you are essentially dependent on the thoroughness and genuineness of the client's report. Such reporting can be laced with bias, selective deletions, editing, or even fabrications. These distortions or omissions may or may not be intentional. Clients may perceive you as an authority figure and, as a result, be motivated to present a (more) favorable picture to avoid being negatively judged. This is known as "social desirability" (Rubin & Babbie, 1993).

Regardless of how forthcoming the client appears, it can be difficult to know precisely what is going on in his or her life between sessions or prior to engaging with the client in a professional setting. A client may deem selected information or events as insignificant or irrelevant and thereby minimize or omit such discussion. Additionally, each person is endowed with only one point of view, so in reality there may not be such a thing as an unbiased story. Through no fault of the client, you may, at best, be hearing only *half* of a story. As important as it is to be aware of these potential distortions/omissions, make an effort to avoid taking a persistent suspicious stance. Try to listen to each story/response with an open mind. You can always assess the quality of the accumulating information as things advance.

Emotions and level of attention (while an incident is occurring) can also influence the way that events are "recorded" and then later "played back." As such, in certain circumstances, with the client's consent, it may be useful to gather supplemental information in order to build a more comprehensive image of the client and his or her situation. This can help tune the assessment and intervention plan accordingly. Such ancillary information may involve gaining authorized access to medical or mental health records, consultation with other providers, or including other significant people in the process (McClam & Woodside, 1994).

For example, a teen may summarily report that his or her parents are unreasonable—the parents monitor/screen phone calls, refuse to allow the client to have Internet access in his or her room, and enforce a sundown curfew even on weekends. Without collateral information, it may seem as if these parents are unfair or overprotective, have no sense of boundaries, do not understand age-appropriate behavior, or perhaps have something to hide. With the consent of the client, however, including the parents in a joint session may reveal useful supplemental information, such as a history of the client's legal problems, substance abuse, decaying grades, and hanging out with a disreputable cohort. As a rule of thumb, consider the information that clients provide as worthy, but also keep in mind that more information, legitimately obtained, can help paint a fuller picture.

Involvement

Friends and family have great latitude in terms of the scope and nature of contact that they can have with each other. For instance, an individual who is involved in a problematic marriage may gain essential support from a friend in the form of late-night calls to process feelings and thoughts and make decisions. Friends may also offer a sofa to temporarily reside on, a means of meeting new people, someone to swap stories with, and so on. As valuable as these gestures are, they are essentially beyond the level of involvement that you would provide as a social worker.

Continuing with this example, your role as a social worker would be quite different. You may be working with the client in the form of offering appropriate supplemental supportive services, which may include processing the facts and feelings at hand or discussing viable alternatives subject to the client's desires (e.g., mediation, couples' therapy, trial separation) while maintaining appropriate boundaries.

At times, a client who is feeling vulnerable may turn to a friend to make potentially life-changing decisions for him or her (e.g., "Should I stay, or should I go?"). While a friend has the privilege to voice an opinion and even facilitate the execution of that decision (e.g., by picking up the phone and booking an appointment with a divorce attorney), as a social worker your role is quite different. As opposed to making decisions for the client, no matter how familiar you may be with that client, the more appropriate course of action might be for you to work with the client, helping him or her cognitively and emotionally explore and weigh the advantages and disadvantages of remaining in the relationship compared with terminating it. In the interest of fostering the client's sense of independence, self-determination, and empowerment, you would ultimately sanction the client with the privilege and responsibility of making such decisions on his or her own behalf (National Association of Social Workers, 1996).

The notion of putting the power of decision making in the client's hands should be laced throughout all aspects of your professional work. Despite your best intentions, each time you feel tempted to do something for a client that he or she could (and should) do for him- or herself, you rob the client of the opportunity to develop a more robust skill set, a sense of independence, and self-direction.

In your social contacts, naturally, there are implicit norms and standards of conduct that you apply when dealing with friends, family, and others; however, there can be considerable breadth with respect to your dealings with such individuals. For example, Jane may recommend, demand, or even threaten John into doing or not doing something.

Though you may likely be perceived as an authority figure, as a social worker you are ethically committed to not abusing your power or (en)forcing your opinions. When appropriate, you do have the privilege to provide clients with feedback and recommendations that you consider suitable for them; however, you are not in a position to unilaterally impose such recommendations. Coercion, threats, or other forms of manipulation are inappropriate means within the professional realm. Despite your good intentions and deep sense of caring, keep in mind that, as a social worker, you are committed to gathering an understanding of the client and his or her circumstances and providing viable options. The ultimate decision as to how to proceed is in the client's hands. The client may choose to go with your recommended options, implement a modified version of your recommendation, or come up with options of his or her own, or the client may choose none of the above and do nothing. Ultimately, the client holds the privilege to choose his or her actions and inactions and the consequences related thereto. Though at times it may be challenging for you to accept, the client holds the privilege to refuse treatment or care at will, despite what you consider best for him or her (National Association of Social Workers, 1996).

Topic of Conversation

In social settings, conversations are free to emerge from virtually any topic. Such discussions may remain on topic. Conversely, subject matter may suddenly switch or gradually blend from one idea to another. In casual conversations, there is nothing inherently wrong with this sort of shifting.

When communicating with clients, the entry point to such conversations is somewhat more purposeful. Typically, the subject matter is relegated to issues pertinent to the client's problem or his or her efforts to advance toward a meaningful goal. In terms of subject shifting, naturally, it is appropriate to provide adequate space for clients to expand ideas and thoughts as the conversation advances; however, you are also committed to detecting potential nonproductive departures from the topic at hand. Such departures are not atypical—professional communication can differ substantially from social conversation in that social conversations typically consist of discussing issues that the participants freely *want* to talk about, whereas communication taking place in the professional realm may involve verbalizing notions that are emotionally uncomfortable or cognitively complex but essential to advancing the process (Kadushin, 1990). Part of your responsibilities as a professional social worker involves recognizing and tactfully acknowledging such departures and then appropriately redirecting the client back to more clinically relevant processing. As with other communication techniques, there are few absolutes— the realm of working with clients is an environment of self-discovery wherein one thought or feeling may naturally lead to another. Although focus is important, try to avoid being too rigid or impatient. Allow for some leeway with respect to natural variability in the conversation—valuable information or feelings may be revealed. Techniques for effectively directing sessions (*focusing* and *specificity*) are covered in more detail in Chapter 2.

Social conversations can vary substantially in terms of the verbal exchange ratio depending on the personalities, topics, circumstances, and individuals involved. Among friends, there may be conversations where you would do 90% of the talking, whereas other times you would do 90% of the listening.

In the professional setting, nobody should be delivering monologues (Egan, 2006). Aim for about a one-third–to–two-thirds talking ratio, wherein you do about one third of the talking and two thirds of the listening. Naturally, there can be variation in this suggested ratio—explaining an essential concept to a client may require more words. Conversely, traditional Native American clients, particularly in early session, will expect to do most of the talking in order to help you understand the basis of their problem (Barcus, 2003). Some self-monitoring can be useful, but do not feel as if you need to resort to anything as precise as word counting. From time to time, ask yourself, "Who's doing most of the talking in these sessions?" If you find yourself crossing the 50% line, you may want to spend more time listening or building more concise messages. Remember: You already know what *you* have in mind—make an effort to comprehend and tend to what the *client* has in mind.

Advice

Socially, friends and acquaintances may freely and regularly exchange advice on virtually any topic, ranging from restaurant selection to complex life issues. In some ways, close friends and family members have an advantage over you, as a social worker, when it comes to offering advice, as they have the benefit of knowing each other deeply over time. Such comprehensive knowledge of another person as a whole can provide valuable guidance in terms of assembling and offering suitable advice. Thus, in social settings, giving advice may appropriately come relatively early in the conversational process.

Conversely, serving as the social worker, you may not (yet) possess such thorough knowledge of the client's personality or life goals and the characters in his or her life; therefore, with respect to offering advice or guidance, you would typically proceed at a more conservative pace. This would enable you to purposefully gather and weigh relevant information about the client (e.g., goals, concerns, interests, education, social setting, belief systems, prior similar experiences, level of motivation, physical health, emotional factors) and explore the availability of appropriate resources prior to offering advice, even if the client directly requests advice. Advice that is hastily delivered is likely to be a poor fit to the client's characteristics and overall situation. Such poorly informed advice is less likely to be followed.

In social relationships, the quality of the advising is not necessarily the foremost concern—friends may offer advice based on personal experience, something encountered in popular media (e.g., online, on a television show, in a magazine), word of mouth, empirical research, an insightful hunch, or even a spontaneous "what-if" proposition.

Whereas friends are free to provide advice based on anything (or nothing), as a social worker you are obliged to constrain your range of recommendations to those with appropriate credibility. It would be inappropriate for you to offer advice or a referral that was not adequately researched in advance. Most agencies have a list of reputable support services or a resource guide detailing the services available in a given area. In cases where you do not have adequate information to provide meaningful advice or referrals, avoid the temptation to offer incomplete or inappropriate information. Alternatively, consider summarizing your comprehension of the issues at hand, and discuss the need for you and the client to research options collaboratively.

Socially given advice can also vary substantially in terms of the manner in which such advice is given. Among friends and family, advice may range from gentle recommendations (e.g., "I wonder how you'd look with shorter hair") to firm demands or threats (e.g., "You better never do XYZ again, or else I'll . . . "). Depending on the context and social norms among the individuals involved, either may be an acceptable form of communication in social settings.

In your capacity as a social worker, you need not be meek. You do have the privilege to offer relevant recommendations. Keep in mind, however, that you are not in a position to order a client to accept or act on any piece of advice that you give. You are committed to honoring the client's decisions and fostering his or her self-determination (National Association of Social Workers, 1996). There may be times when the client's decision as to how to proceed or not proceed will differ from your ideas as to what is best for the client. Despite your best efforts and intentions, the client's choices, actions, inactions, and consequences related thereto are ultimately in his or her hands. In short, each person owns his or her life and, as such, has the privilege to decide what will or will not be in that life and what he or she will or will not do. There may be times when you will not agree with the life decisions that a client may make. As a social worker, you are entitled to voice your concerns and recommendations; however, ultimately, you are obliged to honor (though not necessarily agree with) the client's right to choose.

To summarize, it may be useful to envision yourself as a consultant working on behalf of the client. As you gain an understanding of the client's current status and goal(s), you may assemble what you believe to be an effective plan of action and deliver this plan, detailing your rationale, expected benefits of following through, and foreseeable consequences associated with not following through, but the choice to accept, reject, or modify this plan ultimately lies in the client's hands. Additionally, the client is responsible for the outcome, and you are not—be it positive, neutral, or negative.

Though social relationships are typically benevolent, there are no hard rules regarding who the beneficiary of the advising might be. For example, Bob may offer Dusty advice or guidance that is designed to benefit Bob or someone else.

In a social work setting, advice and the overall treatment plan must be geared toward advancing the quality of the client's life or the lives of those specified by the client (e.g., sibling, spouse, significant other). In accordance with ethical principles and legal rules, as the social worker you cannot be the beneficiary, primary or otherwise, of professional interventions (Ivey, 1983).

Professionalism

Legal

Members of casual relationships are not beholden to specific laws detailing appropriate conduct. Unfortunate occurrences, such as failing to show up, showing up late, last-minute cancellations, disloyalty, rudeness, and dishonesty, may have unpleasant *social* consequences (e.g., damaged rapport, hurt feelings, sense of mistrust, possible collapse of the relationship); however, there are no *legal* consequences, per se.

In a professional setting, however, there are specific laws that govern the client–social worker relationship. When working with clients, you are required to maintain thorough case notes. Such documentation typically includes the client's initial application for services, signed informed consent, fee agreement, assessment notes, diagnoses, collateral information, care plan, and progress notes. Professionally, you are also required to adhere to guidelines detailing the safeguarding of such documentation, including protocol for safely and confidentially managing paper and electronic files, client and third-party access to client files, and when appropriate, properly disposing of such records. Parenthetically, although *deleting* a file or record from a computer system or backup medium makes the data inaccessible using conventional software, more sophisticated users may have little difficulty retrieving residual content. If you are storing client information on a computer system, make a point to confer with an information technology expert regarding practices for safeguarding client data using appropriate security measures (e.g., passwords, file encryption, access protocols, locks, properly expunging data).

Depending on the state laws governing professional privilege, your notes may be subject to subpoena or court order, and depending on the case, you may be called to testify in a court of law.

Social workers must also comply with legal regulations involving mandated reporting. These laws vary from state to state. For example, in some states, social workers are required to comply with the Tarasoff law, which involves compulsorily breaching the client's confidentiality in instances wherein the client expresses a threat to inflict harm against an identifiable target (individual). In such cases, you would legally be required to notify those that are the target of a client's threat and also report the same information to local law enforcement authorities (Tarasoff warning; Kagle & Kopels, 1994).

In your professional capacity, you are legally mandated to submit a formal report to the appropriate authorities in situations wherein you have reason to believe that the client has engaged in, or has knowledge of, the abuse or neglect of a child, a dependent, or an elderly individual (Hepworth & Larsen, 1993). Legally, those who submit such reports in good faith are protected from legal recourse from those named therein (Lindsey, 1994).

From a professional standpoint, you must be familiar with the laws in the state in which you practice with respect to properly responding to subpoenas, depositions, and court orders. Such limitations to confidentiality should be included in the informed consent agreement that clients sign upon their entry into a professional relationship. Additionally, such issues may be discussed explicitly with clients prior to or at the onset of your professional contact.

Unlike social relationships wherein mutual consent among adults is all that is required to embark on an intimate encounter, laws and professional ethics strictly forbid social workers from engaging in intimate/sexual relations with (current) clients and those closely associated with clients (National Association of Social Workers, 1996). In terms of having sex with ex-clients, as in terms of confidentiality, laws vary considerably from state to state. You are responsible for knowing and complying with the laws pertaining to social work practice in your state.

Confidentiality

In relationships with friends and family, confidentiality is regulated by social standards as opposed to legal rules. For example, Johanna is free to tell George of her day spent with Charles, detailing their activities, conversations, and subjective impressions. Additionally, Johanna may choose to tell Charles one of George's secrets. Though Johanna's indiscreet disclosure may cause her to be perceived as untrustworthy among her friends when it comes to secrets, she has not broken any laws.

As a social worker, you are legally and ethically required to maintain client confidentiality, meaning that with the exception of legally mandated reporting (e.g., mandated abuse/neglect reporting, court orders, Tarasoff warnings where applicable), you should not disclose any client information without the client's written permission. The contact between you and your client is considered a privileged relationship, meaning that information pertaining to each client is confidential and can be disclosed only with the client's written consent, with the exception of instances designated by law (Kagle & Kopels, 1994; National Association of Social Workers, 1996). For example, suppose you receive a phone call requesting information regarding a client. Whether you recognize the client's name or not, you would be right in stating, "I can neither confirm nor deny any knowledge of this person without his or her signature on an appropriate consent form. Here is my contact information should you wish to submit such a (signed) form," or words to that effect, and then end the call. You would also be entitled to notify the client that such an inquiry was made.

As a social worker, you have the privilege to engage in peer or supervisory consultations without the client's written consent, provided you do so in a manner that protects the client's identity, disclosing only those details necessary to address your clinical question. For example, in the interest of better masking the client's specific identity, saying, "I'm working with Arlene, a 43-year-old client who is the principal of a local high school . . ." might be better stated as "I have a female client who's in her 40s and works in education . . ." Such consultations should be conducted in a confidential setting as opposed to public spaces wherein others might overhear.

Take precautions to protect client confidentiality using a variety of means and media: Contact with clients should be conducted in a sound-protected setting. Some facilities provide music in waiting rooms to help mask confidential dialogue that may otherwise leak into that area. Acoustic noise generators may be placed outside of office doors or be strategically placed in hallways to reduce the potential for eavesdropping.

Paperwork related to clients should be stored in a secured fashion (e.g., a locked file cabinet, a locked desk, a locked office). Computer records should be encrypted or at least password protected. If the computer is portable, when it is not being used it should be stored in a secured containment, such as a locking file cabinet, a locking desk, or a safe. This applies to backup media as well. Client information that has been authorized for release may be transmitted by e-mail; however, e-mail is *not* a direct route. Such messages may pass through multiple servers en route to their designated destination. As such, any number of less-than-ethical system operators or clever programmers may have the opportunity to view this e-mail message (and attachments) as it migrates from one system to another. Encryption software, wherein a password directs an algorithm to scramble and unscramble attached data files, is considered a reasonable precaution when transmitting such data. Naturally, the decryption password should not be included in the body of that e-mail.

In addition to physically protecting client information, as a social worker you are also responsible for maintaining confidentiality regarding the identity and details related to current, ex-, and deceased clients. Aside from legal consequences, inadvertent breaches in maintaining client confidentiality can cost you and your colleagues the trust and support of clients and compromise the public opinion of such services (Crenshaw, Bartell, & Lichtenberg, 1994). Concerns regarding confidentiality may be particularly critical to traditional Asian clients with whom the stigma of mental health issues reflects unfavorably, not only on the individual client but also on the family as a whole (Gaw, 1993).

Documentation

In social settings, one may choose to keep a diary, periodically journaling one's private experiences, observations, and impressions on a subjective basis. The therapeutic setting differs in that documentation is essential as opposed to optional. When writing clinical notes, keep in mind that such documentation may at some point be disclosed to the client, other clinicians, or legal entities, so consider these "ABC" guidelines when composing case notes:

Accuracy—The information included in the chart must be authentic. Do not omit, alter, exaggerate, or fabricate data.

Brevity—Use concise sentences that get to the point. Including approved abbreviations may be useful.

Clarity—Use appropriate grammar, syntax (sequence of the words within a sentence), and punctuation. Errors in sentence construction can compromise your intended meaning. When handwriting notes, tend to your penmanship. Illegible notes are useless. Also, be certain to sign your notes and avoid leaving blank lines.

Some organizations will use free-form notes, whereas others may have forms or databases to make entries. A common system of documentation used in professional settings is the "**SOAP**" format wherein case notes are divided into four sections:

Subjective—Information gathered from the client (e.g., his or her current condition, employment status, living conditions, socialization practices)

Objective—The clinician's observations of the client

Assessment—Diagnostic information, which can include mental status examination (MSE) findings (p. 144), mental health diagnoses (as per the *Diagnostic and Statistical Manual of Mental Disorders*, or *DSM*) (p. 126), and (external) psychological testing

Plan—Intervention plan, goals, and expected outcome (Kettenbach, 2004)

Scope of Practice

Among social contacts, there are no enforceable limitations with respect to what services friends might offer to each other. For example, with no particular research or expertise, one may individually, or with the cooperation of a friend, choose to experiment with such things as aromatherapy, acupressure, hypnosis, or herbal remedies.

Though such holistic interventions may seem inherently helpful or, at least, harmless, as a social worker you are committed to providing only those services and interventions for which you have specific training, certification, or licensure (National Association of Social Workers, 1996). The principle of providing care within one's scope of practice cannot be waived by a client's request or even demand for a service that you are not qualified to provide. In instances where you feel that the client might benefit from such supplemental care, you do have the privilege to provide the client with appropriate referrals to reputable service providers.

Clients may, of their own volition, choose to include any number of additional components in their care regimen. Some African Americans may access folk healers who might offer curative herbs, teas, and traditional rituals to address physical or mental problems (Baker & Lightfoot, 1993; Wilkinson & Spurlock, 1986). Latinos may confer with religious leaders to aid in the resolution of selected mental health issues (Dana, 1993; Ho, 1992; Martinez, 1993). Similarly, Native Americans may seek guidance from culturally significant individuals, including tribal leaders or elders, when dealing with family issues (Paniagua, 2005).

Boundaries

Within personal relationships, social norms and personal values provide the implicit boundaries in determining what constitutes acceptable topics of conversation. For some contacts, this may include discussions relegated to a fairly narrow scope, such as school, career, or finances, whereas conversations with others may involve details of one's private life, wishes, desires, or secrets. Similarly, in social settings one may engage in different activities depending on the structure of the relationship. This may consist of one or several types of activities (e.g., dining buddy, travel companion, love interest, dance partner). Social relationships can remain relatively stable, or they may be flexible over time (e.g., friends can evolve into best friends, travel companions may become roommates).

When working with clients, there is less variability in terms of boundaries. Your professional contact should adhere to meeting at the agreed-upon location at the designated appointment time and should not involve outside contact. As your contact with clients progresses, a sense of closeness, familiarity, and in some cases liking or admiration may develop. None of this is wrong or inappropriate; however, unlike social relationships wherein it might be appropriate to consider taking the relationship to the "next level," in your role as a social worker you must maintain a sense of professionalism when working with clients. Moving from being the client's social worker, a perceived expert/authority figure, to being a client's social friend would likely carry an inappropriate power difference, which could unintentionally lead to intimidation or abuse.

Your purpose as a social worker is to coordinate with clients in efforts toward improving the quality of their lives. While maintaining positive rapport facilitates the working relationship, it is important that you keep your personal life separate from the client's. Predictability, stability, and robust boundaries have been shown to be key elements in terms of clinical effectiveness, building and maintaining the professional relationship, and carefully balancing the separateness and independence of each individual within the context of a collaborative setting (Epstine, 1994).

Respecting the client's boundaries also pertains to the topics processed in the professional arena. If a client refuses or strongly resists discussing selected issues that you consider particularly relevant, you are entitled to explain your rationale for wanting to proceed along these lines. This may include your concerns regarding potential consequences related to dodging issues that you consider critical. Ultimately, however, in keeping with the social work principle of self-determination, the client has the final say-so, with respect to which topics will (or will not) be discussed and to what depth (National Association of Social Workers, 1996).

As essential as it is to establish and maintain professional boundaries with the client, it is important to be flexible in order to effectively accommodate relevant cultural factors. For example, when working with Latino clients, the initial therapeutic relationship may, over time, evolve from addressing clients in a formal manner (*formalismo*) (e.g., Mr. Gomez) to a more personal form (*personalismo*) wherein clients would be addressed on a first-name basis (Bernal & Gutierrez, 1988; Ho, 1992; Martinez, 1993). Some Latino clients may offer you a modest gift as a traditional sign of gratitude. Though social workers typically would not expect or encourage such gift giving, refusal of such a gesture could be perceived as insulting per the *personalismo* practice, hence degrading the professional rapport (Paniagua, 2005).

Time

Casual relationships offer a great range of flexibility in terms of time. Though it is not uncommon for friends to set the *start* time for an encounter (e.g., "Let's meet for dinner at 6:00"), less often is there a designated *end* time. There are also no hard-and-fast limitations regarding the total number of, duration of, or time between contacts. Such contacts may involve prearranged scheduling, or they may be spontaneous. Friends also have the advantage of engaging in relationships with no specified limitation in terms of duration. Social friends may keep in contact over months, years, or a lifetime.

The realm of your contact with clients is more rigid with respect to time. Appointments are typically once per week for 50 minutes. It is expected that sessions will begin and end on time (Kadushin, 1990). Traditionally, the treatment consent provides details regarding the agency's cancellation policy. Clients are usually required to provide 24-hour notice should they need to cancel or move an appointment. The policy may also specify the total number of appointments that a client may miss or cancel.

As motivated as you might be to assemble appointment schedules that maximize efficiency when it comes to serving clients during business hours, it is equally important to recognize and accommodate mediating cultural factors. For example, some Latino clients would consider it inappropriate or rude to abandon a task, such as helping a friend, in order to keep a fixed appointment (Martinez, 1986; Sue & Sue, 2003). Similarly, some traditional Native Americans consider time a naturally occurring event as opposed to a phenomenon that controls their lives (Barcus, 2003; Ho, 1992; Sue & Sue, 2003).

Termination

Aside from exceptional circumstances (e.g., impending geographical relocation, onset of a serious illness, layoffs), we seldom think about termination in our personal lives. It is natural to presume that our relationships with friends, family, and peers will endure over time.

The professional relationship differs in that clients typically seek the services of a social worker in order to address a particular need. In most cases, such relationships are meant to be temporary.

Social workers who provide traditional therapy may, for selected clients, implement a form of short-term therapy. Short-term therapy, usually consisting of 1 to 20 sessions with an average of about 6, was developed in the early 1960s as an alternative to the psychoanalytic method, which is administered over an extended period (Bloom, 1997). Termination is an integral component in the short-term method: The therapist, a respected authority figure, reasonably asserts that the client's problem is adequately addressable within the allotted time, hence helping establish a positive (time) framework for achieving the specified goals (Garfield, 1989).

Short-term therapy has demonstrated effectiveness in as few as the first three sessions, wherein gains tend to be the greatest in the early sessions of therapy (Barkham, 1989). There is evidence showing that longer-term therapy can provide greater improvement, but with diminishing returns over time (Howard, Kopta, Krause, & Olinsky, 1986), and that therapeutic gains tend to endure regardless of the length of the therapy (Lambert & Ogles, 2004; Nicholas & Berman, 1983).

Regardless of the type of professional services that you provide, relationships with clients are typically conceived as temporary. Nevertheless, as facts and feelings are exchanged, it is natural and expected that some mutual emotional connections will be built. As a result, even in the professional setting, the process of termination can bring some sense of loss to both you and the client (Leigh, 1998). Termination of the professional relationship provides a valuable opportunity for clients to build proficiency in coping with the multiple losses that occur as part of the natural process of living (Maholick & Turner, 1979).

Discussion of termination need not be relegated to the final minutes of the last session. If termination is foreseeable (e.g., 10 sessions are allotted), it can be beneficial to raise the topic of termination progressively, providing opportunities to evaluate the client's progress made to date, recognize and reinforce progress achieved thus far, reassess, and, if indicated, adjust the treatment to best utilize the remaining time. Chapter 7 provides more comprehensive discussion regarding the process of effective termination.

Respect

Social relationships can vary in terms of the level of respect expressed between members. Communication between friends and family members may range from supportive and loving messages to degrading behavior and language that may include such things as taunting, teasing, sarcasm, criticism, judgmental attitudes, rude behavior, ignoring, or not taking the other person seriously. Though harsh, such conduct may be considered appropriate, depending on the nature of the relationship and social norms.

Respect can be thought of as holding someone else's feelings, beliefs, and thoughts in high regard—actively recognizing and honoring the other person's perspective as valid and valuable to him or her, even if it does not match your own belief system. It is essential to convey respect toward clients in all phases of your contact with them (National Association of Social Workers, 1996). This means taking the client seriously and being open to the possibility that the client may choose to reject your recommendations in favor of his or her own plans, which you may not necessarily agree are in the client's best interest. In keeping with the ethical principle of self-determination, as a social worker you are obliged to respect the client's right to choose; however, respect does not imply that you are required to sit idly by, pretending to agree. Quite the contrary. Even in your professional role, you are entitled and obliged to engage the client to discuss your concerns regarding the nature of the client's proposed plan (or lack thereof), pointing out such things as potential conflicts in the treatment plan or evidence-based practice (effective interventions that are based on the outcome of rigorous social science) and detailing better alternatives, expected consequences, and so on. After engaging in such discussion in a nonjudgmental, nondegrading fashion, the final decision as to how to proceed (or not proceed) ultimately lies in the client's hands. This presents one of the greatest challenges to social workers and healthcare providers in general: respecting the client's inherent right to self-determination, even when you do not agree with the client's decisions.

Positive Regard

Relationships among friends can consist of a natural ebb and flow of circumstances and feelings. Depending on the events, even the best of friends can experience negative feelings leading to corresponding angry expressions, such as disappointment, jealousy, resentment, raised voices, accusations, insults, outright rejection, or physical confrontations with each other.

Among the greatest challenges that helping professionals face is the commitment to maintain a standpoint of positive regard, honoring the value and worth of the client at each phase of the helping process (Rogers, 1957). This is not always easy, considering that within the context of providing social work services, clients are challenged to set and pursue substantial and worthwhile goals. In circumstances wherein the implementation is delayed or less than fully successful, your dedication to the principle of positive regard does not mean that you are committed to dodging discussion of such happenstances; nor would it be appropriate to take a punitive stance. Rather, more appropriately, such issues should be systematically addressed in a nonaccusatory fashion. Instead of assigning blame or delegating fault for failure, the preferred strategy would be to address this in a more positive fashion, collaboratively and constructively identifying the roadblocks that were encountered and seeking solutions to meaningfully address such encumbrances. Such an approach could be employed to encourage the client to try again using a more refined method. Maintaining a genuinely positive attitude toward the client serves to strengthen the collaborative nature of the professional relationship (Nugent, 1992). As the social worker, a perceived knowledgeable figure, your genuine conveyance of an "I know you can do this" attitude can instill hope, thereby enhancing the client's potential to persevere toward the accomplishment of meaningful goals, especially when obstacles are encountered.

Education

Some people might regard marching proudly to "Pomp and Circumstance" to claim their well-earned diplomas as the conclusion of their education. While donning your cap and gown upon the successful completion of a social work degree is indeed a momentous occasion, it should by no means signify the end of learning. Certainly, the rigors of the bachelor or master of social work program challenges one at many levels, including academic mastery, development of clinical skills, time management, and managing your personal life. Yet, even if you managed to earn all As, it would be naive to think that you now know all that there is to know about the richly diverse field that is social work.

As a professional social worker, you must be committed to continuing to improve, update, and broaden your education throughout your career (National Association of Social Workers, 1996). Your employment setting or career goals may suggest the direction that your continuing education should take in order to build expertise in a particular specialized area of care (e.g., bereavement counselor, organ transplant social worker, foster care social worker, medical social worker, adoption social worker, policy administrator, social service agency manager/ director, school social worker, senior center social worker) (Wittenberg, 2002).

Your ongoing education, plus the corresponding implementation of evidence-based practice, which involves the development and dissemination of best-practice guidelines, can help reduce the guesswork in the postgraduate realm and facilitate more effective and efficient interventions, thereby affording clients the best opportunity to improve their quality of life. For a social worker, good intentions and intuition are essential ingredients when working with clients, but they are not always enough. A lesser-informed social worker may unknowingly utilize intervention methods that have been demonstrated to have neutral or possibly negative outcomes.

Evidence-based practice, in a realistic sense, is not intended to make for "cookbook care" wherein a client presenting with diagnosis X automatically receives treatment Y. As important as it is to honor a cogent external knowledge base, it is equally important to attend to the impressions and knowledge that you glean from each client when it comes to proposing and implementing treatment plans. Sackett, Rosenberg, Gray, Haynes, and Richardson (1996), writing from a medical standpoint, recommend a blended approach, honoring both external validated findings and the judgment of the practitioner:

> Good doctors use both individual clinical expertise and the best available external evidence, and neither alone is enough. Without clinical expertise, practice risks becoming tyrannised [*sic*] by evidence, for even excellent external evidence may be inapplicable to or inappropriate for an individual patient. Without current best evidence, practice risks becoming rapidly out of date, to the detriment of patients. (¶ 3)

When working with clients, consider building interventions based on a three-dimensional integrative model: (1) empirical social science research, (2) your comprehension of the client's biopsychosocial characteristics, including problems and resources, and (3) your existing knowledge base and perspective. To reify this, one might reasonably expect a theoretically robust intervention to hold little chance of being successfully implemented (as is) if it entails aspects that are profoundly unpalatable to the client. In such a case, one might consider collaboratively assembling a customized version of the intervention or perhaps an alternative approach, which may consist of a unique hybrid of interventions.

With respect to formal academic training, a survey of 62 master of social work programs revealed that only 31.4% include courses detailing the implementation of evidence-based practice (Weissman et al., 2006). In terms of actual application, the argument has been made that the conditions under which evidence-based practice research is conducted involve hand-selected clients studied under controlled circumstances. This sort of methodology fails to reproduce the "real-life" characteristics of clients presenting with multiple dynamic issues and fluctuating symptoms in a variety of settings. As a result, practitioners regard the treatment recommendations rendered by such social science scholars as essentially unusable in the "real world" (Maier, 2006). Despite this potential discontinuity, it has been found that when clinicians are provided with access to evidence-based practice literature, such clinicians tend to include the treatment recommendations when conceiving and implementing treatment plans for appropriate clients (Stewart & Chambless, 2007).

The adversarial nature of the relationship between the social science researcher and the social work practitioner is not new. Social science researchers tend to focus on overall (as opposed to individual) outcomes, involving such things as clinical trials and statistical findings. In contrast, social work practitioners tend to focus on knowing each client on an individual basis and dynamically tending to subjective data, such as subtle but significant changes in mood or attitude, incremental advances in coping, and positive accomplishments. The goal is ultimately to merge these two worlds via mutual trust and respect, honoring the skills, education, and professional perspectives of both the researcher and the practitioner (Garland, Plemmons, & Koontz, 2006). In an effort to bridge the gap between the lab and the field, a novel approach has been devised: As opposed to the traditional "top-down" approach, wherein social science researchers conduct studies and then disseminate their findings, which may or may not be applicable, to social work practitioners, a collaborative "bottom-up" method has shown promise. The process begins with the researchers respectfully conferring with social work practitioners in order to comprehend their realm, which includes characteristics of the client population, each client's identified goals or problems, and the intervention methods currently being applied. The social science research team then works with the social work practitioners to devise appropriate means of measuring the effectiveness of their interventions, ultimately providing meaningful feedback to tune and derive more effective interventions and methods (Sullivan et al., 2005).

When considering the dynamic environment of health and human services, you cannot realistically expect that you will be able to provide the best care possible based solely on yesterday's knowledge. There is a substantial difference between having 10 years of evolving experience and having 1 year of experience and then merely repeating it nine times.

Your ongoing education may include a variety of aspects, which may involve working collaboratively with social science researchers, clinical supervision, peer consultations/networking, keeping abreast of literature published in relevant reputable journals, and selecting and satisfying pertinent CEU (continuing education unit) requirements.

Self-Disclosure

Social conversations are typically characterized by a free and open exchange of ideas and stories between the parties involved, wherein individuals readily swap personal details about themselves and their opinions about a variety of topics in an open and spontaneous manner. These sorts of conversations, which seamlessly include two-way self-disclosure, are a natural way for people to mutually engage and connect with each other.

In your service as a social worker, self-disclosure is more of a one-way path, wherein the client tells his or her story to you; however, there is no single opinion regarding your use of self-disclosure when working with clients. For example, social workers who provide clients with psychotherapy may be guided by their theoretical orientation when it comes to regulating self-disclosure. If you were a humanistic therapist, you would deliberately use self-disclosure as a means to facilitate authenticity. Alternatively, if you subscribed to a psychodynamic orientation, you would depend on the use of *transference*, wherein the client readily *transfers* his or her emotions associated with a significant person in his or her life (e.g., parent, sibling, spouse, friend, boss) onto you, a receptive neutral figure. Under this particular orientation, your self-disclosure(s) may confound the client's ability to superimpose the emotional cloak of another onto your distinct frame. From a psychodynamic standpoint, self-disclosure may pollute or ultimately confound the transference potential (Goldfried, Burckell, & Eubanks-Carter, 2003).

Two forms of self-disclosure, specifically *implicit self-disclosure* and *professional self-disclosure,* are typically considered customary.

Implicit Self-Disclosure

Despite your deliberate efforts to focus your attention on understanding your clients and their stories, clients may, out of natural curiosity, derive some impression of you regardless of how little you verbalize about yourself. Without feeling self-conscious, it can be helpful to be aware that clients may gather clues as to your personal identity by correlating readily observable characteristics, such as your gender, race, ethnicity, estimated age, grooming style, and clothing. Your accoutrements (e.g., wedding ring, other jewelry, watch, agency badge) may provide additional clues as to the client's estimate of who you are. Additional personal characteristics that may be notable to clients include your mannerisms, conduct, physical appearance (e.g., body structure, stature, posture, facial expressions, eye contact, hand gestures, body movements), and vocal characteristics (e.g., language, volume, tempo, warmth, vocabulary, expressions, accent).

If you see clients in an office setting, clients may also take note of your working environment, noting such elements as photos, artwork, books, décor, neatness or clutter on your desktop or work area, diplomas, licenses, and certificates, which may guide the client in forming some impression of who you are.

Professional Self-Disclosure

Another generally accepted form of self-disclosure involves providing relevant details regarding your professional qualifications where applicable. For example, a client may reasonably inquire about your education, years of experience, or history of working with clients with characteristics similar to his or her own. You may, without direct inquiry, find it appropriate to cite your specific expertise in a clinically relevant field. Suppose one of your internships was at a geriatric care facility. When working (in the present) with an elderly client who is concerned about potential memory loss or other cognitive deficits, few would argue the appropriateness of briefly mentioning the relevant expertise that you gained via your internship and associated research.

Advantages of Self-Disclosure

Studies indicate that using a moderate, as opposed to a low or high, level of self-disclosure during initial sessions results in higher return rates to future appointments (Simon, 1988; Simonson, 1976) and that sharing personal thoughts and feelings provides the client the opportunity to know the person with whom he or she is dealing, thus developing the professional relationship (Shulman, 1977).

Selectively using self-disclosure to demonstrate that you have personally dealt with issues similar to the client's can promote a sense of normality, demonstrating that the client is not the only one who has faced such a problem. The client may deem you uniquely qualified to comprehend his or her circumstances, and you may, as such, instill a sense of hope as the client utilizes you as a viable role model to follow (Bandura, 1986).

Your use of self-disclosure can also result in a reciprocity effect, wherein the client's perspective is "You told me some of your story, so now it's time for me to tell you some of my story." This relaxed style of mutual sharing is characteristic of the kind of social (nonclinical) conversations to which clients are accustomed. As such, it may set the tone to enable the client to more naturally embark on meaningful self-disclosure, thereby advancing the process (Doster & Nesbitt, 1979).

According to a survey (Anderson & Mandell, 1989), professionals tend to use self-disclosure as a means of enhancing the client's awareness of options, encourage the client's self-disclosure via modeling, reduce anxiety, and communicate authenticity. Among the professionals studied, the most disclosed topics included personal history and current relationship. The least disclosed topics included sexuality and money.

Disadvantages of Self-Disclosure

Should you choose to engage in self-disclosure to clients, you are faced with the running questions regarding the optimum content (e.g., backstory, detailed facts, depth and range of facts, feelings, beliefs) that is pertinent.

Persistently revealing personal details about yourself may lead to role confusion on behalf of the client. A client who comes to know you on a personal basis may develop a sense of selective sympathy toward you with respect to your disclosures. For example, if the client senses that you are experiencing some personal difficulties or believes that raising a certain topic might be distressing to you, he or she may feel hesitant to speak from a genuine place. Out of respect for you, the client may reduce, alter, or strategically omit relevant issues from his or her discussion—in essence, your level of disclosure may negatively influence the client's level of disclosure. Additionally, if through excessive self-disclosure the client has developed a sense of compassion toward you, the client may feel compelled to cushion your feelings by falsely reporting that your interventions have been successes when in fact there may be problems in the design or implementation of the treatment plan. Such disingenuous feedback can cause both you and the client to miss the essential opportunities to reevaluate and tune the intervention that may have occurred had the client offered more genuine feedback.

Though presenting a genuinely friendly and accepting attitude toward clients can serve to foster rapport, persistently engaging in self-disclosure may cause a blurring of boundaries. The client may begin to see your contact with him or her as more social than professional. As a result, the client may begin to wonder why you have not taken the relationship to the next level (e.g., lunch engagement, going out for drinks together), or the client may feel spurned should you decline a social invitation.

Despite your best intentions, self-disclosure may not necessarily transfer to the client in the manner in which you expect. For example, suppose a client discusses his or her addiction to prescription medication, to which you disclose your prior use of marijuana in order to more authentically lead to a discussion of recovery options. The client may have any number of unexpected adverse reactions: The client may feel that the drugs and reasons for using them are very different in nature, so you really do not have much in common along those lines. The client may hold a negative judgment against you for using mind-altering/illegal/"street" drugs. The client might question your credibility, wondering whether you were high while you were a student, an intern, or working with other clients. The client might reasonably be distracted by concerns about the continuity and quality of your professional service to him or her should you relapse.

In cases where the client reveals a problem that you have personally dealt with effectively, with all good intentions it can be tempting to summarily state the solution that you used, implying that the client should simply reproduce your prepared formula. Though you may (privately) reflect on your past experiences when working with clients, merely handing prefabricated solutions over to a client may be a disservice to him or her in a number of ways: The client forgoes the opportunity to learn essential problem-solving skills that may apply to this and other situations. Also, the prompt delivery of complex answers, the origin of which may be elusive, may foster an inappropriate controlling-dependent relationship between you and the client, wherein the client inappropriately comes to conceive you as the exalted advice guru, prompting him or her to implicitly assume the passive role of the uncertain fool. The client's unique attributes (e.g., personality, skill set, preferences, talents, intellect, social systems, values, belief systems, spirituality, access to resources) may be substantially different from yours; hence, the client may require a unique adaptation or perhaps an entirely different approach when it comes to solving the same problem.

Paradoxically, disclosing your personal success pertaining to the client's present problem may lead him or her to reason, "Of course you solved this—it'd be easy for you—you're successful, and I'm not. I could never do this," thereby laying the groundwork for the client to fail in order to fulfill his or her presumption (Mann & Murphy, 1975).

Instead of issuing methodical directives, consider engaging the client in a collaborative manner to address the problem from a perspective that is suitable to the client. This offers the client the opportunity to evolve his or her problem-solving skills, contributing to the client's generalizable skill set, sense of independence, and empowerment.

Under certain circumstances, your use of self-disclosure may give the client the impression that your methods are being guided more by subjective personal opinions than by more robust professional standards. For example, suppose a client reveals severe distress in that he or she is not attracted to the opposite sex, and the client's goal is to achieve heterosexual attraction. Further, suppose that you, as the client's social worker, are lesbian, gay, or bisexual, and in your benevolent quest to help this client, you reveal your own sexual orientation and your comfort with it. From there, you go on to explain that efforts to alter one's sexual orientation are essentially futile and that the proper course would be to work along the lines of accepting and ultimately embracing the nature of the client's own, unique sexual attraction. True: This message does in fact concur with social work ethical values and the contemporary (nonpathological) psychological conception of sexual orientation; however, since this information is couched in the form of the clinician's personal anecdote, the client may perceive the message as stilted, biased, or perhaps even an effort to recruit.

Depending on the theoretical orientation to which you subscribe, your use of self-disclosure may corrupt the communication pathway with respect to transference. Transference involves the client, perhaps unintentionally, super-imposing (*transferring*) his or her emotions for a significant person (e.g., parent, authority figure, spouse, sibling, friend) onto you, the neutral clinician (Breuer & Freud, 1955). Such expressions can provide both you and the client access to the client's feelings, thoughts, and nature of his or her relationships with others. If your goal is to facilitate effective transference, you should essentially present as an unbiased blank slate (tabula rasa). Excessive self-disclosure may lead the client to build a distinct, concrete image of who you are, thereby confounding his or her ability to readily *transfer* the emotional cloak of another onto your unique, possibly incompatible frame (Basch, 1980).

Time is also a consideration with respect to self-disclosure. For example, suppose you have a standing 50-minute weekly appointment with a client. These are the *client's* 50 minutes, not *yours*. In essence, each minute that you spend talking about yourself is a minute taken away from the client. Should you indulge in frequent or lengthy self-disclosure, the client may resent that you are con-suming his or her time and money by talking about yourself. Additionally, in all humility, it is important to consider that no matter how compelling or helpful you may consider your self-disclosure to be, the client may perceive your story as tedious or even irrelevant; hence, it may be wise to utilize self-disclosure sparingly and keep your message as concise as possible.

There is also the possibility that a client may take advantage of your self-disclosure as a welcome detour, offering a convenient departure from discussing and processing his or her own challenging issues, potentially derailing the focus of the process (Hill, Helms, Speigel, & Tichener, 1988).

It is possible that your well-intended spontaneous discussion of your own emotionally laden issues may trigger an unexpected array of feelings within you (e.g., vulnerability, hurt, anger, confusion), thereby possibly destabilizing you and the overall professional environment (Ulman, 2001).

Self-Disclosures Should Be Honest

Occasionally, you may wish to provide some encouragement or well-founded advice to a client in the form of self-disclosure yet lack a matching experience. As tempting as it may be to fabricate a story or appropriate someone else's story, this is ill advised, as this practice constitutes lying. From an ethical standpoint, misleading the client or misrepresenting yourself, even if your intentions are good, is a violation of the standards of the social work (or any professional) relationship (National Association of Social Workers, 1996).

Deceptions that begin small have the potential of snowballing over time (Peck, 1998). In order for a lie to stand as plausible, it must typically be presented within an environment of supplemental lies that support the initial false assertion. For example, suppose a client mentions that he or she drives a public bus for a living, and recent routing changes have made the job more stressful. Then, with no such experience in your own history, you falsely state that as a former bus driver yourself, you understand just how stressful that job can be. Having opened this door of (false) self-disclosure, it is not so easily shut. The client may engage you in discussions wherein you may be called upon to provide further reasonable details regarding your bus-driving experience. You may find yourself in a position wherein you will need to spontaneously conjure up further fake remembrances, which may include the name of the bus line, supervisors' names, coworkers' names, city and routing characteristics, the type(s) of busses you drove, stories regarding memorable passengers and incidents, licensing requirements, salary range, or dates of training and employment. Not only must these lies be spontaneously created and performed plausibly in real time, but you would also be responsible for memorizing your falsehoods to facilitate continuity for future discussion, which may require further bogus elaboration. In terms of complications, it can be challenging to assemble a set of facts that would sound plausible to someone who actually *is* an experienced bus driver. You would also be risking such things as timeline conflicts (e.g., How could you have been a bus driver in Eastville during the years when your diploma says that you were at Western University?). There are also any number of ways that the client may discover inaccuracies in your story through simple outside research, such as contacting your old bus company. Fabrication and maintaining a system of lies is a poor use of your cognitive capabilities as it detracts from the attention that you can pay to the client's real issues. Moreover, lying compromises the quality of the foundation of any professional relationship—trust.

A better approach would be to openly admit that you have no such experience and ask the client to provide you with details regarding the rigors of being a bus driver. This adaptation has many advantages: It is honest. It enables the client the opportunity to articulate and process the facts and feelings that are troublesome. It provides you with an opportunity to do what you need to do to be helpful—to focus on listening attentively in order to better understand the client.

Self-Disclosure Guidelines

Despite the array of advantages and disadvantages related to clinical self-disclosure, there are no universal rules. As such, the following guidelines are proposed as a framework when considering using self-disclosure in your professional settings:

1. ***Assess how comfortable you feel disclosing this particular piece of information.*** No matter how useful you believe your self-disclosure might be in serving the client, the higher order of business is how *you* feel about it. If you feel that such a disclosure could compromise your sense of comfort, dignity, professionalism, or safety, you are entitled to withhold such information. Self-disclosure is merely one of many means by which you may help clients—if self-disclosure is not right for you, you will undoubtedly find another way to be helpful. In your service as a social worker, you are not required to sacrifice your sense of privacy. You are entitled to keep your personal life personal.

2. *Reflect on how beneficial this self-disclosure would be to the client.* Your self-disclosure should be geared toward providing something meaningful to the client and should not be used as a vehicle for serving your own needs (Evans, Hearn, Uhlemann, & Ivey, 1993). Prior to embarking on such disclosures, take a moment to reflect on your motivation: Is your primary goal to add something facilitative to the session on the client's behalf, or might you be seeking an opportunity to process your own feelings, thoughts, or experiences? Venting and processing are natural parts of the human social experience, but consider the wisdom of sharing your experiences with your client as opposed to others in your life.

3. *Keep self-disclosures genuine.* Self-disclosures should be honest. Avoid borrowing, inflating, or inventing stories.

4. *Consider using self-disclosures sparingly.* Self-disclosures should be purposeful, concise, focused, and pertinent to the client's situation. Try to avoid engaging in supplemental storytelling, wherein one story leads to another. Return focus to the client promptly. Your job is to be there for the client, not vice versa.

As with other aspects of the process, it is your responsibility to decide on the extent to which you will choose to disclose aspects of yourself in your mission to benefit clients, while taking into account that such disclosures are completely voluntary on your behalf. Some of the factors that may guide your decision to self-disclose include your comfort with the subject matter, your personal perspective (e.g., sense of privacy, values, belief systems, feelings), professional factors (e.g., sense of rapport/commonality with the client, setting, facility policies, cultural norms, nature of the client's problem, client's diagnosis, sense of dangerousness), or any number of other relevant ineffable influences.

Determining the appropriate usage of self-disclosure is among the many subjective judgments that you will make in your provision of quality care to clients. Trust yourself to make competent decisions, taking into account the needs of the client yet favoring your own feelings when it comes to considering injecting your personal information into the mix.

CHAPTER 1 EXERCISES

CONCEPT REVIEWS

Explain each concept in your own words. Where applicable, provide a case example without disclosing identifying information.

1.1   Selection (p. 2)

What are some of the criteria that may be used in determining a client's eligibility or ineligibility for care at a social service agency?

1.2   Personal contact (p. 3)

What is the rationale for avoiding dual or multiple relationships with clients?

1.3   Involvement (p. 5)

What advantages do you have with personal friends that you do not have with clients?

1.4   Topic of conversation (p. 6)

What are some of the differences between conversations that you may have with friends and conversations that you would have with clients?

1.5   Advice (p. 7)

Offering advice in casual relationships may vary from the way that advice is administered in a professional setting. What are some of the differences in terms of timing and style of delivery?

1.6   Legal (p. 9)

List some of the laws guiding the practice of social work that a new client might be unaware of.

1.7   Confidentiality (A) (p. 10)

What is needed (from the client) in order to disclose privileged information?

1.8   Confidentiality (B) (p. 10)

Under what circumstances are you legally mandated to break client confidentiality and disclose selected privileged information without the client's consent?

1.9   Documentation (A) (p. 11)

What sort of information should be included in the client's case file?

1.10   Documentation (B) (p. 11)

What is the rationale for maintaining client documentation?

1.11   Scope of practice (p. 12)

How does adhering to one's "scope of practice" serve clients?

1.12   Boundaries (p. 12)

How does maintaining professional boundaries facilitate the professional relationship?

1.13   Time (p. 13)

Compare the difference between how time is managed in your personal relationships and how time is managed with your clients.

1.14   Termination (p. 14)

What are some of the ways in which dealing openly with termination in a progressive fashion (not just in the last session) can be used to facilitate your contact with clients?

1.15   Respect (p. 15)

Briefly give your definition of *respect* and how it can be used to facilitate your professional relationship with clients.

1.16   Positive regard (p. 15)

What is meant by "positive regard," and how might this benefit the client?

1.17   Education (A) (p. 16)

While enrolled in your social work academic program, what are some of the sources of your education?

1.18   Education (B) (p. 16)

List some reasons for continuing to educate yourself beyond graduation.

1.19   Self-disclosure (A) (p. 18)

Compare the differences between *implicit* and *explicit* self-disclosure.

1.20   Self-disclosure (B) (p. 18)

What do you consider appropriate guidelines for regulating self-disclosure (your ideas may differ from those detailed in this text)?

DISCUSSION POINTS

Discuss among your peers how you might handle these circumstances. Document the opinions expressed using a "+" or a "−" to indicate whether you agree or disagree with each opinion.

1.1   Were we meant for each other?

Upon completing your initial assessment, you determine that the client is eligible for services at your facility. The client, who is of a cultural/ethnic background that is unfamiliar to you, asks if you will be his or her social worker.

1.2   Tennis anyone?

The client, having noticed a photo of you on a tennis court, invites you to play this weekend.

1.3   What's mine is yours

Your client has begun bringing food to sessions—more than enough for one person, insisting that you partake and keep the leftovers since he or she is not going directly home. The client has recently made inquiries regarding your favorite foods.

1.4 Confidentially speaking

In the initial session, the client asks, "Hypothetically, if I told you that I was having an affair, could you keep this off the record—no notes—and not tell my spouse or anybody?"

1.5 Time after time

You have a client who repeatedly shows up late for appointments. He or she has started to ask for time extensions on those days.

1.6 I'm one; are you?

The client has expressed concerns that being a single child has affected the way that he or she relates to others. The client makes inquiries regarding your family structure—in particular, how many siblings you have and the nature of your relationships with them.

1.7 I've got a secret

A client states, "I want to tell you something, but you have to swear you won't tell anyone, ever, no matter what."

1.8   Job 1 or job 2?

Your client, who is employed, has recently been offered a different job, but he or she is having trouble deciding which job to select. The client wants you to make the decision "since you are smart."

1.9   Questionable cuisine

A client brings in a menu plan detailing a diet that appears to consist of very poor nutrition and indicates that he or she intends to begin this diet on Monday.

1.10   Client or class?

Three weeks from now, a professional seminar pertaining to your practice specialty is being offered locally; however, it coincides with several appointments.

ROLE-PLAY 1.1 TOO MUCH PRESSURE

Note: Guidelines for role-play implementation, feedback, and documentation can be found in the "Overview of Exercises" section (p. xiii).

Brooke has recently been diagnosed with high blood pressure and is motivated to manage it effectively. Brooke's physician has prescribed appropriate medication and has recommended a stress reduction intervention. Having never been hospitalized or diagnosed with any significant health conditions, Brooke is moderately anxious. Brooke reports having many "acquaintances" and only one supportive friend.

Client

- Ask the social worker to assess your sleeping arrangement at home to see if it looks suitable for rest and relaxation.
- Request that the social worker include aromatherapy in your treatment and offer to provide the fragrances.
- Ask the social worker whether or not you should continue your volunteer work.

Social Worker

- **Involvement** (p. 5)—If Brooke requests you to become involved in contact outside of the clinic, explain that this is inappropriate and discuss alternatives.
- **Scope of practice** (p. 12)—If asked, explain that you are not necessarily against aromatherapy but that you are not trained to provide that service. Discuss alternatives (e.g., Brooke may confer with an outside expert).
- **Advice** (p. 7)—If Brooke requests advice regarding volunteer work, consider discussing the nature of what is involved (e.g., hours, overall negative and positive emotional impact). Encourage Brooke to make an appropriate decision. If necessary, consider discussing the notion of self-determination.

Role-Play 1.1 Self-Evaluation

(1 = needs further work, 5 = excellent)

1	2	3	4	5	Involvement
1	2	3	4	5	Scope of practice
1	2	3	4	5	Advice
1	2	3	4	5	_____
1	2	3	4	5	_____

Role-Play 1.1 Case Notes

_____

_____

_____

_____

_____

_____

_____

_____

_____

_____

_____

_____

_____

_____

_____

_____

_____

_____

_____

_____

_____

_____

_____

ROLE-PLAY 1.2 SOBERING THOUGHTS

Devin has recently been working a lot of overtime, which has the advantage of providing some much-needed extra income; however, the long hours are tiring, leaving little time for leisure activities or contact with family and friends. Devin admits to drinking more than usual in order to manage the stress.

Client

- Discuss your concerns regarding the drinking, but in a guarded fashion.
- Without giving much detail, mention that you have been considering other (less legitimate) ways of earning extra money, but express your hesitation to talk about this.
- Ask the social worker if he or she has ever had a problem with drinking or drugs.

Social Worker

- **Topic of conversation** (p. 6)—Make an effort to assess Devin's drinking (recent and prior), use of other substances, recovery efforts, and possible relapses. If there is resistance, explain your rationale for asking, but ultimately, Devin will decide how much to reveal.
- **Confidentiality** (p. 10)—If Devin seems concerned about you reporting potentially illegal behavior, review the laws and ethics regarding client confidentiality.
- **Self-disclosure** (p. 18)—If Devin makes inquiries regarding your experience with substance or alcohol abuse, you may wish to discuss your professional expertise (if applicable). Consider the advantages and disadvantages of disclosing information regarding your experience with your own addictions or lack thereof.

Role-Play 1.2 Self-Evaluation

(1 = needs further work, 5 = excellent)

1	2	3	4	5	Topic of conversation
1	2	3	4	5	Confidentiality
1	2	3	4	5	Self-disclosure
1	2	3	4	5	_____
1	2	3	4	5	_____

Role-Play 1.2 Case Notes

ROLE-PLAY 1.3 NEW IN TOWN

Lane recently moved to this area and has been having considerable trouble finding work, friendships, and appropriate social outlets. Lane is starting to lose hope, which is leading to isolation and excessive daytime sleeping.

Client

- For your next appointment, request the last appointment of the day so that, afterward, the social worker can take you on a tour of the town—offer to buy dinner.
- Since you have lots of free time, ask for 2-hour or daily sessions. You might state that money is not an issue.
- Present as moderately hard on yourself for being unemployed, having no friends, being uncertain about how to resolve things, and so on.

Social Worker

- **Personal contact** (p. 3)—If Lane requests contact beyond the scheduled appointment, tactfully explain that ethical principles and agency policies preclude this. Discuss alternatives that may more appropriately fulfill the client's desire for socialization.
- **Time** (p. 13)—Should Lane ask for more than one 50-minute session per week, explain the agency's policy (e.g., sessions are 50 minutes, a maximum of two sessions per week).
- **Positive regard** (p. 15)—Gather information about Lane and point out things that you find genuinely admirable (e.g., courage to move to a new place alone, prior successes, motivation to seek help, positive personality characteristics).

Role-Play 1.3 Self-Evaluation

(1 = needs further work, 5 = excellent)

1	2	3	4	5	Personal contact
1	2	3	4	5	Time
1	2	3	4	5	Positive regard
1	2	3	4	5	_____
1	2	3	4	5	_____

Role-Play 1.3 Case Notes

PART II

Mutual Understanding

2

Fundamentals of Communication

This chapter provides an introduction to the basic skills for communicating effectively with clients both cognitively and emotionally. For a more comprehensive array of such skills, please refer to the text *Therapeutic Communication: Developing Professional Skills* (Knapp, 2007).

Principles

Fostering Sensitive Disclosure

Unlike casual conversations, which may vary substantially in depth, complexity of the story, or sensitivity of the issues at hand, the realm of the professional social worker is an environment of client self-examination and processing problems, which may involve potentially sensitive or embarrassing details of the client's personal life. As such, it is important to recognize that simply expecting clients to provide truthful and thorough disclosures to you—a stranger/authority figure—is not enough. You, as the social worker, need to do your share in creating an environment that is conducive to the client making such disclosures.

Researchers have assembled models representing the processes that individuals use when responding to questions (Cannell, Miller, & Oksenberg, 1981; Tourangeau & Rasinski, 1988). One such four-step model may be useful in helping you understand the factors that may lead a client to disclose, distort, or withhold details:

1. Comprehension—understanding the instruction or question

2. Retrieval—accessing pertinent memories

3. Judgment—assembling the retrieved memories in a meaningful order

4. Response—delivering an apt reply

Although this process appears logical, other (emotional) mediating factors may short-circuit this model, particularly when it comes to inquiries involving potentially sensitive topics (Tourangeau, Rips, & Rasinski, 2000). For example, if a client perceives a question as an invasion of privacy, he or she may leap from Step 1 (comprehension) directly to Step 4 (response), intentionally providing a deceptive reply.

In terms of gathering accurate and thorough responses, the sensitivity of the questions may mediate the amount and type of responses that are provided. For example, asking someone about his or her favorite breakfast food is a fairly mundane question whose answer you would expect to be forthcoming and honest; asking about a person's favorite sexual activity, however, is considerably more sensitive, so one might expect hesitation, refusal to respond, or possible deception.

Evaluation of the sensitivity of a question and how such inquiries will be dealt with are mediated by (a) social desirability, (b) sense of privacy, and (c) concerns of disclosure to third parties:

(a) Social desirability is "the tendency of people to say or do things that will make them or their reference group look good" (Rubin & Babbie, 1993, p. 156). People have concerns about being negatively judged. A client may feel embarrassed to provide honest disclosures wherein he or she risks revealing such things as unpopular beliefs, odd habits, and uncommon tastes or desires, hence leading him or her to substitute with more commonplace responses.

(b) The client's sense of privacy may influence responses involving issues that depart from everyday discussion (e.g., religion, financial information, sex, legal issues, certain bodily functions). Although a client may not feel ashamed of his or her answer, the question itself may be perceived as intrusive. For example, a client may be proud of his or her financial standing; however, asking how much cash the client has in the bank or on his or her person may be sensed as an unwelcome invasion of privacy (Willis, 1997).

(c) A client may fear consequences should his or her disclosures be revealed to third parties not directly related to his or her care (e.g., legal authorities, employer/coworkers, family, community). Accordingly, a client may selectively withhold or sanitize disclosures based on his or her sense of (mis)trust (Couper, Singer, & Kulka, 1998; Singer, Mathiowetz, & Couper, 1993).

Taking these factors into account, it is clear that, even as a trustworthy and well-intended social worker, it would be presumptuous to reason, "I'm a professional, so you can just tell me the truth." As such, the question remains: "How much truth can I expect clients to disclose?" A large predictor in answering this question involves the nature of the rapport that is built between you and your client. In a nutshell, the client's level of disclosure is regulated by the client's sense of safety. A client who feels comfortable will likely reveal more honestly than a client who feels fearful. Figure 2.1 presents this notion graphically, as the fear/honesty teeter-totter.

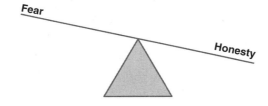

Figure 2.1   The Fear/Honesty Teeter-Totter

In this model, the client's level of fear (inversely) controls the client's level of honesty. To demonstrate this concept, consider this relatively extreme example: Suppose Mel serves Sandy a piece of cake and, holding her at gunpoint, asks, "What do you think of my new recipe?" Referring to the fear/honesty teeter-totter model, Mel's use of a life-threatening weapon brings Sandy's fear to its maximum level (fear of losing one's life), thereby pushing honesty to a minimum. Sandy has no choice but to deliver an affirming response: "This is the most delicious cake I've ever eaten!" Conversely, suppose Mel had approached Sandy with no weapon and politely said, "I've been experimenting with this recipe—I'm not sure if it's there yet. You've got a good sense for these things. Could you taste this and tell me what you think?" Obviously, using this more neutral approach, the fear/honesty teeter-totter tips the other way: Fear would be low; hence, honesty would ride higher. As a result, Sandy would offer a more genuine reply, which may involve some constructive criticisms.

To reify the notion of fear mediating honesty, take a moment to consider this brief back-solving exercise: Think of the last time that you lied. This may have been an explicit lie, wherein you said something that you knew was dishonest or only partly true, or it may have been an implicit lie, wherein you had an opinion but deliberately chose to say nothing. Now reflect on the *fear* that motivated your deception. This fear likely consisted of you trying to avoid loss, hurting yourself, or hurting another. Think in terms of "I was afraid that . . . , so I . . ." (e.g., "**I was afraid that** my friend's feelings might be hurt, **so I** said her outfit looked nice," "**I was afraid that** I might have to work on Saturday, **so I** told my boss I'd be out of town"). Essentially, people alter the truth in order to reduce the risk of experiencing or causing hurt or loss.

Consider this brief example involving a client's sensitive disclosure:

Cl: *I don't know exactly why, but I've been wanting to do this for a long time: See, I've had this cowboy hat for years, and well, nobody was home. Anyway, there's a full-length mirror in the bathroom, so I locked the door, and I finally got to see what I look like wearing the cowboy hat . . . only.*

Sw_1:   *So, what other bizarre stuff do you do in the bathroom?*

This social worker's judgmental reaction communicates to the client that pursuing this line of discussion will be an emotionally costly, uphill endeavor and that, in the future, the client really needs to watch what he or she says. Reflecting on the fear/honesty teeter-totter, this social worker's judgmental reaction would likely instill a sense of fear in the client, thereby reducing the level of truth that the client would disclose. Concerned about having to incur further negativity, the client may react by abandoning this topic and shifting to or inventing a more mundane issue that would be less likely to elicit a negative reaction.

At this point, it can be difficult to know the client's true purpose in raising such an issue: The client may genuinely want to discuss this naked-with-the-cowboy-hat story in further detail. Alternatively, it is possible that the client may have been using this story, genuine or not, as a means of testing the waters to see the social worker's reaction. Based on this social worker's judgmental reaction, the client may resist disclosing further sensitive information, which may or may not involve issues of nudity or sex.

When the client feels fearful, there is the risk that he or she may edit or withhold his or her disclosure. Each time this happens, something genuine and potentially valuable is lost, thereby compromising the content and direction of the encounter.

Alternatively, think about the client's potential reaction had the social worker responded differently:

Sw₂: [Smiles warmly] *So you finally had the opportunity to safely make the leap from fantasy to reality. Every cowboy hat has a story. What was it like for you?*

This social worker's more open reply carries no negative or judgmental reaction, essentially communicating, "This all sounds normal to me. I'd like to hear more about this." This more accepting reply further suggests that the client need not be as fearful when considering raising further sensitive issues. Reflecting back on the fear/honesty teeter-totter, as fear falls, honesty has the chance to more fully emerge. The more honest the disclosure, the better the chance for you and the client to identify and address the genuine issues in need of attention.

Your efforts toward facilitating a professional yet comfortable setting are a beneficial service to all—and, in particular, to those whose race, culture, or ethnicity differ from your own. Specifically, per the history of African Americans, which includes such adversities as slavery, racism, and discrimination, some such individuals may present with an appropriate *healthy cultural paranoia* (Ho, 1992; Smith, 1981). Similarly, Native Americans, with their history of being maltreated and deceived, may initially feel hesitant in fully trusting a Caucasian social worker (Barcus, 2003).

As diligent as you may be in presenting a genuine accepting attitude toward clients, understand that the client is the other side of the rapport equation. The client may have his or her own time frame for establishing trust and feeling comfortable with you. During this time, a client may (rightly) regulate the boundaries of his or her conversation, producing a middle-of-the-road effect, wherein the client dodges both insignificant and highly sensitive topics (Farber, 2003). In such cases, you may express appropriate curiosity regarding potentially more substantial issues, but your willingness to work effectively with what the client is prepared to discuss can be inherently beneficial. Time and quality of the relationship are key factors in building the professional relationship. Comfort cannot be rushed, so try to be patient. The duration and strength of the alliance between you and your client contributes to his or her willingness to engage in the disclosure process (Farber & Hall, 2002).

Rapport

One can think of rapport as the nature of the contact between the social worker and the client—how you engage with each other. A practical definition of *rapport* is the feeling of relationship (Hayes & Stratton, 2003). The nature of the rapport can be the difference between a harsh relationship, wherein the client may withhold sensitive information for fear of being (emotionally) punished, and a warmer, safer, more accepting setting, wherein the client can be confident that his or her disclosures will be met with appropriate professional engagement that is conducive to (further) disclosing and processing of sensitive topics (Mahoney, 1991).

Alliance between you and your client, which is facilitated by rapport, consists of three interdependent factors: (1) setting goals (Step II—Goal), (2) designating the tasks that the client and you will perform (Steps III and IV—Objectives and Activation), and (3) professional attachment (Steps I–V) (Bordin, 1979). Rapport and alliance are not just a matter of making friendly professional contact. Research has revealed a positive correlation between the quality of the client–social worker alliance and the client's outcomes and goal achievement (Horvath & Symonds, 1991).

Rapport is not something that is built once. As a key characteristic of the dynamic professional relationship, rapport is a matter of ongoing concern beginning with your initial presentation. In telephone contacts, clients will attend to audio factors, such as the quality of your voice and background sounds, as well as other elements, including your professionalism (e.g., courtesy, sense of organization/efficiency, patience, demeanor, responses to questions). If your initial contact is in person, additional visual factors, such as your appearance, eye contact, and general physical presentation, may also be taken into account. Presuming a self-confident but not authoritative stance should enable you to make an appropriate professional impression.

It is not uncommon to be concerned that initial impressions may also be influenced by differences between you and the client in terms of race, ethnicity, or other cultural factors. The universalistic hypothesis states that your ability to provide quality care is more a matter of cultural sensitivity and understanding than an actual match to the client's race and ethnicity (Baker, 1988; Tharp, 1991). Your familiarity with various cultural characteristics, practices, and belief systems can help you form an adaptation that is appropriate to the client's unique social attributes; however, nobody expects you to know everything. This does not necessarily mean that you should refuse to provide services to a client based on the differences in your backgrounds. For example, suppose a potential client is a Native American, and with the exception of some "book knowledge," you have not had much experience dealing with members of that group. You may consider stating this openly and respectfully in the initial session, indicating your willingness to provide service while enjoying the privilege of coming to know the client's ways. In such cases, early in the process, you may respectfully request an overview of some of the client's core values and beliefs, as well as ask that he or she point out any errors or omissions that you may unintentionally make throughout the course of providing care (Richardson, 1981). This practice principle can help you build rapport with members of other diverse populations while expanding your professional versatility.

As important as rapport is in promoting the professional relationship, your role is not merely to sit by, mindlessly nodding throughout the course of providing care. As you come to know your clients, you will have thoughts, feelings, recommendations, and questions that may be less than comfortable to air. Does this mean that you should politely hold your tongue in the interest of preserving rapport? No. This means that you should proceed in a purposeful yet respectful manner. There will also be times in which the client expresses beliefs or goals that depart substantially from your way of thinking. In the interest of rapport, does this mean that you are obliged to sit by, smiling, when you feel that you have a relevant question, concern, or opinion to express? Again, no. As a social worker, your role is to fully utilize your education, experience, feelings, and understanding of each case to help the client identify and advance toward accomplishing goals that are significant to him or her, even though, at times, your input may conflict with the client's modality. If your contribution is met with resistance, this is worth discussing, but ultimately, it is important to persistently recognize—and even verbalize to the client—that the decision as to how to proceed or not proceed ultimately rests on the client (National Association of Social Workers, 1996).

Rebuilding Rapport

Even with the best of intentions and education, it is entirely possible that your benevolent efforts may transfer to the client in a less-than-idyllic manner, hence compromising your rapport. This does not necessarily mark the demise of the professional relationship. As in friendships and other social relationships, reparative efforts are appropriate. When you feel that rapport has slipped, it is essential to address it in a prompt and direct manner. This is known as *rebuilding rapport*. The process consists of three straightforward steps:

1. Identify the problem. If the problem is unclear, ask about it.

2. If you have made an error, own it and apologize one time.

3. Solicit the client's feedback and move on.

Sw: *It looks like you've been pretty banged up. What happened to you?*

   (1) Ask about the problem.

Cl: *I don't want to talk about it.*

Sw: *Did your boyfriend hit you?*

Cl: *What? I can't believe you said that! How could you say that? You don't even know him! How dare you judge him like that! Just because we're not getting along doesn't mean he hit me. For your information, I was in a car wreck. Some stupid drunk driver hit me and totaled my car, and that's why I'm all "banged up," and that's also why I was late today—because I had to take the damn bus, so that's what you're looking at here . . . some stupid drunk driver who smashed into me, not my boyfriend! In fact, he's been great through all this. Here's a copy of the accident report . . . see! I can't believe how insensitive you are!*

Sw: *I'm sorry. I didn't mean to accuse your boyfriend. You're right; I don't know much about him. The only reason I asked is that I remember you telling me how violent your father was with you when you were a kid, and sometimes, without meaning to, even bright people can reproduce those sorts of relationships later in life with their own partners. Honestly, seeing your injuries and knowing your history, it just seemed like a relevant question. I hope you understand; I'm only concerned for your safety. I'm actually relieved to know that your boyfriend is helping you through this.*

(2) If you have made an error, own it and apologize for it one time.

Cl: *OK, I get it.* [Pause] *I guess I've heard of stuff like that happening sometimes—people going from one bad relationship to the next—but you've got to know: I'd never hook up with someone who'd hit me . . . ever.*

Sw: *Right. I believe you. I'm glad you wouldn't. Your safety is everything.* [Pause] *How are you feeling right now?*

(3) Solicit the client's feedback and move on.

Cl: *Well, to be honest, my arm and neck still hurt, but between us? Yeah, we're OK.*

Nonjudgmental Attitude

Every individual is endowed with his or her own unique personality, tastes, and preferences. Since it is not possible to simply switch off your perspective, it is important to recognize that you are perceiving each client and his or her circumstances through your own particular "life lens." As such, it is important to monitor your own potential biases. Ideally, the professional realm should be as free as possible of judgmental attitudes, feelings, reactions, and biased opinions. The principle is to provide an implicitly accepting stance with respect to the client's characteristics, including such attributes as age, race, gender, sexual orientation, ideology, religious/spiritual beliefs, intellect, and socioeconomic status (National Association of Social Workers, 1996).

Through your contact with clients, you may encounter cultural practices or belief systems that are unfamiliar to you. Occasionally, such customs may seem unreasonable or implausible to your way of thinking. Nevertheless, it is essential to honor the significance that clients assign to them. For example, some Latinos may assert that mental or emotional disorders are attributable to evil spirits or witchcraft, for which they may confer with a folk healer for (supplemental) help. In the interest of serving your clients, as well as promoting your own professional growth, try to keep an open mind. Set your personal judgments aside long enough to accommodate cultural or spiritual elements that may be foreign to you but are relevant to the client (Martinez, 1986).

Maintaining an open and nonjudgmental attitude also serves to help you assemble a more accurate image of the client and his or her problems, strengths, resources, and potential solutions, as opposed to relying exclusively on your less-informed presumptions. Also bear in mind that issues raised in the professional setting may differ from topics raised in casual conversations. The subject matter that you process with clients is likely to involve challenging feelings (e.g., hurt, guilt, anxiety) related to the problem(s) at hand. As a result, the last thing the client needs is for you to put more weight on those harsh feelings by expressing negative judgments (Ivey, 1983).

Persistently presenting with a genuine nonjudgmental attitude may be more of a challenge for some than others. Even for the most accepting person, there may be circumstances that are not conducive to engaging in an effective professional relationship. For example, regardless of your qualifications and professional attitude, an elderly client may not trust the wisdom of a young social worker. In such a case, you would be within your right to respectfully acknowledge the client's concerns as valid but also to provide the client with an overview of your education, experience, and willingness to work with him or her. If, ultimately, the client chooses not to work with you, that is his or her privilege. Depending on the agency's policy, the client may be offered an alternate social worker or appropriate referrals to receive care at a different facility.

In reality, maintaining a nonjudgmental attitude may not be plausible in all circumstances. Consider a case wherein a client who strongly embraces the beliefs and practices of a hate group is paired with a minority social worker. Unlike the previous example characterized by a unilateral sense of discomfort on the client's behalf, this case presents the potential for mutual resistance. Though this pairing would undoubtedly be mutually uncomfortable in the beginning, such a combination could potentially provide an opportunity for the social worker to challenge the client's prejudice attitudes. Nevertheless, with the exception of certain compulsory treatment arrangements, the client would rightly be afforded the privilege to refuse to work with this social worker.

Skills

Listening

Your efforts should be designed and implemented in such a way as to help clients advance toward improving the quality of their lives. With this in mind, consider your position in relation to the client's. In terms of knowing the landscape of the client's life, the client has seniority over you. The client should be viewed as an expert witness to the history, current status, and desired direction of his or her life and, as such, should be considered an authority on the subject of his or her life. As a result, the most powerful tool that you can hope to master is the ability to listen and try to understand the client.

As a temporary guest in the client's life, your entry point is somewhere in the middle of the client's story; hence, it is your job to start where the client is. Make what is important to him or her important to you. Your receptiveness, curiosity, and attentiveness will help you comprehend the client's history, draw meaningful links between people and events in the client's life, and better understand the client's emotional and cognitive perspective.

As enticing as it may be to expediently embark on problem solving, make an effort to resist the temptation to jump in too fast. Just as a tailor must take multiple measurements before endeavoring to build a custom-fitted suit, the solutions that you propose will be useful only if they are tailored to the multidimensional biopsychosocial (biological, psychological, and sociological) characteristics that uniquely form each client's life. Advice that pays no heed to the client's unique circumstances and ways of doing things is likely to be as useless as an ill-fitting suit, constructed using no measurements taken from the intended wearer. Advice that is incompatible to the individual is seldom followed. These "measurements" are taken by listening attentively and learning about the client through cogent communication using the fundamental skills detailed in this chapter.

Matching

Each person has his or her own style of communication. With respect to speech, some of the parameters that can vary from person to person are wordiness, level of detail, precision of language, vocabulary, and concrete or abstract expressions, along with the auditory characteristics of the voice: loud or soft, fast or slow, articulate or slurred, and so on. In addition to listening to the client's meaning, pay attention to the *way* the client communicates, and make an effort to meet the client on his or her linguistic ground.

For example, a client who speaks using a scholarly vocabulary and thoughtful analogies would likely respond well to your appropriate expression of sophisticated verbal engagement. Conversely, a client whose communication style consists of simple but well-assembled words, conveying concrete notions, would likely feel uncomfortable, confused, or intimidated should your messages contain arcane language or polysyllabic words. With a little thought, any complex concept can be expressed in simpler terms. Without sacrificing meaning or "dumbing down" concepts, do what you can to tune your use of language to approximate the level and style of the client.

To exemplify this point, consider this mismatched interaction:

Cl: *I get scared so easily. Like two nights ago, I woke up totally terrified because I heard this awful sound. Later, in the morning, it turned out that the wind had just blown down a planter outside, but at night, the sound really scared the hell out of me, and my heart started racing, and when stuff like that happens . . . well, I hate that it takes me forever to get back to sleep!*

Sw₁: *It sounds as if spontaneous nocturnal auditory anomalies trigger an amplified startle response within you, accelerating your metabolic processes, thereby inhibiting your ability to promptly resume your slumberous cycle. You find these circumstances personally unsatisfactory and unsettling.*

Clearly, this social worker's grasp of the client's message is accurate; however, the use of scientific language could be sensed as distant, impersonal, or even intimidating. This sort of mismatched communication could potentially compromise the rapport. Additionally, the unnecessary use of elaborate language can make it difficult for the client to follow and comprehend—it is hard to pay attention to something that you do not understand. Considering this social worker's style of communication, the client may reasonably hesitate to discuss sensitive personal issues. Who would want to hear his or her deeply emotional problem reduced to such cold scientific jargon?

Alternatively, consider this response:

Sw_2: *Nighttime sounds can catch anyone off guard. It sounds like you're looking for a way to feel a little more relaxed, especially at night.*

This message effectively communicates the social worker's comprehension of the client in a manner that more seamlessly matches the client's style of communication. This more compatible mode of dialogue implies that the client need not alter or upgrade his or her communication style in any way—the client is free to speak in a spontaneous, unedited fashion. Building an environment that is conducive to such genuine disclosures, including the freedom to speak naturally, serves to advance the disclosure process. Remember: Each time a client edits his or her message, something genuine is liable to be lost, thereby confounding your ability to understand and ultimately provide targeted services to the client.

As with many communication skills, when it comes to matching, no single approach is universally applicable to all clients. A study involving medical patients (Swenson, et al., 2004) showed that most of the patients preferred a patient-centered style of communication wherein their physician demonstrates a genuine personal interest in them, as opposed to a clinical style of communication that focuses predominately on the medical aspects of the case. Conversely, older patients tended to prefer the opposite. Just as there is no single communication style that suits all medical patients, each client should be assessed on an individual basis and addressed in a manner that uniquely suits him or her.

Probing

As a social worker, your mission is to help. In order to help, you must try to understand the client. Whenever you need to gather more information or you do not understand, it is time to ask a question.

Close-Ended Questions

Close-ended questions are requests for a specific, typically brief response, such as yes, no, or a number (e.g., "Are you a student?" "Do you have a valid driver's license?" "How old are you?" "Do you smoke?"). The advantage of close-ended questions is that they can be useful for concisely getting an answer to an objective question. The disadvantage of such questions is that the client's responses may lack subjective details that may have provided additional useful information.

Despite the fairly objective nature of close-ended questions and the usually brief responses associated with such questions, some valuable subjective details may be gathered depending on *how* those brief answers or nonverbal responses are delivered. For example, suppose you ask, "Are you pregnant?" and the client replies, "Yes." The manner in which the "Yes" is delivered may be revealing. An enthusiastic "Yes" is very different from a soft-spoken, tearful "Yes." Listen beyond the text. Even in a single-syllable response, great detail may be conveyed if you are open to it.

Open-Ended Questions

In terms of gathering subjective details, open-ended questions reach beyond the realm of the yes and no responses characteristic of close-ended questions, implicitly allowing for the inclusion of subjective details (e.g., "How are things going at home?" "What was it like growing up in a town of 852 people?" "You mentioned that you were on the radio for a while—tell me a little about that"). The responses to such questions may include richly detailed storytelling, elaboration, or an array of feelings, or the client's response may provide an unexpected bridge to another relevant topic. Open-ended questions can offer you the opportunity to know the client more deeply.

Semantically, notice that not all open-ended questions need to be phrased so as to end in a question mark. An open-ended question may be submitted as a respectful request for more information or elaboration on a point (e.g., "You mentioned that you were on the radio for a while—tell me a little about that").

To better illustrate the contrast between close-ended and open-ended questions, consider Table 2.1, detailing both forms of the same question.

Table 2.1   Close-Ended Versus Open-Ended Questions

Close-Ended Questions	**Open-Ended Questions**
Did you go home after work?	*What did you do after work?*
Are you on any medications?	*What drugs do you use?*
Are you employed?	*What sort of work do you do?*
Are you depressed?	*How are you feeling?*
Do you have a brother?	*Tell me about your siblings.*

Suppose you had asked a client the first close-ended question on this list ("Did you go home after work?"), and the client replied, "No." The continued use of close-ended questions could expectedly start to sound like a tedious guessing game:

Sw₁: *Did you go home after work?*

Cl: *No.*

Sw₁: *Did you go bowling?*

Cl: *No.*

Sw₁: *Did you take a walk?*

Cl: *No.*

Alternatively, consider how this dialogue might be different just by converting the close-ended question "Did you go home after work?" into an open-ended version of the same question: "What did you do after work?"

Sw₂: *What did you do after work?*

Cl: *Well, since I got off work a bit early, I decided it was time to roll down the windows and go for a nice, long drive. I called my best buddy, and we met for dinner at that greasy little burger shack at Pico and Sepulveda. We talked and laughed so hard; we nearly got thrown out of the place! It's like my whole life went from neutral to high-gear in under an hour . . . and on a Wednesday! So, I figure, why wait till Saturday to enjoy life? Anyway, we decided we need to make this a weekly thing—for next week, we're going to invite the whole crew!*

Clearly, the open-ended version of the question rendered richer details that could not have been derived from any lengthy combination of close-ended questions.

Both open- and close-ended questions have their place in the interviewing process. Your selection of open- or close-ended questions should be guided by the nature of the information that you need to gather. As a rule of thumb, when you are seeking a concrete, succinct (*yes* or *no*) response, a close-ended question will likely serve you well (e.g., "Are you thinking of hurting yourself?" "Did someone hit you?" "How long have you been sober?"). More often, though, open-ended questions are preferred, as they allow for deeper factual and emotional elaboration. If you find yourself often resorting to close-ended questions, prior to verbalizing your next close-ended question you may wish to take a moment to compose an open-ended adaptation of the same question. If you feel it is appropriate, consider using the open-ended version of the question.

Despite your efforts to use open-ended questions, the client may still provide brief (one-word) responses. If this persists and you feel that you need some further details, you may wish to make a more explicit request for elaboration.

Open-Ended Requests

Open-ended requests are similar to open-ended questions, as they both open the door to soliciting further details. An open-ended request involves phrasing a question so as to suggest that there is *more* information for the client to reveal, as opposed to *none*. Consider this first example, which fails to use an open-ended request:

Cl: *Even though I'm grounded, I stopped by Ponty's Grill on the way home for a quick bite.*

Sw₁: *And then you went right home?*

Close-ended request

Cl: *Uh huh.*

Perhaps in an effort to present a supportive attitude, the social worker's reply ("And then you went right home?") suggests to the client that there is a right answer here—that the client *did,* in fact, go home after stopping at Ponty's. This social worker may have unintentionally missed an important opportunity: Since the client had already admitted to bending his or her grounding penalty, perhaps the social worker should have been a bit more curious, seeking what *other* liberties the client may have taken. In this second example, the social worker uses an open-ended request as opposed to providing a convenient "offramp":

Cl: *Even though I'm grounded, I stopped by Ponty's Grill on the way home for a quick bite.*

Sw_2:   [Friendly voice tone] *What else did you do before you got home?*

Open-ended request

Cl: *Well, after Ponty's, I met up with Clay and Clarisse. My parents hate them just because of how they dress—they're so narrow-minded! Anyway, Clay loaned me his cell phone so at least we can talk after the parent monsters are tucked safely into bed at 9:00. Anyway, after Ponty's, we headed down our favorite alley—there's this gourmet French bakery that throws away tons of perfectly good food, all boxed and bagged about once a week. . . .*

In this example, it becomes clear that by simply shifting from a close-ended request ("And then you went right home?") to the open-ended counterpart ("What else did you do before you got home?"), a wealth of details are revealed, involving information as to what happened before the client headed home. Additionally, further clues related to the nature of the client's norms, values, resourcefulness, attitude toward (possibly unfair) authority figures, friends, socialization, family relations, and sense of fun are seamlessly revealed.

Naturally, not all such inquiries will lead to such richly revealing disclosures. The client's elaborate truthful reply to this open-ended request may have been more limited (e.g., "Just Ponty's, and then I went home"). As a rule of thumb, consider forming questions that open the door to *more* information and feelings rather than *less.*

Ask One Question at a Time

Occasionally, in your enthusiasm to understand the client, more than one question may come to mind at a time. While it is OK to assemble a provisional sequence of questions, try not to ask questions in a combined fashion. Compound questions, also known as "double-barreled" or "stacked" questions, consist of two or more distinct questions bundled into what seems like one inquiry, to which it can be tough to respond:

Cl: *I'm working two jobs.*

Sw_1:   *What jobs, and how many hours?*

Although this social worker has asked a compound question, the client may not sense that two different *types* of questions have been combined: The first question ("What jobs [do you work]?") requires a subjective textual response, whereas the second question ("How many hours [do you work]?") is asking for an objective numeric response. In an effort to be cooperative, the client may make a futile attempt to assemble a single, all-encompassing response to the two related but very different types of questions.

Another less subtle form of compound questioning consists of multiple discrete questions delivered back-to-back in a single volley:

Cl: *I grew up in a military family, so when I was a kid, we moved around a
         lot.*

Sw$_2$: *Did you have trouble making friends? Were you close with your siblings?
         Did you ever live out of the country, and if so, what was it like?*

Though none of the social worker's questions is out of line, submitting multiple questions simultaneously is inefficient in that it unnecessarily taxes the client in a number of ways: The client must begin by trying to figure out which question he or she ought to answer first—the first question? The last question? The most important question? The easiest question? While responding, the client must inefficiently expend some cognitive energy to maintain a mental list of the other question(s), which can subtract from his or her ability to deliver the answer at hand. Persistently pitching compound questions at a client may unintentionally cause him or her to feel like the subject of an intimidating inquiry as opposed to being afforded all the respect that clients are due.

Should multiple questions occur to you at once, ask what you consider to be the most relevant (single) question, and let the client's response guide your next question or comment. You can always ask follow-up questions, one at a time.

Verifying

As a social worker, your ability to provide properly targeted aid is mediated by the extent to which you understand the client. Misconceptions or confusion may emerge from a variety of sources, such as the client's use of ambiguous or unfamiliar words or expressions, partial or distorted information, skipped parts of a story, or disorganized or vague presentations. There are a variety of skills for verifying and correcting your perception of the client's story and conditions: (a) clarification, (b) reflection/paraphrasing, (c) summarizing, (d) generalizing, and (e) identifying and resolving discrepancies.

Clarification

Clarification should be a fairly familiar skill that you have likely used in a variety of social and academic settings. Clarification involves requesting further details to help you better understand vague, confusing, or disjointed storytelling.

Though at first it may feel like an exercise in humility to admit that you do not understand, keep in mind that you cannot effectively help if you do not understand the client's story. Never pretend to understand when you do not. Consider adopting the following position: "I'm here to understand. When I don't understand, I need to ask a question." A gap in your comprehension may involve the client's use of a word, an expression, a phrase, or syntax (the sequence of the words in a sentence) that is unique to a particular cultural background (Wilkinson & Spurlock, 1986).

If it is not immediately clear from the context precisely what the client means, request clarification promptly.

Cl: *I have this new supervisor at work. Such a schmendrick!*

Sw: *Schmendrick? How do you mean?*

The term "schmendrick" is unfamiliar to the social worker. At this point, there is not enough context to discern the client's impression of this supervisor, so before the client advances any further, the social worker asks.

Cl: *He's a jerk! He stands next to me and watches me work and asks the stupidest questions: "What's this? What's that? How do you do this?" There's nothing worse than having a new supervisor who has no idea how the business works and what I do—and this guy is supposed to supervise me? As if I'm supposed to be able to go to him for answers. Schmendrick!*

Sw: *OK, I get it now.*

Clarification can also be used when the client's storytelling has taken a leap that loses you (e.g., the client skips from A to B to D). If this happens, identify the nature of your confusion and tactfully request appropriate details (e.g., "Just a moment; I'm a little lost here: OK, I understand that first A happened, which led to B, but I'm not getting how we got from B to D.").

Remember: Your primary goal is to *try to understand.* Whenever you feel that your understanding is starting to slip or if you want to gather deeper, more detailed information about something, you need to rescind your ego and tactfully ask questions until you *do* understand.

Reflection/Paraphrasing

Reflection, sometimes referred to as *paraphrasing,* entails using your own words to play back your understanding of the client's message in a provisional manner, essentially implying, "This is what I'm understanding; am I right?" Reflection, used in a progressive fashion, serves multiple purposes: It demonstrates that you are attentively taking in the client's story and provides an opportunity for the client to offer corrections along the way. Reflection may also prompt the client to provide further details regarding a particular point. Additionally, it offers the client the chance to hear what he or she is telling you and to reflect on the content of his or her story. Reflection may also be used as a means of requesting further details on a point that may have been discussed in a prompt or seemingly superficial manner.

Although at times you may reiterate the client's words verbatim to emphasize a particular point, persistently using this "parroting" form of reflection can begin to sound repetitive and thoughtless. Instead, consider presenting a concise restatement of the client's words in a provisional manner, wherein your understanding of the client's statement is subject to the client's validation.

Cl: *I ended up spending half of my vacation in the hospital.*

Sw: *You were in the hospital for a week?*

Cl: *Two weeks! And the food there stinks!*

The client corrects the social worker's time misconception.

Sw: *You couldn't eat the food?*

Cl: *The food stinks . . . literally. I couldn't eat anything—they had me on this I.V. nutrition thing, but three times a day, when they brought the meal trays by, it smelled disgusting!*

Again, the client provides the social worker with more detailed corrective information.

Sw: *So no eating for 2 weeks?*

Cl: *I'm just glad it's over and I didn't get one of those awful hospital infections that you always hear about. I'm so relieved that the X-ray cleared.*

The absence of corrective comments suggests that the social worker's reflection was on target.

Sw: *The X-ray cleared?*

The social worker uses reflection to prompt for further details regarding the X-ray.

Cl: *Yeah, no more bowel obstruction—and no surgery! Everything's working now.*

In retrospect, it may seem as if this dialogue got off to a bumpy start, as the client provided repeated corrections to the social worker's statements. Instead of thinking of this as a communication fumble, this dialogue should be regarded as exceptional. Each time the client offered corrective information, the social worker gained access to critical supplemental information, thereby painting a more accurate picture of the client's actual condition.

Summarizing

Whereas reflecting involves submitting your understanding of one or several sentences, subject to the client for validation or correction, summarizing enables you to do the same thing for larger blocks of the client's story.

Since the client holds the first-person perspective on his or her story, the client should be considered the expert. As with reflection, make an effort to phrase your summarizations speculatively as opposed to authoritatively, as if you are implying, "It sounds like this is what happened; am I right?" Additionally, your summarization enables the client to hear the content of his or her story played back from another source, potentially providing an additional perspective on the same information.

Cl: *Last week, while I was shopping, this guy came up to me and just started talking to me. He knew my name, where I grew up, where I went to school, all about my family, what the inside of my old house used to look like. Not only didn't I recognize him, but when he told me his name, I still had absolutely no idea who this guy was. It was bizarre.*

Sw: *So this stranger, who knew your whole history, really caught you off-guard?*

The social worker assembles a few words to represent the content of the story thus far.

Cl: *Right. It was spooky. So then he starts rattling off this list of places that I've worked, where I went to school, cities I've lived, favorite foods, favorite music, and so on. I mean, he was friendly enough, but now I'm starting to get scared.*

The client explicitly confirms the social worker's summary and elaborates further.

Sw: *It sounds like he really threw you with all this personal information.*

The social worker summarizes the client's feelings related to the events of the story.

Cl: *Well, it turns out he was friends with my cousin, who he met up with about a year ago at a class reunion. Apparently, he'd been over to our house a few times for family holiday occasions, and it turns out he had a crush on me. Of course, since he is 2 years older than me, we never had any classes together and never really talked. Anyway, now, after more than 10 years, he actually asked me out.*

Sw: *It seems like you made quite an impression to be remembered in such detail.*

The social worker continues the summary, citing facts and feelings.

Summarizing is a versatile skill that can be used to address your perception of the facts and feelings embedded in the client's story. Summarizing can be particularly useful when working to follow a storyline that becomes complicated or otherwise hard to follow (e.g., extensive or sparse details, multiple characters, shifting timelines). If you find yourself becoming lost or confused, consider respectfully pausing the client's storytelling, summarize your comprehension up to that point, and then continue to summarize incrementally as the client resumes the storytelling.

Generalizing

Generalizing involves identifying and articulating patterns or trends in the client's life. Such patterns may involve the client's actions, inactions, emotions, thoughts, or recurring events in the client's life. Your objectivity may provide you with a unique perspective, enabling you to recognize patterns that may have eluded the client due to multiple confounding factors (e.g., being emotionally involved in the event, the chronological remoteness of such events, other dissimilarities). Even a difference in venues may mask a potentially insightful generalization. For example, a client may consider instances in his or her home life separate from instances in his or her work life, when, in fact, repeating themes common to both domains may become apparent to you.

Although possible, assembling generalizations would typically not happen early in the process. Certainly, a generalization may be based on elements drawn from a single session, but more often, you may find yourself reflecting on meaningful fragments spanning several sessions. Typically, you need to know enough of the client's history in order to identify trends or repeating themes in the client's life.

Astute generalizations may be useful in tuning the clinical process. Correlating a pattern of symptoms or problems may suggest meaningful adaptations with respect to building or modifying the treatment plan. Further, generalizations may point toward an overarching problem, thereby suggesting a worthy goal.

When looking for generalizations, be aware that not all patterns are dysfunctional or pathological. Consider seeking recurring patterns characterizing positive coping, resilience, effective problem solving, leadership, levelheadedness, adaptability, and so on. Citing positive generalizations can encourage forward progress, engender hope, and be useful in building effective strategies based on what has worked in the past (e.g., "You seem to have a reputation for finishing what you start," "It sounds like people have come to depend on you when it comes to XYZ").

Consider using the following guidelines when proposing generalizations:

Be Specific. Generalizations that provide specific, concrete details are more effective than vague statements or broad assertions. Proclaiming, "You are just late all the time!" lacks a supportive basis; hence, it is easily refutable. Consider the impact of using a more detailed approach (e.g., "I remember you mentioning that you missed an important enrollment date and then had to settle for some second-rate choices. You also talked about having problems in your relationship—being late for dates—and the conflicts that you've had with your supervisor, about not having your figures ready for the Friday morning meetings. It seems like there's something of a pattern here"). Citing specific instances provides support for more robust generalizations. Additionally, specificity helps keep your efforts focused on the client's actual conduct, as opposed to making it seem as if you are merely pitching a barrage of unfounded criticisms.

Use Tentative Language. Try to avoid the use of such words as *always* and *never.* Since you do not have access to the client's comprehensive life record, you are not truly qualified to use such words, and as a result, the client may likely cite one exception, defensively refuting your assertion. Additionally, the use of extreme language could inappropriately suggest that the client's condition is permanent—that the client has *always* been this way and *always* will be. Social work is about facilitating change. The use of such extreme language is counterproductive in that it implicitly denies the client's potential malleability. Instead, an approach that uses more tentative phrasing can be more accurate, and using such words and phrases as *typically, usually, tend to, sounds like, seem like,* and *there's a history of* carry less of an authoritative stance. Remember: The nature of a generalization is to suggest the presence of what seems to be a pattern, subject to the client's consideration, as opposed to making unilateral (accusatory) declarations.

Avoid Accusations. While it would be wrong to water down or neglect discussing the client's propensity to think or behave in a manner that is conducive to negative outcomes, there are ways of effectively discussing such patterns without assigning blame to the client. For example, "You just can't get anything to happen on time" has an accusatory tone, whereas "It sounds like you want to meet deadlines, but it seems like something gets in the way" delivers this message positively without sacrificing the meaning. As opposed to the first statement, which would likely be met with a defensive reaction, the second approach opens the door to concretely discussing the specific confounds that the client has encountered, which could ultimately lead to constructively building appropriate problem-solving strategies.

Encourage Exploration and Elaboration. Bearing in mind that the client knows more about his or her life than you do, engage the client to reflect on related incidents. Help the client think broadly over time for matching experiences that may or may not have been discussed yet. Such active engagement may help the client see the depth and breadth of a problem and that addressing this issue may benefit a number of other circumstances. Such insights may serve as a motivation to change, whereby embarking on resolving the problem of being late could have a positive multiplier effect, potentially resolving a number of problems in a variety of seemingly unassociated domains, such as work, school, family life, or social life.

Discuss History. In the interest of gathering details of additional similar events, encourage the client to discuss his or her history (e.g., "When was the last time you did XYZ?" "When was the first time you did XYZ?" "Can you remember other times when you resorted to doing XYZ?"). Through such inquiry, you may find that some antecedent event causes a particular behavior (e.g., "ABC seems to be a trigger for you doing XYZ"). In such cases, you may consider discussing ways to avoid or minimize ABC, learning to interpret ABC in a different way, coming up with an alternate way of coping when ABC happens, and so on.

Relate Finding to Goals. Whenever possible, link your generalizations to the client's goals in a meaningful way. Generalizations may provide guidance in shaping the treatment plan or goals. For instance, it may be revealed, through thoughtful generalizations, that the client's lateness is due to the client saying yes to other people's requests too often. This propensity to overcommit may suggest a meaningful addendum to the treatment plan. A new (sub)goal may involve helping the client build his or her "no" muscles through some form of assertiveness training or self-esteem building in order to promote the priority of his or her own projects ahead of others'.

Cl: *I'm feeling kind of stressed—my boss has been hinting that I haven't been on time for a while. Anyway, she said that the next time I'm more than 15 minutes late, she'll have to write me up.*

Sw: *I remember you mentioning how hard it's been getting to work on time. This makes me think of a few other things we've talked about: your son's anger at you for being an hour late to his school play, your Tuesday night bowling team—how they make you buy the snacks for being late and holding up the play—the conflicts that you've had with your landlord about not getting the rent check in on time. I'm just wondering if there might be something that links these together.*

Discuss related specific incidents using tentative language and a positive attitude.

Cl: *So you're saying I'm irresponsible?*

The client has taken a defensive stance. It's time to clarify the reasons for providing this "laundry list of lateness."

Sw: *Actually, I think you're a very responsible person. An irresponsible person wouldn't be stressed about these sorts of things—he or she just wouldn't care. I'm just wondering if there might be something drawing these things together. Can you think of a time in your life when being late wasn't much of an issue—a time when you were more punctual?*

Avoid accusations. Encourage exploration and elaboration.

Cl: *Well . . . I'd say this all started about 2 years ago.*

Sw: *What was going on 2 years ago?*

Follow the client's lead—discuss history.

Cl: *Me and my family—we were living on the other coast. It's just that it's so different here—the climate, the people, the way traffic moves, the way the roads are laid out . . . I guess after all this time, I'm still not used to it. Actually, I really kind of hate it.*

The client provides valuable contextual (perhaps causal) details.

Sw: *You know, I think we're on to something here. Let's think about this for a bit. I'm thinking we should spend some time talking about how you feel about being on this coast. We might also come up with some adaptations to your travel stress too.*

Relate findings to the client's goals.

When administered thoughtfully, generalizations may reveal patterns that may be stemming from a common (problematic) source.

Identifying and Resolving Discrepancies

Throughout the course of the client's discourse, conflicting information may emerge. This is not exclusively attributable to the client intentionally lying. Any number of circumstances may lead to inconsistencies. For example, the client may have intentionally or unintentionally omitted or understated some information; alternatively, the client may have used a word or an expression in an unclear or ambiguous manner.

Other sources of potential discrepancies lie within you: Considering the vastness of the emotional and factual communication exchanges endemic in their contact with clients, even the most skillful social workers may forget selected details of the client's story. This can happen regardless of how thorough your case notes are and how often you refer to them. It is also possible that you may have misconstrued part of the client's story as it was being conveyed; hence, future related storylines may seem inconsistent with your memory.

Inconsistent or conflicting information may take a variety of forms:

Factual Conflicts: "I remember you telling me that you had no children, and now you're telling me about how you celebrated your son's birthday."

Timeline Conflicts: "I'm remembering that during your teen years, you lived in a rural community, but now you're telling me that you went to high school in an urban setting."

Action Conflicts: "You mentioned that you wanted to shorten your work commute, but now you've applied for a job that's farther away."

Emotional Conflicts: "I'm noticing that whenever you talk about how much you love your sister, you clench your fists and your voice sounds stressed."

Thought Conflicts: "You've told me a lot about how bad it gets when you live with someone, and now you're talking about bringing in a roommate."

Discrepancies left unresolved can become the source of confusion, frustration, and possibly misguided efforts. When you identify inconsistencies or conflicts in the client's story, it is important to identify them and make an effort to engage the client in resolving them in a nonaccusatory, nonjudgmental fashion.

Consider the following guidelines for addressing such instances:

Be Specific. As when proposing effective generalizations, make an effort to phrase your questions regarding conflicts as specifically as possible. You may cite or paraphrase quotes or summarize relevant segments of dialogue, pointing out one discrepancy at a time. A simple tool for citing such incongruities is the "You said . . . , but . . ." method (e.g., "***You said*** you were independently wealthy, ***but*** now I'm hearing that you're having trouble affording groceries") (Hackney & Cormier, 2000). In cases where more than one conflict emerges at a time, select the one that you consider the most significant and address it first—its resolution may serve to resolve other discrepancies. Additionally, inundating the client with multiple discrepancies simultaneously may bring about confusion, embarrassment, anger, or frustration on the client's behalf.

Encourage Exploration/Elaboration. Upon presenting conflicting information to the client for clarification, provide him or her with a reasonable opportunity to respond. Further details, explanations, or clarifications may resolve the issue.

Try to remain open to the possibility that the client did not intentionally lie or mislead you.

Avoid Accusations. As stated earlier, not all conflicting information that emerges is necessarily attributable to the client lying. In cases where the client's expressions seem inconsistent or implausible, you need not be meek. The purpose of identifying discrepancies is not to punish the client; rather, you are seeking to advance to a clearer, more accurate understanding between you and the client. Keep in mind: Your overarching mission is to try to understand. As objectively as possible, without blaming the client, state your observations in an open manner, as if to say, "This is how I'm understanding this. I'm not sure I'm fully clear on it, though. Could you help me understand it better?"

Present Confrontations Tentatively. At times it can be difficult to be certain if the source of the discrepancy is the client—in the form of intentionally or unintentionally omitting, distorting, or fabricating information—or if you are failing to comprehend or fully recall essential details. As a result, it is important to use phrasing that suggests, "This is how the information appears to me" as opposed to "You said XYZ, and that can't be right!" Phrase your confrontations so that you are open to the possibility that this discrepancy may resolve with the proper explanation. Certainly, there is the possibility that the client will admit to having lied, but try not to make that your sole assumption.

Solicit the Client's Discussion. Openly inviting the client to discuss the nature of the conflict provides the client with the opportunity to offer supplemental information that may serve to resolve seemingly inconsistent or implausible information. Alternatively, the client may use this as an opportunity to retract prior statements in favor of more genuine information and perhaps engage in discussion as to what initially motivated him or her to provide less-than-honest disclosure(s).

Cl: *Two days ago, I got to see my kids again. They're so great.*

Sw: *You got to see your kids? I remember you telling me that you didn't have any children.*

The client's discussion of seeing his or her kids is in conflict with a prior statement. As a result, the social worker identifies the conflicting information.

Cl: *Of course. Yes, I did say that. See, I don't have any kids of my own, but I'm a godparent to my best friend's kids, and since they have just their father . . . well, over the years, they've just kind of come to think of me as a parent who just doesn't live with them. I mean, that's just how we all think about it. It's all good—and they love me too.*

The client clarifies the godparenting role, thereby resolving the conflicting semantics.

Sw: *I get it. OK, that makes sense now.*

The social worker's statement implies gratitude to the client for clarifying the situation as opposed to chastising the client for failing to use more precise language (kids/godkids).

In other instances, the client may be placed in a situation wherein a previous lie is no longer compatible with other information that has emerged through the process:

Cl: *I'm a little worried . . . I think I might have picked up an STD.*

Sw: *A sexually transmitted disease? I'm not sure I understand—I'm remembering you telling me that you haven't had sex in over a year.*

The social worker points out the implausibility of the client's statement.

Cl: *Yeah, well . . . not at home . . . see, I've been having an affair.*

The client corrects a prior lie (of omission) and reveals more information.

Sw: *Oh, OK. We can talk about this. I think we should also talk about getting you to a physician.*

Cl: *Yeah. I don't know why I didn't tell you before.*

The client may have been fearing a negative reaction from the social worker, or the client may have been afraid that the information would be leaked to the spouse.

Sw: *It's OK. These sorts of things aren't always that easy to discuss at first. I'm glad you're telling me now. Maybe you're feeling a little more comfortable here.*

Notice that the social worker integrates the client's revelation into the conversation in a nonpunitive manner, as opposed to saying or implying, "I got you! See what happens when you lie to me?" Conversely, the social worker implicitly normalizes the client's corrective disclosure and thanks the client for providing this more accurate information. The social worker's open attitude essentially communicates an array of constructive messages: "I'm not upset that you lied; in fact, I'm grateful that you found the courage to discuss this more honestly, despite your discomfort. Maybe you're coming to trust our relationship more. Maybe you're feeling more comfortable talking about these sorts of things. You know, if you want, you're always welcome to go back and correct anything else we've talked about—we don't punish here." Though implied, it may be warranted to actually articulate part(s) of this message aloud.

As your contact with each client advances, rapport and feelings of trust will hopefully follow. Ideally, clients will, in their own time, come to know that you do not have a judgmental or otherwise punitive attitude. As the client's sense of comfort increases, he or she may find it necessary to correct information given earlier. Your persistent open and nonjudgmental attitude can help facilitate this evolving process.

Directing

As important as it is to provide the client with the opportunity to proceed through his or her storytelling in a continuous manner, it is equally important to recognize the need for providing direction. Whereas social conversations have the freedom to drift from topic to topic in an unfettered manner, it is important to be able to recognize significant departures from purposeful topics and be prepared to guide the dialogue back to more meaningful tracks. Two skills that can be used to provide (re)direction are *focusing* and *specificity*.

Focusing

As your contact with the client advances, expect one idea to naturally lead to another related idea, feeling, or memory. Additionally, people have more than one thing going on in their lives at a time—circumstances in one aspect of the client's life can naturally overlap into others. For example, a client may raise issues regarding contention with an authority figure, such as a supervisor at work, which may also lead him or her to discuss similar stressful relationships outside of work (e.g., home, recreation, other authority figures). While such discussions can serve to provide valuable contextual information regarding the issues at hand, it is also possible that such tangential storytelling may diverge to the point that it derails the process.

Despite your potential wishes to embark on resolving multiple problems simultaneously, since each circumstance is unique the better strategy is to identify and hone down the number of topics raised and to focus on one issue at a time. Clients report more improvement on issues that are the focus of clinical efforts than on those that are not (Blizinsky & Reid, 1980). One way to conceptualize this is that *the effectiveness of your intervention is inversely proportional to the number of topics being discussed.* In other words, the more topics that are raised, the less depth each one can have. As more and more topics are included, the more divergent ideas and feelings are likely to be present, which can result in randomly shifting from one half-baked topic to another, essentially disorganizing the intervention process.

In instances wherein more than one topic emerges at once, share your recognition of this with the client and solicit the client to select which topic he or she wishes to process first. In order to maximize the effectiveness of the client's session, you might help guide the client toward prioritizing and selecting substantial issues.

Cl: *This last weekend, my old roommate, who was clean and sober for about a year, stopped by my place totally drunk and wants to move back in. Sure, I need a roommate, but I don't know—this sort of just isn't the time for something like this. I don't know if I want to go through that all over again. Plus, there's been talk about layoffs at work, and on top of all that, my computer's been acting up, and now my résumé's a mess!*

Item 1: Relapsed roommate returned

Item 2: Layoff threat

Item 3: Computer trouble

Item 4: Résumé needs work

Sw: *You've got a lot going on. Just to summarize: Your roommate's relapsed and wants to return, you might be facing a layoff, your PC's unstable, and your résumé is corrupted. Which one would you like us to address first?*

The social worker recaps the client's issues and requests that the client select the first one to process.

Cl: *[Sighs] I guess my ex-roommate is the main thing, really. You know, last time around, that just sucked up so much of my life. I swore I'd never go through that again. I mean, I'd feel awful about turning my back on a friend, but I just can't go down that road again. Last time, I nearly lost everything.*

Sw: *It sounds like you've pretty much made up your mind on what needs to happen here.*

Cl: *Yeah . . . It's not easy, but I guess I just need to do it.*

Sw: *We can talk about this.*

Cl: *And as for my computer and screwed-up résumé, I'm thinking of calling my cousin—she's great with that stuff. Feed her some chocolate, and she'll fix anything!*

Despite your efforts to guide the client to address (more) substantial issues, the client may, nonetheless, opt for alternate topics. Certainly, you can voice your rationale for how you are prioritizing the multiple topics; however, ultimately, it is the client's choice as to what will and will not be discussed and in what order.

You need not be passive when it comes to helping the client select topics to focus on. Referring to the prior dialogue, one technique that you might consider using is to enumerate the issues mentioned and prompt the client to select the most relevant topic (e.g., "I want you to try something. Go back to a time before we were working together. Now, which of these topics might you consider booking an appointment with a social worker to process: A relapsed roommate who wants to return, work stress, or a faltering PC with a mangled résumé?"). Given this context, clearly the computer and associated file recovery stands as the least likely selection to pursue with a social worker.

Another technique to help clients identify and select substantial issues involves recapping the list of problems and then asking something along the lines of "If you had a genie who could grant only one wish, which one problem would you want to see fixed, permanently?" or "If you could just push a button and make one problem go away forever, which one would you choose?" Presumably, the client will want to get the most out of this one magical opportunity, thereby thoughtfully promoting the most substantial issue to the top of the list.

Specificity

Your efforts, as a social worker, are meant to facilitate meaningful changes in the client's life. This involves actively working toward assessing the client's circumstances (Step I), and from there, appropriate goals (Step II) and objectives (Step III) can be combined and activated (Step IV). In order to meaningfully initiate this process, both you and the client must be able to precisely identify the issue(s) that will become the focus of the change efforts.

To conceive the importance of specificity in more concrete terms, imagine that you are an auto mechanic. Which work order would you prefer to receive?

Work order A	Work order B
Car's all screwed up.	*When cold, as car is accelerating, low-pitched repetitive slapping noise is heard under the hood on the driver's side. Also, dashboard lights dim.*

The vagueness of work order A makes it virtually impossible to speculate as to the nature of the problem; hence, the efforts and resources required to affect repairs would be equally elusive. In fact, reparative work cannot reasonably begin until (much) more information regarding what is and is not working is gathered. Conversely, work order B provides valuable multidimensional information detailing the specific nature of the problem (e.g., thermal conditions, velocity, type and orientation of the problematic sound, dashboard lighting affected), thereby better directing your reparative efforts.

Vagueness on the client's behalf can make it equally difficult to assemble and implement meaningful treatment plans. When the client's expressions seem imprecise, unclear, or otherwise confusing, it is essential to solicit specificity.

Cl: *My life is such a mess!*

Though this statement conveys the client's sense of dissatisfaction, it does not suggest the nature of the problem(s).

Sw: *What are some of the things that are making your life so messy?*

This messy life might consist of any number of things (e.g., one or several problems, feeling overwhelmed, instability, general sense of disorganization, confusion). The social worker appropriately requests that the client elaborate on what constitutes this "mess."

Cl: *Oh, well, my doctor said my cholesterol is too high, so I'm supposed to be on this diet, but really, the foods that I like just aren't there. I mean, how am I supposed to get by with nothing good to eat? Having a good meal is one of the few pleasures I have in life—how am I supposed to just give all that up? Sometimes I feel like I just want to go shopping so I don't have to think about it, but I just got out of debt, so I know that's wrong . . . it all just stinks.*

The client has appropriately moved from a vague but genuine expression to articulating four distinct but interrelated problems involving high cholesterol, dietary noncompliance, emotional distress, and the temptation to spend unnecessarily.

Whereas little can be done to constructively work with a vaguely stated problem ("My life is such a mess!"), through the social worker's prompting the client is able to provide more specific information. This can lead to exploring the relative weights, relationships, and priorities among these problems. From there, it becomes possible to move forward in a more meaningful fashion.

Emotional Aspects

Emotional Language

The text thus far has focused primarily on skills for effectively processing content consisting of mostly factual verbal exchanges. As essential as it is to comprehend the *facts* of the client's story, the *emotional* track that runs parallel to the facts is equally important.

When placed within a limited context, the emotional meaning of a word can be unclear, as in the following succinct example:

Sw: *How are you doing today?*

Cl: *Fine.*

Though the client responded, "Fine," in the absence of knowing the context of this word it can be difficult to interpret the client's emotional meaning. Additionally, without the benefit of observing the client's visual cues (e.g., facial expression, eye contact, posture, body language, gestures) or vocal characteristics (e.g., volume, tone, intensity, inflection), it can be difficult to know if the client means he or she is "fine" in a genuine sense or, conversely, if the client is speaking sarcastically, implying that he or she is absolutely not "fine." Since the meaning of an emotional word can be so strongly influenced by the manner in which it is expressed, arranging such a list of words by magnitude is not plausible; hence, the feelings adjectives presented in Table 2.2 are simply arranged alphabetically within each group.

Awareness of such groups of words can help you facilitate your comprehension of the client's emotional track. For instance, suppose a client expresses that he or she feels "stuck" and provides no further details. Referring to the feelings table, *stuck* is a synonym for *frustration*. Frustration is experienced when a goal is delayed or encumbered. Hence, you may form a question that addresses the source feeling (frustration) (e.g., "You say you're feeling stuck. I'm wondering if you might be frustrated—as if something or someone might be in your way"). Such a question could naturally lead the way to deeper exploration of relevant facts and feelings, as well as the change(s) that the client hopes to achieve.

Table 2.2 is divided into two sections: positive feelings and negative feelings.

The positive feelings are arranged into two categories: strength and happiness.

Strength. Feelings related to personal surety, solidity, and certainty.

Happiness. Feeling satisfied that one's needs and desires are being met.

The negative feelings are divided into five groups: frustration, anger, depression, anxiety, and guilt.

Frustration. Frustration is felt when one is unable to gratify a desire or satisfy an urge or a need. In other words, when one is blocked from achieving a goal or otherwise fulfilling his or her wishes, the resulting feeling is frustration (Sutherland, 1996).

Psychiatrist David Viscott (1976) offers a useful framework for comprehending a continuum of negative feelings—anger, depression, anxiety, and guilt—as a function of how one processes, or fails to process, hurt and loss.

Anger. Anger is the expected emotional reaction to hurt, loss, or disappointment. Expressions of anger can take many forms, ranging from a slight sense of irritability to a burst of physical violence. Depending on the client's culture, belief system, or personality attributes, anger may not be so obvious to detect. Some consider expressions of anger primitive or socially inappropriate, suggesting that a loss of composure is in bad taste. Others may resist openly expressing their anger for fear of appearing harsh, weak, out of control, vulnerable, unlovable, or undeserving of respect. Some people may attempt to suppress their anger out of fear of what others may think of them or how others may treat them.

Depression. Depression is anger (due to hurt or loss) that the client fails to process. Depressed clients are fearful of what might happen if they express their anger; therefore, they keep it inside. In terms of emotional energy dynamics, depressed people must spend an equal amount of (positive) energy to quell the volume of unprocessed hurt (anger) that they store within themselves; hence, they have less energy available to conduct their daily lives. As a result, depressed people present as having low energy. They tire easily, move slowly, give up early, and lack the stamina to try hard or to try again.

Sadness is not depression. Whereas depression involves rerouting hurts so that they are banked *within*, sadness involves an appropriate *outward* expression of loss or hurt. Stated another way, depression is an *interruption* in the expression of negative feelings, and sadness is the appropriate *flow* of hurt feelings. The advantage of sadness over depression is that, in sadness, the outward expression of a negative experience allows for the feeling to be vented and processed, enabling the person to soon return to a normal level of functioning. Conversely, in depression, such feelings are not directly expressed. Instead, they are stored within and pooled with other unresolved hurtful feelings in a cumulative fashion, adding to the overall weight of the depression and corresponding energy depletion.

Anxiety. Anxiety is caused by anticipating hurt or loss in the future. Anxious clients feel as if their safety or well-being is at risk—as if something bad is going to happen to them at some point in the future. The more substantial the anticipated hurt or loss is estimated to be, the higher the anxiety.

Table 2.2   Feelings List

Positive Feelings

Strength: *Feeling positive about oneself and circumstances*
Aggressive, Attracted, Capable, Certain, Charged, Competent, Confident, Determined, Durable, Energetic, Forceful, Hopeful, In charge, Independent, Motivated, Powerful, Proud, Safe, Secure, Solid, Super, Sure, Tough, Trusting

Happiness: *Feeling that one's needs and desires are being met*
Accepted, Affectionate, Amused, Belonging, Calm, Cheerful, Clear, Comfortable, Complete, Composed, Content, Delighted, Ecstatic, Elated, Excited, Exhilarated, Exuberant, Fantastic, Fine, Free, Fun, Glad, Good, Great, Hopeful, Joyous, Loving, Overjoyed, Peaceful, Playful, Pleased, Positive, Proud, Ready, Refreshed, Relaxed, Relieved, Respected, Rested, Safe, Satisfied, Secure, Thrilled, Together, Up, Warm, Wonderful

Negative Feelings

Frustration: *Feeling that a goal is delayed or encumbered*
Baffled, Bewildered, Blocked, Bothered, Confused, Disorganized, Disoriented, Displaced, Divided, Foggy, Impatient, Insecure, Lost, Misplaced, Mixed up, Perplexed, Puzzled, Split, Stuck, Torn, Trapped, Troubled, Uncertain, Unclear, Undecided, Unsure, Weird

Anger: *Initial reaction to hurt, loss, or disappointment*
Aggravated, Aggressive, Agitated, Annoyed, Betrayed, Defensive, Disappointed, Disgusted, Dismayed, Enraged, Fed up, Fuming, Furious, Hateful, Incensed, Inconvenienced, Irate, Irritated, Jealous, Mad, Mean, Nervous, Outraged, Put out, Put upon, Repulsed, Resentful, Sick of, Spiteful, Strained, Suspicious, Tense, Tired of, Upset, Uptight, Vengeful

Depression: *Anger that is trapped or held in*
Abandoned, Apathetic, Bad, Beaten, Blah, Blue, Bored, Crushed, Defeated, Dependent, Desperate, Disappointed, Discontent, Dissatisfied, Distressed, Down, Drained, Exhausted, Grief-stricken, Heartbroken, Helpless, Hopeless, Hurt, Ignored, Incapable, Inferior, Lazy, Left out, Lifeless, Listless, Lonely, Lost, Low, Miserable, Numb, Overwhelmed, Rejected, Rotten, Run-down, Sad, Shaky, Sick, Sleepy, Sorrowful, Tired, Trapped, Troubled, Uncomfortable, Unhappy, Unwanted, Upset, Useless, Vulnerable, Worthless

Anxiety: *Feeling that hurt or loss is looming*
Afraid, Apprehensive, Cautious, Concerned, Distraught, Dreading, Edgy, Fearful, Frightened, Horrified, Hysterical, Insecure, Jittery, Miserable, Nervous, Panicky, Pensive, Petrified, Reluctant, Scared, Shaken, Shocked, Shy, Tense, Terrified, Threatened, Timid, Uncertain, Uncomfortable, Uneasy, Unsettled, Unsure, Uptight, Worried

Guilt: *Feeling a discrepancy between how one is and what one conceives as acceptable*
Embarrassed, Humiliated, Regretful, Remorseful, Shameful, Sorrowful

---

Guilt. Guilt is caused by the belief that something about oneself is unacceptable. Believing that one's actions, inactions, thoughts, impulses, or feelings are wrong induces feelings of guilt. In quantitative terms, the magnitude of the guilt is the discrepancy between what one *conceives* as right and how one *actually* is. For example, consider a client who strongly believes that his or her proper weight should be 150 pounds (about 68 kilograms); as his or her actual weight departs from that idealized target, guilt increases.

One's sense of guilt may be based on the client's personal set of standards, or it may be imposed by a perceived authority figure. Guilt leads an individual to believe that he or she is bad in some way and deserves to be punished. The client may resort to punishing him- or herself, or the client may behave in such a way as to induce others to administer punishments. The most common source of client guilt involves feeling that he or she has done something harmful to him- or herself or another.

Guilt is not always easy to detect. Clients who feel guilty may avoid discussing related issues, fearing that such open discussion may confirm that they are, in fact, bad.

Empathy is the preferred skill for effectively acknowledging and working with the spectrum of emotions that arise throughout the course of contact with clients.

Empathy

Just as skills, such as *summarizing* and *reflection/paraphrasing,* are useful in tracking the *facts* of the client's story, empathy is used to follow the *feelings* that the client is expressing.

The term *empathy* comes from the German word *einfühlen*, whose literal translation is "grasp," meaning "to feel." More specifically, the notion of empathy means not only seeing the world through the client's eyes but also making an effort to perceive the client's feelings from his or her point of view (Basch, 1988).

Whereas skills like *summarizing* and *reflection/paraphrasing* involve providing the client with your perception of the *facts* that he or she is presenting, subject to his or her confirmation or correction, appropriate use of empathy involves communicating your impression of the client's *feelings/emotions* from his or her standpoint, subject to his or her confirmation or correction (Bohart & Greenberg, 1997).

Effective use of empathy has been shown to facilitate the clinical relationship, helping bridge gaps between clients and clinicians from different ethnicities (Carkhuff & Berenson, 1977; Traux & Mitchell, 1971). Empathetic communication has also been shown to reduce clients' premature termination (Bohart, Elliott, Greenberg, & Watson, 2002).

Regardless of how objective and professionally detached you are as a social worker, it is entirely possible that some elements of a client's story may move you emotionally. Other times, you may find yourself understanding the client's plight and comprehending the client's facts and feelings, but you may not necessarily feel much emotionally. You need not feel compelled to attempt to conjure up a copy of the client's feeling within yourself in order to respond empathetically. Just as summarizing and reflection/paraphrasing are not about telling *your* story, empathy is not about conveying *your* feelings, per se. Empathy involves acknowledging your perception of how the *client* is feeling in a provisional manner.

Empathy is different from sympathy. Sympathy involves pitying the client in accordance with hurt feelings or harsh circumstances. Though initially this may seem appropriate, sympathy is limited in that it only focuses on negative feelings, whereas empathy is more versatile. Empathy can be used to address a great array of emotions (e.g., "It looks like you're feeling a bit low today," "This is the most excited I've ever seen you"). Sympathy, which focuses exclusively on the client's hurt feelings, may unintentionally serve to intensify the client's negative feelings, thereby potentially worsening his or her emotional condition.

Alternatively, empathy (provisionally) acknowledges the client's (positive and negative) feelings and opens the door to further processing of the issues at hand (Egan, 1994).

Observe the following dialogue example, wherein the social worker responds using sympathy:

Cl: *My grandmother passed away last night.*

Sw₁: *Oh, that's so sad. The poor lady. How awful. You must feel terrible.*

        Sympathy

Upon initial read, the social worker's sympathetic response seems warm and goodhearted; however, closer inspection reveals that this response carries an array of potentially faulty messages:

1. *Oh, that's so sad.* This statement naively assigns a singular feeling to the situation as a whole. It is possible that the client may have more than one feeling at this time, which may or may not include sadness (e.g., loss, confusion, numbness, disbelief, relief, exhaustion). Additionally, the blanket statement "That's so sad" assigns a singular universal feeling to the experience—implying that the client and all others involved (e.g., family, friends) are or should be experiencing only one emotion: sadness. This narrow assignment ignores the diverse and dynamic system of feelings that can naturally flow and vary within and between individuals, especially in times of loss.

2. *The poor lady.* This statement inappropriately shifts the clinical focus from the client to the deceased grandmother. With all due respect to the client's deceased grandmother, the session is meant to be about the client and his or her experiences and feelings, not the grandmother. Additionally, at this point we do not have enough information regarding the grandmother in order to know if referring to her as "the poor lady" is appropriate—she may have enjoyed a beautiful, long life filled with loving people and intriguing experiences; hence, this statement may inappropriately conflict with the client's image of his or her grandmother. Further, this statement fails to take into account the client's spiritual belief system regarding his or her conception of death—whereas some conceive death as an end to existence, others see death as a transition to another form of being.

3. *How awful.* Narrowly defining the grandmother's death as awful ignores a variety of other viable means of conceiving death: Perhaps the client sees the grandmother as having had all the years that she was supposed to have and that it was a gift that she died peacefully in her sleep. Alternatively, the grandmother may have been suffering from a progressive cognitive decline or a debilitating/painful disease process. As such, death may be viewed as a welcome relief from such suffering.

4. *You must feel terrible.* This statement presumptuously assigns a specific (negative) feeling, which may not reflect the client's actual feeling(s) at this time. The client may be experiencing any number of feelings that are not *terrible,* such as anger, frustration, denial, disbelief, confusion, numbness, or satisfaction. Assigning a feeling may serve to emotionally confuse the client or

unintentionally induce a sense of guilt—for example, a client who may be feeling relieved that his or her grandmother's suffering is finally over may now be cued to feel guilty that he or she is not feeling bad (enough) per the word of the social worker, a perceived mental health expert.

Consider this variation wherein the social worker responds empathetically:

Cl: *My grandmother passed away last night.*

Sw$_2$:   *Yeah. I could see that you seemed kind of down when you came in today.*
        Empathy

In this example, appropriate compassion is expressed without resorting to pity. This social worker's statement indicates his or her perception of the client's emotional state, demonstrating acute attentiveness to the client's feelings. It is clear that the client's feelings have not gone unnoticed, and the social worker will presumably proceed in an appropriately sensitive fashion.

Notice that this statement includes "I could see." In accordance with the principle of delivering effective empathetic messages, you are talking about how *you* are perceiving the client's emotional state, subject to his or her feedback. This is the heart of what empathy is—expressing *your* perception of the client's feelings at this time. "You seemed" is also a useful component in this delivery. This phrasing indicates that this is your provisional understanding of the client's emotional state, whereas using more definitive language, such as "You are," authoritatively assigns a feeling to the client (e.g., "You are sad today"). Delivering empathetic expressions in a speculative manner demonstrates that you are perceiving the client's feelings, subject to his or her acceptance, correction, or elaboration. Just as the client should be considered an authority with regard to the facts of his or her story, the client should also be considered the most qualified person to provide details regarding his or her feelings. Remember: Your goal as a social worker is to understand the client; this includes his or her facts and feelings.

The following dialogue demonstrates some additional uses of empathy:

Cl: [Subdued affect] *My brother and his family are coming into town this week.*

Sw: *You sound a bit down when you talk about your brother.*

        Empathy: The social worker pitches his or her perceived change in the client's emotions as this brother is mentioned.

Cl: *I mean, I love his kids—all of my nephews are just so great, and my sister-in-law—she's so dear—but my brother—he's just hard to be with. He always has been. The stuff he does and says . . .*

Sw: *When you talk about your nephews, I can see how prideful and joyful you look—I also get that you have some warm feelings for your sister-in-law, but when you shift to talking about your brother, your mood seems so much darker.*

Empathy: The social worker notes how the client's feelings seem to shift, depending on the family member being discussed.

Cl: *Yeah, that's kind of how it is. I almost wish I could just spend the weekend taking my nephews around and just enjoy them, but that'll never happen. My brother just needs to control everything and everyone. So many arbitrary rules and regulations, the penalties and the yelling, tons of threats and punishments. There's just never any peace when he's around. Maybe I'll just tell them that I'm busy with work or something. It's just sad. It's like having no family.*

Sw: *It sounds like your harsh feelings for your brother trump your loving feelings for your nephews.*

Empathy: The social worker reflects his or her understanding of the emotional balance that the client has expressed.

When responding empathetically, it is neither required nor appropriate to say, "I know [exactly] how you feel." In order to provide empathetic support, you need not necessarily find or produce a matching feeling within yourself, though at times, this may happen. Additionally, one cannot plausibly state that he or she has the same feeling as another—that one knows (exactly) how another person feels. Even with a seemingly straightforward feeling, such as sadness, there is no way to verify that your sense of sadness is a proper match to the client's in terms of depth, intensity, sense of hopelessness, and so on.

Empathy can be presented in more tangible terms, as in this example involving a physician preparing to examine a patient who appears to have a broken bone:

Dr: *I can see that you're in some pain. I'm going to need to feel for a possible break, but I'm going to do this as gently as I can.*

Like the social worker, this physician need not be experiencing the pain that is normally associated with a broken bone. Perhaps this doctor has never even had a fracture. Nevertheless, awareness and validation of this patient's (physical) pain can provide essential guidance in handling this patient in an appropriately sensitive manner.

Self-Awareness

In addition to your cumulative knowledge of social sciences, you will use yourself as a thinking and feeling instrument in order to comprehend and process the client's conditions. Despite your professional commitment to serve the client in an objective manner, it is unrealistic to think that it is possible to completely switch off your life history and personal perspective when working with clients. As you engage with clients in processing the multiple aspects of their lives, it is reasonable to expect that selected elements of their stories may resonate with various components in your life history.

While it is essential to track the facts and feelings entailed in each client's story, it is equally important to keep tabs on your own emotional awareness, actively monitoring your reactions as to how you are receiving, processing, and responding to clients in light of your own cognitive and emotional point of view.

In order to promote your effectiveness as a social worker, actively tending to your self-awareness may suggest relevant opportunities to advance your own growth, not only as an evolving professional but also as a whole person.

Recognizing Your Perspective

As with any person, you are endowed with a unique set of values, beliefs, thoughts, and feelings, based on a lifetime of experiences. Essentially, you are not an objective being. Through your sense of self-identity, no matter how open-minded you are, there is no denying your own personal perspective: You have a unique set of tastes and preferences. You know what you think is right and wrong. You know what you do and do not believe in. You have your own thoughts and feelings about the world and those in it. You have opinions about how things should be and how various circumstances ought to be handled.

Though it may seem obvious, it is worth pointing out: The only thing you can make a social worker out of is a person. This notion, however, deserves some attention. Endowed with the above attributes that constitute who you are as a person, it is not plausible to presume that all of who you are can or should be left behind when it comes to dealing with clients. It is through your personal experiences as a feeling, thinking human being that meaningful connections are built between you and the client in the form of cognitive and emotional understanding. Your lifetime of experiences enables you to relate meaningfully to the client and his or her condition.

Since you have immediate access to the feelings and events that make up your compendium of experiences, working with clients can, at times, feel like a delicate balancing act—working to keep your personal feelings in check while effectively using your emotional antennae to function in an empathetic manner with clients (Brammer, 1993).

Monitoring Your Feelings

As you engage with clients, naturally you will be focusing on the flow of the client's facts and feelings. It is equally important to devote some fraction of your attention to your own emotional self-awareness. Look for instances wherein you find yourself having strong or unexpected feelings, either positive or negative, before, during, or after your contact with clients. In such instances, it can be useful to ask yourself, as honestly as possible, what might be setting off such strong feelings within you. Some of your reactions may be triggered by countertransference. To explain: Transference occurs when the client super-imposes his or her emotional conception of another in his or her life (e.g., a parent, friend, supervisor) onto you. For example, a client may perceive one or more of your characteristics (e.g., demeanor, attitude, appearance, vocal characteristics, conveyance style, position of authority) as similar to those of someone else in his or her life, such as a parent. From there, the client may *transfer* (a copy of) the emotions that he or she has for that parent onto you and, perhaps unknowingly, begin to interact with you in a way that is similar to the way that he or she would interact with his or her parent.

Countertransference occurs when you, perhaps unknowingly, do this to the client. For example, suppose you were raised with a sibling who persistently presented as immature, demanding, self-centered, volatile, and manipulative—essentially, a spoiled brat. Through your years of living with that difficult sibling, you would naturally have formed an opinion, an emotional stance, and possibly a system for dealing with this sort of difficult personality. For the sake of this example, let us suppose that you developed a fairly curt adaptation when confronted with this sibling. Now, suppose that in the present day, you find yourself working with a client who behaves in an impulsive, immature, self-serving, and manipulative manner, moving from one petty crisis to another. It is entirely possible that your contact with this client may (emotionally) remind you of your childish sibling. Such circumstances may lead you to *(counter)transfer* a copy of the feelings that you have for that sibling onto this client. You may even find yourself addressing this client in a manner similar to the way you would address your sibling. This is countertransference.

Make an effort to be aware of strong (positive or negative) feelings that may emerge within you. Be aware of some of the reactions that social workers and other health and human service professionals commonly experience:

Feeling anxious about or looking forward to your time with a client

Feeling a strong sense of hatred or affection toward a client

Feeling that you want to cut a session short or go into overtime

Strongly longing for or dreading/avoiding termination

Managing Countertransference

Recognizing that your reactions, either positive or negative, are unusually strong is the first step in effectively managing countertransference. Monitor your emotional reactions during sessions in order to pinpoint which components of the client's conduct (e.g., words, behaviors, subject matter, general presence) are correlated with your strong(est) feelings (Goldfried & Davison, 1994). Consider reflecting on your findings as they occur. Also, consider asking yourself some introspective questions outside of the session environment:

What is it that is making me like or dislike this client (so much)?

What issues do I really want or not want to process with this client?

What is making me feel so uncomfortable?

Is there someone else about whom I feel this way?

Does this client remind me of myself?

Honestly and patiently responding to questions like these may help you identify unresolved relevant feelings regarding people or experiences that dwell within you. Such insight may be sufficient to separate your personal feelings from your professional contact with the client.

A supplemental approach might involve conferring with a colleague, an instructor, a supervisor, or another healthcare professional to help you identify and resolve residual personal issues that may be resonating within you as you engage with clients.

Naturally, the clearer your "emotional pallet," the more professionally available you can be for clients. Regardless of how emotionally robust and nonjudgmental you consider yourself to be, it is still possible that you may encounter a particular population, client issue, or diagnosis that you find yourself unable to effectively work with. In such cases, it is advised that you provide the client with an appropriate referral, along with your rationale, as opposed to providing potentially biased or substandard care (Hepworth & Larsen, 1993).

Coping With Prejudices

Though the NASW code of ethics prohibits discrimination with respect to clients (National Association of Social Workers, 1996) and implicitly discourages prejudicial attitudes, it is implausible to presume that people do not have preferences. Such preferences may be extreme (e.g., hateful attitudes toward members of a particular minority group), or they may be more benign (e.g., preferring to converse with particularly bright people). It can be a subtle distinction between such preferences and outright prejudicial attitudes, wherein prior to encountering and evaluating an individual based on his or her unique characteristics, one automatically inflicts his or her preconceptions onto that individual, based on preexisting feelings toward the group that he or she appears to be associated with. Such preconceptions, both negative and positive, can be virtually unlimited in scope. Prejudicial attitudes may be associated with such factors as gender, age, stature, attire, general appearance, socioeconomic class, vocal characteristics, sexual orientation, marital status, educational level, race, color, or religion.

With such a wide array of elements that could potentially set off prejudicial attitudes, one might rightly ask, "How might one undo such prejudicial attitudes?" A study of prejudicial attitudes among mental healthcare providers may hold a clue: This survey revealed that regardless of educational level, homophobic attitudes were inversely related to the level of contact that the clinician had with homosexuals. That is, lower levels of homophobia were found among clinicians who had a history of contact with homosexuals, such as acquaintances, family members, peers, coworkers, and supervisors, whereas clinicians with less such contact were characterized by higher levels of homophobia. This correlative study also revealed lower levels of homophobia among clinicians who, themselves, had undergone prior psychotherapy (Berkman & Zinberg, 1997).

These findings suggest that one strategy for reducing prejudicial attitudes might be to seek out opportunities to engage directly in meaningful contact with such individuals (Cook, 1978). Brief, impersonal, or infrequent contact is unlikely to produce the desired effect (Brewer & Brown, 1998).

Actively monitoring your sense of discomfort with respect to clients and related subject matter can serve as a compass to guide your personal and professional development. Working to recognize and reduce your levels of biases and prejudices can serve to expand your professional versatility in terms of the range of client characteristics and subject matter that you can competently address.

CHAPTER 2 EXERCISES

CONCEPT REVIEWS

Explain each concept in your own words. Where applicable, provide a case example without disclosing identifying information.

2.1 Fostering sensitive disclosure (p. 42)

Clients may feel uncomfortable, fearful, or embarrassed when it comes to discussing certain issues. What are some of the things that you can do to help facilitate the client's disclosure?

2.2 Fear/honesty teeter-totter (A) (p. 43)

Provide an overview of the fear/honesty teeter-totter model.

2.3 Fear/honesty teeter-totter (B) (p. 43)

What is your impression of the fear/honesty teeter-totter model?

2.4 **Rapport (A) (p. 45)**

Explain what is meant by "rapport."

2.5 **Rapport (B) (p. 45)**

What purpose does rapport serve?

2.6 **Rapport (C) (p. 45)**

What are some means for facilitating quality rapport?

2.7 **Rebuilding rapport (A) (p. 47)**

Why might you need to rebuild rapport?

2.8   Rebuilding rapport (B) (p. 47)

Explain how you would go about rebuilding rapport.

2.9   Nonjudgmental attitude (p. 48)

Describe how presenting a genuine nonjudgmental attitude can facilitate your work with clients.

2.10   Listening (p. 49)

Describe the value of listening attentively.

2.11   Matching (p. 50)

Explain what matching involves and how it can enhance the communication process.

2.12   Close-ended questions (A) (p. 51)

Describe what a close-ended question is and the purpose that such questions serve.

2.13   Close-ended questions (B) (p. 51)

Write three close-ended questions.

2.14   Close-ended questions (C) (p. 51)

What advantages do close-ended questions have over open-ended questions?

2.15   Open-ended questions (A) (p. 52)

Describe what an open-ended question is and the purpose that such questions serve.

2.16   Open-ended questions (B) (p. 52)

Write three open-ended questions (if possible, write the open-ended versions of your responses to Concept Review 2.13).

2.17   Open-ended questions (C) (p. 52)

What advantages do open-ended questions have over close-ended questions?

2.18   Open-ended requests (p. 53)

Describe an open-ended request. Include an example.

2.19   Open-ended requests (p. 53)

Explain the rationale for submitting an open-ended request.

2.20 Ask one question at a time (A) (p. 54)

Describe the rationale for asking one question at a time.

2.21 Ask one question at a time (B) (p. 54)

Explain what is meant by a "compound question" (also known as a "double-barreled question" or "stacked question"). Include an example of a compound question.

2.22 Ask one question at a time (C) (p. 54)

In the event that a compound question comes to mind, explain how you would handle it.

2.23 Clarification (A) (p. 55)

Explain the purpose of clarification.

2.24   Clarification (B) (p. 55)

Under what circumstances might you use clarification?

2.25   Reflection/paraphrasing (A) (p. 56)

Describe what reflection/paraphrasing is.

2.26   Reflection/paraphrasing (B) (p. 56)

How can reflection/paraphrasing facilitate communication?

2.27   Summarizing (p. 57)

How does summarizing differ from reflection/paraphrasing?

2.28   Generalizing (A) (p. 58)

What is needed in order to assemble meaningful generalizations?

2.29   Generalizing (B) (p. 58)

Describe the manner in which a generalization should be delivered.

2.30   Generalizing (C) (p. 58)

How might meaningful generalizations serve the client?

2.31   Identifying and resolving discrepancies (A) (p. 61)

What are some of the factors that can lead to discrepancies (discuss factors pertaining to the client and also the social worker)?

2.32   Identifying and resolving discrepancies (B) (p. 61)

Describe the technique for tactfully identifying and resolving discrepancies.

2.33   Focusing (A) (p. 65)

What is meant by "focusing"?

2.34   Focusing (B) (p. 65)

Describe the purpose that focusing serves.

2.35   Specificity (p. 67)

In what way(s) can soliciting specificity be useful?

2.36   **Emotional language (A) (p. 68)**

Describe the emotional dynamics of (a) frustration, (b) anger, (c) depression, (d) anxiety, and (e) guilt.

2.37   **Emotional language (B) (p. 68)**

What is the difference between sadness and depression?

2.38   **Empathy (A) (p. 71)**

Compare empathy to sympathy.

2.39   **Empathy (B) (p. 71)**

Describe how empathy can facilitate discussions involving emotional issues.

2.40   Recognizing your perspective (p. 75)

Describe how your own (personal) perspective may help or hinder your contact with clients.

2.41   Monitoring your feelings (p. 75)

How might monitoring your own feelings serve to facilitate your interactions with clients?

2.42   Managing countertransference (A) (p. 76)

Describe what is meant by transference and countertransference.

2.43   Managing countertransference (B) (p. 76)

What are some clues that might suggest that you are experiencing countertransference?

2.44   **Managing countertransference (C) (p. 76)**

Describe some techniques that you might use to manage your countertransference.

2.45   **Coping with prejudices (p. 77)**

Describe some techniques that you can use to reduce your sense of bias or prejudicial attitudes that you may encounter within yourself.

DISCUSSION POINTS

Discuss among your peers how you might handle these circumstances. Document the opinions expressed using a "+" or a "−" to indicate whether you agree or disagree with each opinion.

2.1   Unspoken truths

During a session, you get the feeling that the client is deliberately dodging what seems to be an important topic.

2.2   I can't believe you said that!

The client has taken strong offense to one of your questions, statements, or assertions.

2.3   Tough tunes

You have positive rapport with a client who explains that he or she listens to music to relax. When you ask about the client's favorite artists and songs, he or she recites lyrics that involve conduct or attitudes that you find offensive (e.g., encouraging violence toward a minority group).

2.4   My #%@&ing parents!

Your client uses vulgar language when discussing his or her parents.

2.5   Brief bits

Your client provides only brief details when discussing a particular issue.

2.6   Bad connection?

Most of your efforts to summarize the client's storytelling are met with numerous corrections, and the client is beginning to exhibit frustration.

2.7   Bundle o' problems

The client is disclosing a multifaceted story in a nonstop fashion, involving numerous characters, story lines, time frames (past and present), settings, and problems.

2.8   Hard for the client, easy for you

The client is discussing issues that he or she finds very serious and emotionally significant; however, to you, it seems as if the client is overreacting to such trivial things.

2.9   Another side of the client

A client with whom you have a robust rapport raises a topic that causes you to suddenly feel very differently toward him or her (e.g., resentment, pity).

2.10   Client conundrum

A client enters the first session wearing jewelry or clothing with the name or symbol of a well-known hate group.

ROLE-PLAY 2.1 NEVER-ENDING STORIES

Note: Guidelines for role-play implementation, feedback, and documentation can be found in the "Overview of Exercises" section (p. xiii).

This is Gerry's first session. Gerry is motivated to provide explicit historical details of people and events (e.g., home, family problems, legal history, failed relationships, work issues, leisure, health problems, travel) spanning many years.

Client

- Shift freely from topic to topic.
- When describing the people in your story, provide little or no details for some and vast details for others.
- If the social worker asks you to adjust your level of detail regarding a story or a person, comply, but after a while, revert back to your prior style.

Social Worker

- **Summarizing** (p. 57)—If the client is speaking incessantly, respectfully request a pause, explaining that you need to make sure that you are understanding the story properly, then provisionally submit your summary and solicit feedback.
- **Focusing** (p. 65)—Keep track of each topic that emerges (you may wish to take some notes). Provide a recap of each topic, and request that the client select which (one) he or she would like to process first.
- **Identifying and resolving discrepancies** (p. 61)—If you notice contradictions or implausible circumstances in the client's story, respectfully ask the client to clarify those issues.

Role-Play 2.1 Self-Evaluation

(1 = needs further work, 5 = excellent)

1	2	3	4	5	Summarizing
1	2	3	4	5	Focusing
1	2	3	4	5	Identifying and resolving discrepancies
1	2	3	4	5	_____
1	2	3	4	5	_____

Role-Play 2.1 Case Notes

_____

_____

_____

_____

_____

_____

_____

_____

_____

_____

_____

_____

_____

_____

_____

_____

_____

_____

_____

_____

_____

_____

_____

_____

ROLE-PLAY 2.2 SAD SAM

Sam has been involved with Jean for several years. Jean recently returned to school, which has reduced the amount of time that the couple can spend together. Sam is feeling abandoned and believes that Jean may be interested in someone at school (e.g., a classmate, an instructor). Sam's thoughts and feelings are persistently interfering with work, leisure, and sleep.

Client

- Present as either heatedly angry or soft and sullen. You may wish to reasonably vary your affect.
- Express regret and self-blaming, wishing that you had never encouraged Jean to return to school.
- Initially, do not provide too many details regarding the changes that you have noticed in Jean's conduct and appearance. If asked, provide some information.

Social Worker

- **Matching** (p. 50)—Adjust your vocabulary and vocal dynamic (tempo and volume) to be compatible with the client's.
- **Empathy** (p. 71)—Acknowledge your perception of Sam's feelings as they emerge. If Sam reacts negatively (e.g., disagreement, confusion), consider requesting clarification.
- **Specificity** (p. 67)—If a key part of Sam's story is vague or does not make sense to you, respectfully explain the nature of your confusion or curiosity and request further details.

Role-Play 2.2 Self-Evaluation

(1 = needs further work, 5 = excellent)

1	2	3	4	5	Matching
1	2	3	4	5	Empathy
1	2	3	4	5	Specificity
1	2	3	4	5	_____
1	2	3	4	5	_____

Role-Play 2.2 Case Notes

_____

_____

_____

_____

_____

_____

_____

_____

_____

_____

_____

_____

_____

_____

_____

_____

_____

_____

_____

_____

_____

_____

_____

_____

_____

ROLE-PLAY 2.3 CAUSTIC COWORKERS

Jo has recently accepted a new job. The work is not hard, but Jo is finding it difficult to establish a comfortable contact with coworkers, which may be related to differences between Jo and the others (e.g., culture, age, ethnicity, gender, education, political affiliation). These circumstances are stressful and are beginning to affect other aspects of Jo's life (e.g., obsessing about work during off-hours, disturbing dreams, general sense of frustration).

Client

- Describe the style of some of your coworkers (e.g., mundane, eccentric, closed-minded) or an unpleasant incident that happened at a recent lunch (e.g., someone forced you to change seats, someone refused to let you order a particular food).
- Include some curious or controversial topics in your conversation (e.g., substance use, odd line of work that you do, a peculiar collection or hobby that you have), but do not provide extensive details unless you are asked to.
- Take (strong) offense to one of the social worker's questions or statements. If the social worker makes an effort to rebuild the rapport, accept it.

Social Worker

- **Open-ended questions** (p. 52)—If Jo raises issues that you would like further details on, use open-ended questions.
- **Reflection/paraphrasing** (p. 56)—As Jo's disclosure advances, periodically reflect/paraphrase your understanding of the story and people involved.
- **Rebuilding rapport** (p. 47)—If Jo becomes angered or offended by something that you said or asked, empathetically acknowledge Jo's reaction and apologize (one time). If Jo was offended by a question that you asked, you may wish to briefly discuss your rationale for having asked such a question.

Role-Play 2.3 Self-Evaluation

(1 = needs further work, 5 = excellent)

1	2	3	4	5	Open-ended questions
1	2	3	4	5	Reflection/paraphrasing
1	2	3	4	5	Rebuilding rapport
1	2	3	4	5	_____
1	2	3	4	5	_____

Role-Play 2.3 Case Notes

_____

_____

_____

_____

_____

_____

_____

_____

_____

_____

_____

_____

_____

_____

_____

_____

_____

_____

_____

_____

_____

_____

_____

_____

VIDEO INTERVIEW SELF-CRITIQUE EXERCISE

Overview

Achieving proficiency in communicating effectively with clients is challenging in that it takes place in real time. You need to learn to think on your feet. As such, it can take some practice to refine your use of the communication skills detailed in this chapter in order to present in a professional and relaxed manner.

Reviewing a video recording of your interactions with a (simulated) client can be a useful tool in terms of helping you identify skills that you are proficient with, as well as those that require further practice.

It is recommended that you complete this exercise twice:

1. Run this exercise upon the completion of this chapter. Use the worksheets on pages 101–111 to document your baseline proficiency with three to five different communication skills. In the post-role-play documentation section, you need not focus exclusively on skills that you feel require further development. It is equally important to cite skills that you implemented proficiently.

2. Toward the end of the academic term or upon the conclusion of your first year, consider shooting a second video role-play. Next, view the first role-play in its entirety, followed by the second role-play. Contrasting the two role-plays will enable you to cite and document improvements in your implementation of the communication skills, as well as areas for further improvement. Worksheets for the second role-play self-evaluation are on pages 112–122.

Setup

Role-Play Partner. With respect to the legal and ethical constraints regarding client confidentiality, do not use an actual client, client's story, name, or persona in your performance(s). Consider casting a willing friend or family member to play the part of the client. Alternatively, for sake of efficiency, you might consider partnering with another student and using this opportunity to record a role-play for you (wherein you play the social worker) and then to swap roles and engage in a second production for your partner to assess his or her skill performance.

Staging. Arrange two chairs facing each other, angled slightly toward the camera. The chairs should be placed so that when the two participants are seated comfortably, their outreached hands can touch fingertip to fingertip.

Place the camera on a tripod or a flat, stable surface. The camera's view should be set to capture a "two-shot" as shown in Figure 2.2. Set up the camera's view so that the full body, from head to toe, of each participant is in the frame. This will enable you to fully observe your physical presence as you interact with the client.

Implementation

Role-Play. As you have likely discovered through running the role-plays provided in this text, you need specify only a few performance parameters in order to engage in an effective role-play experience. You and your partner may choose to use a role-play from this book or invent a scenario of your own. Alternatively, you may mutually agree that the person playing the client will present a story line of his or her own, which may be fictional, based on real events, or some blend thereof.

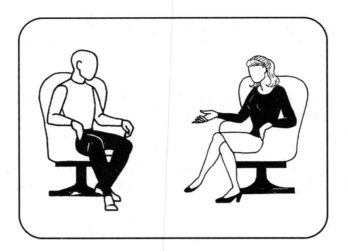

Figure 2.2   Camera's View of Role-Play
SOURCE: Dean Cameron.

In order to gather an adequate sample of your skills, this role-play should run about 15 minutes. It is recommended that you use a countdown timer or a clock placed off camera, within the social worker's line of sight. If you choose to use the clock option, just before starting the role-play, set the clock to 5:45; hence, when the clock reaches 6:00, you will know that 15 minutes have elapsed without having to be continually distracted with time calculations.

Debriefing. At the conclusion of the role-play, stop the recording. Before viewing the recording or embarking on a second role-play, wherein you would swap roles with your partner, take some time to mutually debrief. Consider using the role-play debriefing protocol specified on page xv. Since this role-play exercise is longer in duration than those presented thus far, allow some extra time for the debriefing—try not to rush the process.

Self-Evaluation Guidelines

Begin by reviewing the recording solo. After documenting your initial findings, you may choose to review all or selected parts of the video with a fellow student, instructor, or field instructor to solicit additional feedback.

The following forms will guide you in documenting your video role-play self-evaluations detailing your proficiency with three to five communication skills.

VIDEO INTERVIEW SELF-CRITIQUE #1 DATE ___/___/___

Section I: Characteristics of the Client

Describe the client's attributes (name, gender, approximate age, cultural background, initial demeanor, presenting problem, and so on).

Section II: Goals of the Interview

What was your initial goal of the interview?

Did this concur with the client's goal?

As the interview progressed, what other goals emerged?

Section III: Skills Used

(Complete this section detailing your use of three to five different skills.)

Name of skill (1) _____

Reason for selecting the skill

Example of the use of the skill

Client's response

Effectiveness of the skill

Missed opportunities

How might the interview have been different?

Name of skill (2) _____

Reason for selecting the skill

Example of the use of the skill

Client's response

Effectiveness of the skill

Missed opportunities

How might the interview have been different?

Name of skill (3) _____

Reason for selecting the skill

Example of the use of the skill

Client's response

Effectiveness of the skill

Missed opportunities

How might the interview have been different?

Name of skill (4) _____

Reason for selecting the skill

Example of the use of the skill

Client's response

Effectiveness of the skill

Missed opportunities

How might the interview have been different?

Name of skill (5) _____

Reason for selecting the skill

Example of the use of the skill

Client's response

Effectiveness of the skill

Missed opportunities

How might the interview have been different?

Section IV: Overall Impression of the Interview

Goal achievement

Quality of social worker–client relationship

Flow of the interview (tempo, pauses)

Use of body language or anomalous movements

Interviewing skill strengths

Interviewing skills that have shown improvement

Areas for continued improvement

Plan for improving interviewing skills

Thoughts and feelings regarding evolving interviewing proficiency

Video Interview Self-Critique #2 Date ___/___/___

Section I: Characteristics of the Client

Describe the client's attributes (name, gender, approximate age, cultural background, initial demeanor, presenting problem, and so on).

Section II: Goals of the Interview

What was your initial goal of the interview?

Did this concur with the client's goal?

As the interview progressed, what other goals emerged?

Section III: Skills Used

(Complete this section detailing your use of three to five different skills.)

Name of skill (1) _____

Reason for selecting the skill

Example of the use of the skill

Client's response

Effectiveness of the skill

Missed opportunities

How might the interview have been different?

Name of skill (2) _____

Reason for selecting the skill

Example of the use of the skill

Client's response

Effectiveness of the skill

Missed opportunities

How might the interview have been different?

Name of skill (3) _____

Reason for selecting the skill

Example of the use of the skill

Client's response

Effectiveness of the skill

Missed opportunities

How might the interview have been different?

Name of skill (4) _____

Reason for selecting the skill

Example of the use of the skill

Client's response

Effectiveness of the skill

Missed opportunities

How might the interview have been different?

Name of skill (5) _____

Reason for selecting the skill

Example of the use of the skill

Client's response

Effectiveness of the skill

Missed opportunities

How might the interview have been different?

Section IV: Overall Impression of the Interview

Goal achievement

Quality of social worker–client relationship

Flow of the interview (tempo, pauses)

Use of body language or anomalous movements

Interviewing skill strengths

Interviewing skills that have shown improvement

Areas for continued improvement

Plan for improving interviewing skills

Thoughts and feelings regarding evolving interviewing proficiency (compared with your performance in the Video Interview Self-Critique #1 exercise)

PART III

The Process

3

Step I—Assessment

Where Is the Client Now?

I	II	III	IV	V
Assessment	**G**oal	**O**bjectives	**A**ctivation	**T**ermination

Before you can embark on effectively providing meaningful help, you must first understand the nature of the person whom you endeavor to help. The client and his or her problem(s) exist within a realm of values, beliefs, resources, constraints, social systems, motivators, and priorities that are unique to each client. In order to provide meaningful care that is applicable to the client, you first need to understand the client and the social sphere in which he or she exists from his or her point of view.

This chapter covers the initial phase of the process—assessment—wherein you will be working to orient yourself to the multiple aspects of the client's life. Techniques for professionally welcoming the client and effectively gathering pertinent information before and after your initial meeting are discussed.

Three means for gathering an understanding of the client's multidimensional life system are covered:

1. *Case Review*—Exploring documentation or engaging in consultation pertaining to the client

2. *Written Assessment*—Assembling a biopsychosocial profile detailing the client's physical health, cognitive/emotional status, and living environment (p. 138)

3. *Mental Status Examination (MSE)*—Building a detailed summary of the client's functioning (p. 144)

Before Meeting the Client

Case Review

On occasion, prior to meeting the client for the first time, you may have legitimate access to client-related materials. This may take the form of an application for service, a screening interview profile, prior case files, a court order, a peer consultation, and so on. Such material should be considered valuable in helping you build a preliminary understanding of the client; however, resist the temptation to build a definitive impression. You need to see how the client presents in real life as opposed to how he or she is represented (by someone else) exclusively on paper or by verbal report. This notion will become clearer in the section "Introduction to Diagnosis," later in this chapter.

From a social worker standpoint, a case review should involve a comprehensive biopsychosocial characterization of the client. This sort of written assessment should include not only clinical disorders and problematic issues but also strengths, resources, and (supportive) social systems present in the client's life. Actively identifying such assets are of more than just academic interest. Knowledge of such positive elements in the client's life can serve as a vehicle for change in terms of assembling and implementing effective intervention strategies.

Based on your case review of a client's characteristics and conditions, it is natural to form some ideas regarding a provisional treatment plan; however, it is important not to become too attached to this image. Such planning must ultimately be tailored to meet the client's unique characteristics and willingness to proceed down the proposed pathway. Social work is a collaborative, not unilateral, paradigm.

Although assessment is an essential initial step, it is not a finite concept. As each case advances, your comprehension of the client's condition is likely to advance incrementally. The helping realm is a dynamic environment. Throughout the course of working with clients, some issues may resolve. As rapport and trust are built, the client may reveal additional substantive issues. One might also see the resolution of one issue lead to the resolution or exacerbation of other issues. As such, assessment can be something of a "moving target," serving to guide the direction of the process in a progressive manner.

Introduction to Diagnosis

While it is beyond the scope of this text to teach you how to make cogent mental health diagnoses, it is entirely possible that you may be assigned a client whose paperwork includes diagnostic information. You may also be privy to a professional consultation that involves diagnoses. Alternatively, a client may, at some point, mention one or more diagnoses that have been assigned to him or her in the past. As such, it is important to have a fundamental understanding of the dimensions of diagnostic information, along with resources for further orienting yourself to the meaning of specific diagnoses.

Making a proper mental health diagnosis is an involved undertaking. In the early phase of your social work academic education and fieldwork, you will not be expected to derive or confirm mental health diagnoses. The purpose of this section is to provide you with a basis for understanding how to interpret potentially cryptic diagnostic information. It is not the intent of the author that you fully comprehend or memorize specific diagnostic categories, subcategories, criteria, names, or corresponding codes.

Principles of Diagnosis

A diagnosis is a system for describing the client's condition based on signs and symptoms. Signs consist of observable phenomena that are objectively discoverable by examination. These are things that you can see or hear when you observe a client, such as a muscular tic or stuttering. Symptoms are phenomena that are experienced by the client, such as nightmares, anxiety, or recurring thoughts or feelings, which the client may report (*Webster's New World/Stedman's Concise Medical Dictionary*, 1987).

Just as a person may be assigned one or more valid medical diagnoses at a time (e.g., asthma and broken arm), depending on the client's functioning, one or several mental health diagnoses may be appropriately assigned at a given time.

Some diagnoses can be dynamic. As treatment advances, some conditions may be resolved, hence necessitating the removal of the corresponding diagnoses, whereas other more enduring conditions may remain part of the diagnostic profile. Depending on the client and the diagnoses, you will find that some diagnoses are more amenable to treatment than others.

Mental Health Diagnosis (*DSM*)

A mental health diagnosis provides a profile of the client's biopsychosocial status using the *Diagnostic and Statistical Manual of Mental Disorders* (*DSM*) (American Psychiatric Association, 2000). This manual provides a systematic directory of mental health conditions detailing essential information for each diagnosis, including the name, code number, and criteria necessary to fulfill each diagnosis.

The diagnoses in the *DSM* are arranged in categories (e.g., Mood Disorders, Anxiety Disorders, Somatoform Disorders, Sexual and Gender Identity Disorders, Eating Disorders, Sleep Disorders, Personality Disorders). Specific diagnoses are presented under each category. A category may be organized into subcategories. For example, the category of Sleep Disorders is divided into two subcategories: Dyssomnias and Parasomnias. Dyssomnias include the diagnostic criteria for Primary Insomnia, Primary Hypersomnia, Narcolepsy, Breathing-Related Sleep Disorder, Circadian Rhythm Sleep Disorder, and Dyssomnia Not Otherwise Specified (NOS). The subcategory Parasomnias includes the diagnostic criteria for Nightmare Disorder, Sleep Terror Disorder, Sleepwalking Disorder, and Parasomnia NOS. Additionally, the category of Sleep Disorders includes four other sleep-related diagnoses: Insomnia Related to Another Mental Disorder, Hypersomnia Related to Another Mental Disorder, Sleep Disorder Due to a General Medical Condition, and Substance-Induced Sleep Disorder.

DSM diagnoses are organized using a five-axis array as shown in Table 3.1. This multiaxial *DSM* diagnostic system provides a means for documenting the client's biopsychosocial functioning, as shown in Table 3.2.

Table 3.1   Five-Axis *DSM* Diagnosis

Axis	Diagnostic Information
I	Clinical Disorders
II	Personality Disorders and Mental Retardation
III	General Medical Conditions
IV	Psychosocial and Environmental Problems
V	Global Assessment of Functioning (GAF)

Table 3.2   Biopsychosocial Correlates to *DSM* Axes

Bio	Psycho	Social	Overall functioning
III	I & II	IV	V

Axis I: Clinical Disorders

Clinical disorders, which are coded on Axis I, include the entire *DSM* with the exception of Personality Disorders and Mental Retardation, both of which are documented on Axis II. Each *DSM* diagnosis has a diagnostic name and corresponding numerical code. Some examples of Axis I diagnoses include such diverse conditions as 304.2 Cocaine Dependence, 299 Autistic Disorder, 312.32 Kleptomania, 309.21 Separation Anxiety Disorder, 307.52 Pica, 312.34 Intermittent Explosive Disorder, 292.89 Cannabis-Induced Anxiety Disorder, 307.51 Bulimia Nervosa, 302.4 Exhibitionism, 307.23 Tourette's Disorder, 301.13 Cyclothymic Disorder, 299.8 Rett's Disorder, and 309.81 Posttraumatic Stress Disorder.

If the client presents with more than one clinical disorder, the disorders should be arranged from most to least significant. If the client presents with no clinical disorders, Axis I may be coded V79.09 No Diagnosis or Condition on Axis I. Alternatively, depending on the level of (un)certainty, 799.9 Diagnosis or Condition Deferred on Axis I may be assigned.

Axis II: Personality Disorders and Mental Retardation

Personality Disorders consist of personality traits that are inflexible, enduring, and maladaptive. As with Axis I disorders, if the client presents with more than one personality disorder, the disorders should be organized with the most significant at the top of the list. The category of Personality Disorders consists of 11 diagnoses: 301.0 Paranoid Personality Disorder, 301.20 Schizoid Personality Disorder, 301.22 Schizotypal Personality Disorder, 301.7 Antisocial Personality Disorder, 301.83 Borderline Personality Disorder, 301.5 Histrionic Personality Disorder, 301.81 Narcissistic Personality Disorder, 301.82 Avoidant Personality Disorder, 301.6 Dependent Personality Disorder, 301.4 Obsessive-Compulsive Personality Disorder, and 301.9 Personality Disorder NOS.

Diagnoses involving mental retardation are also coded on Axis II. The *DSM* recognizes four levels of mental retardation, based on the client's IQ score. A fifth diagnosis pertaining to mental retardation is 319 Mental Retardation, Severity Unspecified. This diagnosis would be assigned when mental retardation is expected but the client is untestable using conventional means as shown in Table 3.3.

If the client presents with no personality disorder and no mental retardation, Axis II may be coded V79.09 No Diagnosis or Condition on Axis II. Alternatively, depending on the level of (un)certainty, 799.9 Diagnosis or Condition Deferred on Axis II may be assigned.

Axis III: General Medical Conditions

The diagnostic criteria for Axis III differ from the others as these diagnoses are medical as opposed to psychosocial in nature. These medical diagnoses and

Table 3.3   *DSM* Mental Retardation Diagnostic Criteria

IQ	Diagnosis	
50–55 to about 70	317	Mild Mental Retardation
35–40 to 50–55	318.0	Moderate Retardation
20–25 to 35–40	318.1	Severe Mental Retardation
< 20 or 25	318.2	Profound Mental Retardation
	319	Mental Retardation, Severity Unspecified

their corresponding codes, such as 403 Hypertensive Kidney Disease, 873.73 Tooth (Broken), and 428.1 Left Heart Failure, are contained in the *International Classification of Diseases (ICD)* manual (World Health Organization, 1992). You can think of the *ICD* as the medical counterpart of the *DSM*. Essentially, Axis III should include medical conditions that are pertinent to the diagnoses present on the other four *DSM* axes. For example, a client who has multiple physical injuries, which would be documented on Axis III, may impair his or her activities of daily life and thereby be correlated to a (depressive) mood disorder, which would be coded on Axis I.

From a legal standpoint, as a social worker you are not qualified to make a medical diagnosis as this is beyond your scope of practice. It is essential, when making an entry on Axis III, that you cite the source of such diagnostic information (e.g., "Broken left arm per client's report," "Medical records indicate client had a stroke 6 months ago," "Physician reports chronic renal failure").

Simply seeing the client with an arm cast would not serve as adequate evidence for you to code "broken left arm" on Axis III. That cast may be present for any number of reasons (e.g., strain, sprain, fracture, surgery, hand injury). If the client presents with no physical disorders, "none" should be coded on Axis III.

Axis IV: Psychosocial and Environmental Problems

There are no fixed diagnostic labels or code numbers to look up for Axis IV. This is a free-text field wherein you can briefly document various aspects of the client's social functioning and living conditions. Axis IV information may include a summary of the client's living situation, primary relationships, employment status, legal status, substance use (which may not warrant an Axis I diagnosis), or other notable social or environmental stressors. Axis IV entries should be in the form of one or several brief statements detailing the problematic condition(s) (e.g., recently divorced, unemployed for 6 months, sibling died 1 month ago, homeless for 3 weeks, temporarily living with a friend). More detailed information should be reserved for the case notes.

If there are no significant deficits with respect to the client's psychosocial or environmental status, "none" should be coded on Axis IV.

Axis V: Global Assessment of Functioning

Axis V contains the Global Assessment of Functioning (GAF) score, which is meant to characterize the client's overall functioning using a number between 0 and 100, with 1 representing profound dysfunction and 100 representing ideal functioning (0 will be discussed shortly). The *DSM* provides a description of symptoms associated with levels of functioning in 10-point blocks (e.g., 1–10, 11–20, 21–30 . . . 91–100). Consider the maximum and minimum descriptions of the GAF scale as detailed in the *DSM* (American Psychiatric Association, 2000):

91–100   *Superior functioning in a wide range of activities, life's problems never seem to get out of hand, is sought out by others because of his or her many positive qualities. No symptoms.*

1–10   *Persistent danger of severely hurting self or others (e.g., recurrent violence) OR persistent inability to maintain minimal personal hygiene OR serious suicidal act with clear expectation of death.* (p. 34)

In addition to selecting an appropriate range, the diagnostician will need to determine the actual score within a specific range (e.g., 86, 99, 13). For example, suppose a client meets the criteria detailed in the text associated with the 91–100 score; the person making the diagnosis will need to plausibly select the actual score within that range (91–100) that best represents the client's overall functioning.

A GAF score of 0 is not interpreted (arithmetically) as less than 1. On the GAF scale, 0 indicates "Inadequate Information," meaning that it is not possible to gather sufficient information to make a diagnostic determination. For example, a GAF score of 0 may be assigned in a medical setting, such as an emergency room, wherein the client is unconscious, unable, or unwilling to respond and where supplemental information is unavailable.

Axis V may contain a single GAF score, indicating the client's level of functioning at the time of the assessment. In some cases, Axis V may also contain an additional GAF score indicating such things as highest level of functioning in the past year, or in the case of a (re)hospitalization, Axis V may include the client's GAF score at the time of his or her last intake, discharge, and so on. Such scores would be noted appropriately (e.g., V: 68 current, 82 highest in past year).

Documentation of a mental health diagnosis can be written using either textual or table format as shown in Table 3.4. In the textual format, the notation ΨDx is commonly used. This indicates "psychiatric diagnosis" wherein Ψ, the Greek letter *psi*, symbolizes psychology and *Dx* is the Latin abbreviation for diagnosis.

It should be noted that although the example detailing the table format includes the diagnostic codes (300.4, 307.44, V71.09) alongside the names of the corresponding diagnoses (Dysthymic Disorder, Primary Hypersomnia, no diagnosis), when documenting, clinicians may choose to use the diagnostic code, the diagnostic name, or both. Make it a point to confer with your supervisor as to the style of documentation that is preferred at your facility.

Table 3.4   Textual and Table Formats for *DSM* Diagnostic Documentation

Textual Format

ΨDx: I Dysthymic Disorder, Primary Hypersomnia, II no Dx, III None, IV Academic decline, stress at home re: parents, V = 68

Table Format

I	*300.4 Dysthymic Disorder*
	307.44 Primary Hypersomnia
II	*V71.09 no Dx*
III	*N/A*
IV	*Academic decline, stress at home re: parents*
V	*68*

Advantages of Mental Health Diagnoses

A mental health diagnosis can facilitate multiple benefits as the client proceeds through the five-step (**A GOAT**) model presented in this text:

Step I—**A**ssessment: Collecting and correlating signs and symptoms may suggest an appropriate diagnosis. Such observations can help you better understand the client's condition at this time, thereby suggesting potential intervention pathways. Additionally, social service agencies, insurance companies, and other third-party reimbursement providers may require a mental health diagnosis in order to demonstrate eligibility for reimbursement or access to (continued) care.

Step II—**G**oal: Appropriate diagnoses may serve to focus your collaborative efforts with clients in terms of identifying problems that they may wish to address.

Step III—**O**bjectives: The client's diagnoses can aim you toward relevant literature detailing evidence-based interventions, suggesting appropriate treatment strategies and resources that can be used to achieve the desired goals in an efficient and effective manner.

Step IV—**A**ctivation: Diagnoses may serve as a guide for implementing and tuning interventions per the nature and magnitude of the symptoms. Numerous instruments or scales have been developed to help quantify the client's baseline (starting point) status and track the level of the client's symptoms pertaining to the diagnoses throughout the course of care. Some examples of the diversity of such measurement surveys include the Index of Marital Satisfaction, the Life Distress Inventory, the Family Assessment Device, the Zung Self-Rating Depression Scale, the Achievement Anxiety Test, the Dating and Assertion Questionnaire, the Client Satisfaction Questionnaire, and the Problem-Solving Inventory (Fischer & Corcoran, 1994). Monitoring such trends may suggest the effectiveness of the intervention, potentially indicating the need for adjusting the treatment plan.

Step V—Termination: Achieving full or partial reduction of problematic symptoms may suggest the completion of the process.

Disadvantages of Mental Health Diagnoses

There can be a variety of disadvantages associated with assigning or adopting preexisting mental health diagnoses:

Partial Representation

One of the risks of strongly embracing the client's mental health diagnosis involves potentially conceiving the client as a mere cluster of diagnostic criteria that he or she fulfills. Subscribing to this narrow perspective can block your ability to view the client as a whole person, taking into account the multiple functional roles that the person may play in life (e.g., parent, employee, friend, sports fan, musician) (Andreasen, 2007).

Cultural Bias

In the absence of robust cultural knowledge, there is the risk of overpathologizing when it comes to assessing clients of a cultural background or level of acculturation that differs from your own (Alarcon, 1995). In terms of the multicultural characteristics of the global community, one cannot reasonably consider that one universal set of values or principles is applicable to all clients (Friedmann, 2005).

In addition to familiarizing yourself with relevant multicultural literature, consider reviewing the section of the *DSM* called "Outline for Cultural Formulation and Glossary of Culture-Bound Syndromes" (American Psychiatric Association, 2000). As you consider the client's cultural characteristics, avoid the temptation to stereotype. Make a deliberate effort to orient yourself to the client's cultural identity and his or her unique adaptation to it.

Potential Ambiguity

Even when flawlessly assigned, a diagnosis can carry a level of ambiguity. Consider, for example, the diagnostic criteria for Borderline Personality Disorder, wherein the client must satisfy a minimum of (any) five of the nine symptoms. Hypothetically, it is possible that one client may present with symptoms one through five, whereas another presents with symptoms five through nine. While both clients would independently warrant the diagnosis of Borderline Personality Disorder, without even looking at the (nine) diagnostic criteria one might expect that these two clients would present in very different manners.

The lesson here is that even an accurate diagnosis is not the whole story. Consider the diagnosis as a sort of clinical shorthand. In order to achieve a more thorough understanding as to the client's unique condition and coping adaptation, look beyond the diagnosis. Review the client's chart, which should include progress notes. With appropriate client consent, it can be helpful to confer with others who may have worked with this client. Also, despite the documented diagnosis, try to avoid building a firm preconception of the client. Allow the client's actual presence to make an impression on you.

Not Otherwise Specified (NOS)

Occasionally, you may encounter a diagnosis with the suffix Not Otherwise Specified, or NOS (e.g., Anxiety Disorder NOS, Somatoform Disorder NOS, Personality Disorder NOS). The NOS designation can be diagnostically ambiguous. For example, consider a client who presents with symptoms from several different anxiety disorders but fails to fulfill the full diagnostic criteria for any one diagnosis. This client could appropriately be assigned the diagnosis Anxiety Disorder NOS, essentially meaning "some of the above." Conversely, a client may be experiencing anxiety, but the symptoms, though clinically significant, are not present on the criteria lists for any of the documented anxiety disorders. In such cases, the diagnosis Anxiety Disorder NOS could also be assigned, essentially meaning "none of the above."

In terms of best comprehending the client, consider the diagnosis as the starting, not the ending, point. Look to the case notes, and when feasible, appropriately confer with others who may have knowledge of the client.

Possibility of Misdiagnosis

Not all mental health disorders are evident (early) in the process. There may be insufficient diagnostic clues at the time that the diagnosis is made. This can be due to a variety of factors (e.g., fear, sense of embarrassment, full or partial remission), potentially leading the client to omit, deny, or suppress selected symptoms.

Some disorders manifest over time. Diagnostic indicators may be absent or only partially revealed during the initial visit or even in the short run. For example, Bipolar I Disorder is characterized by extreme mood swings, ranging from deep depression to mania over time. In instances where the client enters therapy in a depressive phase, without additional information the client may be misdiagnosed as having Major Depressive Disorder or possibly Dysthymic Disorder. In such a case, historical information (e.g., prior case file, professional consult, details provided by the client or significant other who might be present in the client's sessions[s]), may reveal recurring incidents of alternating mania and depression, which would help fill in the diagnostic picture. Such vital information could be helpful in assigning a more accurate diagnosis, which would suggest a more appropriate treatment plan (Perlis, 2005).

Single Point of View

When listening to the client, it is important to remember that each person is endowed with only one point of view. Without being suspicious, keep in mind that you may only be hearing half of a story. For example, in isolation an adult client may describe his or her child as antisocial and immature; however, upon meeting this child, it may become clear that the child's behavior is, in fact, age appropriate, but the parent's expectations are out of line. Alternatively, you may discover that it is the parent who has poor coping skills.

Additional Attributes of Mental Health Diagnoses

Eligibility

Social service agencies, such as an outpatient walk-in center, may provide a broad spectrum of services to individuals presenting with a variety of mental health symptoms. Other organizations may offer a more specialized set of services (e.g., substance abuse recovery, bereavement, eating disorders); hence, one's mental health diagnosis may appropriately be used as a means test in order to determine eligibility for such services.

Resolution

Make a point to review the date, setting, and case notes in which the diagnosis was assigned. Problems that were initially documented as clinically relevant may have resolved over time (with or without professional help), thereby making the diagnosis obsolete. For example, a client may have, at one point in time, been strongly fearful of dogs and properly diagnosed with Specific Phobia. Further, suppose that client had been treated effectively with desensitization therapy, thereby neutralizing the phobia. While the diagnosis of Specific Phobia may rightly be part of the client's (historical) record, if the client is no longer exhibiting symptoms that satisfy the diagnostic criteria of that (phobic) disorder, this diagnosis should not be included in the client's current diagnostic profile.

Social Lingo Versus Clinical Diagnoses

Social definitions can differ substantially from formal mental health diagnostic criteria. Diagnostic terms, such as *schizophrenic* and *paranoid*, used in social settings can carry very different meanings than they would in a professional setting.

For example, in a nonclinical setting, seeing a man in a dress might lead you to conclude that he is a transvestite. Socially, this is not a misnomer; however, consider the *DSM* diagnostic definition for Transvestic Fetishism, wherein both criteria A and B must be satisfied in order to warrant the following diagnosis:

Diagnostic Criteria for 302.3 Transvestic Fetishism

A. Over a period of at least 6 months, in a heterosexual male, recurrent, intense sexually arousing fantasies, sexual urges, or behaviors involving cross-dressing.

B. The fantasies, sexual urges, or behaviors cause clinically significant distress or impairment in social, occupational, or other important areas of functioning.

According to these *DSM* criteria (American Psychiatric Association, 2000), suppose that this man, who is in a dress, has a life that is completely functional: He is generally a happy person; has good relationships with his family, friends, and coworkers; is advancing appropriately in his career; and has a satisfying social life. Despite his choice of feminine attire, he is not experiencing "clinically significant distress or impairment" in any of the areas mentioned in criteria B; hence, he fails to fulfill the full diagnostic requirements and therefore would not warrant this diagnosis.

Might a man like this ever seek the services of a social worker? Possibly. Suppose someone close to him passed away. Depending on his reaction, an appropriate diagnosis could be assigned to account for the corresponding changes in his mood or coping (e.g., Bereavement, Adjustment Disorder, Major Depressive Disorder).

While you would have the prerogative to include the client's cross-dressing propensity and functional adaptation to it in the case notes, Transvestic Fetishism would not be included as part of the diagnosis. Since, to this client, his cross-dressing propensity is not problematic (as specified in criteria B), it should not be part of the diagnosis or the treatment plan.

The goal of the diagnosis is to cite problematic areas. For this man, cross-dressing is neither an inherent problem nor a factor in his reason for seeking care at this time. Even when you become proficient at determining and properly assigning mental health diagnoses, avoid the temptation to overpathologize.

After Meeting the Client

Welcome to Therapy: What the Client Needs to Know

Unlike social relationships, which have no formal startup requirements, when engaging with a client for the first time, there are a few initial things that need to happen:

Introductions

Appropriate professional introductions are in order. Depending on your sense of professionalism and the practices at the agency, it may be appropriate to refer to yourself using your first name. Alternatively, more formal introductions may be in order (e.g., Mrs. Doe, Mr. Smith, Dr. Jones). If you are serving as an intern, your agency may also have a policy requiring you to state your role as such, indicating the name of your school, program, and field supervisor.

Greet the client using his or her full name, and ask how he or she wishes you to address him or her. For instance, when meeting your new client, Jonathan Jones, you might ask him if he prefers to be called "Jonathan," "Mr. Jones," or some other name. He may feel comfortable with John, Johnny, or another variation.

In settings where more than one seating position is available for the client, it is advisable that you sit down first, thereby enabling the client to select a seating position that suits his or her distance preference.

Some clients, specifically Latinos, may feel comfortable partaking in some informal warm-up chatting (*la plática*) prior to embarking on more formal discussion (Martinez, 1986). Conversely, Asians may consider such conversation nonproductive and therefore professionally inappropriate (Root, Ho, & Sue, 1986; Sue & Sue, 2003). For some clients, ethnicity and cultural background may provide some guidance in this respect. It can be helpful to familiarize yourself with the multicultural characteristics and the communication customs of those in the community that you serve (Pedersen, Draguns, Lonner, & Trimble, 1996; Sue, 1992). As is always the case, avoid stereotyping. Make a consistent effort to understand and engage each client, taking into account his or her unique style.

Informed Consent and Agency Policies

In the initial appointment, it is essential to review and have the client sign the treatment informed consent. This document specifies such things as the agency's policies, services provided, fee structure, instructions regarding missed and canceled appointments, termination parameters, and other relevant rules and policies. This document may also include information regarding limitations on confidentiality, specifying the conditions under which, in accordance with legal mandate, confidentiality may be breached (e.g., court orders, Tarasoff warnings, incidents wherein the client may have perpetrated or have knowledge of child, elderly, or dependent abuse, neglect, or abandonment).

Confidentiality

The client has the right to know about the handling and flow of information pertaining to his or her case. For instance, during the course of your contact with the client, supplemental information regarding that client may be made available to you in the form of case files, legal documents, relevant peer consultations, medical records, and so on. In the interest of keeping in synch with clients, as promptly as possible it is advisable that you provide the client with a summary of what you have learned, along with your impressions. It can be useful to discuss such information, soliciting the client's feedback. Engage the client to provide corresponding commentary, elaboration, corrections, and addendums. This may provide valuable contextual information.

Depending on your agency's policies, you may also be expected to discuss compulsory disclosures with the client, such as mandated reporting that you may be required to make. Further, should there be any inappropriate or otherwise unauthorized attempts to access the client's information (e.g., a call or message from the client's sibling, friend, or boss requesting a progress report), you may consider disclosing this to the client, assuring the client that no such information was released.

Learning About the Client

As a social worker, your mission is to listen and try to understand. Your primary job is to come to know the client and the multidimensional characteristics of the realm in which the client lives (e.g., family, friends, social system, spiritual base, culture and ethnic identity, core values, emotional perspective). The extent to which you understand your clients largely predicts the quality of the contact that you will have with them. Failure to gain a comprehensive image of who a client is and the domain in which he or she lives will deprive you of essential information to guide your collaborative efforts.

In addition to listening attentively, make a consistent effort to build and maintain a professional, comfortable environment that is conducive to sensitive disclosure. Such an environment entails privacy, genuine respect, trust, compassion, and your desire to be helpful. Maintaining a genuine nonjudgmental, accepting attitude can facilitate the client's disclosures—remember the fear/honesty teeter-totter model (p. 43).

Depending on a number of factors, including cultural influence, sensitivity of the information, the client's emotional state, and the client's sense of comfort in your presence, there can be some variability in terms of how clients embark on their initial clinical disclosures. Some clients may ease into their discussion, starting with some fairly neutral disclosure and gradually blending toward revealing and processing more critical information, whereas others may choose to blurt out the crux of their most pressing issue. Other times, the client may present with silence. This may be due to any number of reasons: The client may be seeking an entry point to a complex or multilayered story. The client may be considering how much backstory to tell in order to place the present issue in a meaningful context. The client may be coping with weighty emotions. The client may be trying to figure out how to tell his or her story without getting him- or herself or others into trouble. Alternatively, the client may be unclear as to what the central problem is or how to articulate it.

Try to be patient in moments of silence. You need not fill all of the silences with words (Neukrug, 2002). When you feel it is appropriate, there are a few phrases that you can use to help get things going:

"Take your time with this." This phrase demonstrates that you are willing to be patient. This may be the first time that the client is telling this story to another person; hence, he or she may be working to arrange the facts and emotional aspects of the story into an order that can be told aloud. There can also be difficult feelings (e.g., fear, regret, embarrassment, guilt) that can appropriately slow the tempo of the client's storytelling.

"How are you feeling right now?" The issues that clients may raise are likely to involve strong emotions. Inquiring about a client's feelings demonstrates that you are aware that he or she may be experiencing some powerful emotions and that you are prepared to receive and handle such feelings in a sensitive manner. A client may prefer to speak of his or her feelings first and then use that discussion as a bridge to disclosing the facts of his or her story.

"What do you want me to know?" If a client is unable or unwilling to discuss his or her *feelings,* a *cognitive,* less emotional entry point may be a viable alternative. This type of question enables the client to begin by discussing facts. From there, the client may begin to include the associated feelings as his or her narrative unfolds.

Briefly State Your Observation(s): "You seem tense." "You look afraid." "I'm noticing your arms and legs are crossed." Empathetically sharing your impressions of the client's physical presentation demonstrates your emotional attentiveness to the client—that you are tuned in and ready to receive the client's story, whatever it may contain. Offering a brief statement of your observations may provide the client with the opportunity to take the first steps toward engaging in the verbal exchanges.

"Start anywhere." Embedded within the client's lifetime of interrelated experiences lies the story that the client wants you to know. Since events in life can naturally blend from one incident to another, it may not be easy to locate the precise entry point of that substory. Enabling the client to "start anywhere" permits him or her to begin the storytelling process with whatever part seems best to him or her, focusing on facts or feelings in the present or the past. The client may choose a moderate entry point, or the client may begin by proclaiming the most critical or sensitive part of the story. Prompting the client to "start anywhere" essentially communicates the message, "It's your story. You're the only one who knows how to tell it. You can include as much backstory as you'd like me to know. Maybe you want to start with whatever part is easiest to talk about right now, or maybe you'd like to begin with whatever's most important to you. If you want, we can always pick up more details and fill things in later." You may even choose to say all or part of this as a follow-up to "Start anywhere."

Throughout the course of listening to the client, resist the temptation to exclusively seek out pathology and dysfunction. Take note of the client's positive characteristics, talents, capabilities, and strengths, as well as such personal attributes as his or her values, belief systems, social systems, skill sets, talents, resilience, and resources. Also, listen for evidence of past and recent successes. Essentially, the strengths, proficiencies, and resources that you and the client actively identify will serve as the "nuts and bolts" in assembling the client's treatment plan.

Though still in the assessment phase, goal identification may emerge at any point during the process. Goals stated early in the process should be taken seriously. Whether goals emerge or not, it is still important to continue to conduct a thorough assessment, aimed at helping you better understand the nature of the client and his or her overall living situation. The more familiar you are with the multidimensional shape of the client's life system, the more qualified you will be to work with the client at each of the next steps of the process:

II—Goal: Does this goal seem synchronous with the client's personality, talents, capabilities, belief system, resources, and so on?

III—Objectives: Does it seem likely that these activities are something that the client is willing and able to do? To what extent will the client have access to the resources necessary to accomplish the goal?

IV—Activation: Does the client have a history of successes or roadblocks that might facilitate or confound the action plan? What can the client do to identify and manage these (potential) encumbrances?

V—Termination: What does the client need in order to function independently?

Your overarching goal is to work collaboratively *with* clients, not *on* clients. Essentially, the better you know your client, the better you will be able to collaboratively craft a customized pathway that is suitable to the client's unique characteristics.

At each step of the process, listen openly and try to understand the content of each client's life and the unique life perspective of each client.

Written Assessment

The principle of assembling a written assessment is to gather a multidimensional understanding of the client in terms of his or her overall health, detailing his or her physical, mental, and social status. Essentially, the written assessment can be thought of as a biopsychosocial profile of the client. In the interest of efficiency, agencies may have prospective clients complete some form of a written assessment prior to their first session. Such documentation may be used as one of the elements in determining the client's eligibility for services. The written assessment enables the client the opportunity to reflect on his or her life system, as well as imparting the prospective social worker with an overview of the client, hence providing something more than a "cold start" for the process.

Other times, you will be called upon to do the written assessment. You may choose to step through each part of the written assessment with the client beginning from the first item. Alternatively, you may wish to engage the client in discussing selected items. Your choices may be cued by items that seem over- or understated, implausible, idyllic, significant, unusual, vague, or otherwise clinically curious.

Unlike the structured format of a *DSM* diagnosis, there is no unified model for assembling a written assessment. The content or level of detail of a written assessment may vary based on the type of setting in which it is administered. For instance, a facility that provides a broad array of care may use a written assessment similar to the model detailed in this section, whereas a facility that focuses on a more specialized clinical issue (e.g., chemical dependency recovery, bereavement, phobias) may include substantially more questions pertaining to those specific areas.

The written assessment may take the form of a self-administered instrument, a semistructured interview, the administration of one or more objective psychometric instruments, or some combination thereof. The following written assessment model consists of 10 categories: self-concept, prior mental healthcare, physical, education, employment, family structure, culture/ethnicity, social, leisure, and legal. Each category also has several subcategories to help spur thorough responses.

Self-Concept

- How do you see yourself in general?
- What are some of your strengths?
- How do you think others see you?
- What problems or concerns have led you to seek care at this time?
- What are you hoping to accomplish throughout the course of care?

Intervention efforts begin from the client's point of view. As such, it can be helpful to gain an initial idea of how the client conceives him- or herself generally with regard to his or her specific strengths, as well as to provide some detail as to how others may conceive him or her. Such questions may provide you with a sense of the client's perspective in terms of self-esteem and sense of empowerment.

Inquiries regarding the client's initial concerns and what the client hopes to accomplish throughout the course of care can suggest both a starting point and possibly the ultimate goal of the process.

Prior Mental Healthcare

- Reason for care
- Provider (e.g., social worker, psychologist, psychiatrist, physician)
- Inpatient or outpatient care
- Start date, end date
- Diagnoses
- Medications
- Treatments or interventions
- Modality (e.g., individual, couple, family, group, peer support group)
- Summary of intervention: status at beginning, intervention, duration, referrals, and so on
- Outcome

Understanding the client's prior access to mental healthcare may provide insights into his or her condition and readiness for services at this time. If the client has had no prior experience in mental healthcare, you may want to take some extra time to orient the client as to what to expect in the form of your professional contact with him or her. Conversely, when working with a more experienced client, in terms of establishing rapport and understanding the client's history, it can be helpful to ask the client to summarize his or her experiences, detailing both positive and negative aspects of his or her care. This can provide insights as to the client's expectations and the extent to which such expectations are reasonable, given the nature of your contact with him or her.

Knowing what has and has not worked for the client in the past may provide guidance when it comes to collaboratively crafting and implementing treatment plans. The client's prior experience may serve as a predictor with respect to how the client may perform with you. For instance, a client who reports numerous unsatisfactory contacts with various providers may be carrying a passive or negative attitude. Such a client may enter with negative expectations, or the client may be expecting you to just fix him or her. On the other hand, a client who has a history of benefiting from such interventions may be prepared to take a more proactive role in working with you.

Physical

- General health
- Disabilities or physical limitations
- Chronic diseases (e.g., diabetes, hypertension, allergies)

- Hospitalizations (medical or mental health): reason for hospitalization, date, length of stay, discharge status
- Prescription medication: reasons, dosages, start date, end date or still taking, effects, side effects
- Other medicines (supplements, over-the-counter medications, herbs, teas): reasons, dosages
- Substance or alcohol use: date started using, amount used, frequency of use, last used, abstaining or still using, problems, recovery efforts, relapses, inpatient or outpatient hospitalizations, intentions (if still using)

Understanding the nature of the client's physical health and how he or she conceives his or her health status can provide key insights with respect to the client's overall treatment plan. For example, a client with a chronic disease requiring multiple unpredictable hospitalizations (e.g., sickle cell anemia, seizure disorder) may face special challenges and adaptations when it comes to fulfilling goals, such as earning a college degree or full-time employment, which requires uninterrupted attendance over extended periods.

As important as it is to understand the nature of the client's physical health, resist the temptation to naively assume that a client's physical health is the chief predictor in terms of setting and accomplishing meaningful goals. For instance, it is possible that a paraplegic client may be more adept at problem-solving strategies than an ambulatory client. Also, each client may have a unique adaptation to the same physical condition. For example, one client with diabetes may see his or her disease as an incidental, manageable attribute of daily life, while another client with the same disorder may conceive the diabetes as a profound disability, persistently confounding his or her life efforts.

It can also be helpful to know what medications the client is using because medications, or combinations of medications, may influence physical, cognitive, and emotional functioning. If medications are coming from more than one source, it can be helpful to ask if any one physician has a comprehensive list of all of the medicines that the client uses, as drugs that are individually beneficial, when combined, may have adverse interaction effects.

Substance and alcohol abuse or dependence may also be critical in terms of selecting goals. Clients who have participated in recovery efforts and are maintaining sobriety may have gained powerful coping skills, which may be applicable in the current setting. Conversely, the client's efforts with you may be substantially hampered in cases wherein he or she has relapsed or is actively using. If the client is using, it can be useful to assess the client's willingness or resistance with respect to including sobriety as a goal.

Education

- Highest degree earned
- Major(s)
- Grades
- Technical training
- Academic and career goal(s)
- Learning disabilities or gifts
- Academic or "street smarts"

The client's level of education and academic interests may be relevant throughout the process. While formal education can be a proxy for one's ability to think abstractly, do not underestimate the client's ability to think, reason, and function effectively in the absence of formal academic achievement. It can be risky to imply too much when considering one's academic major. One may have simply pursued a line of education that was of interest to him or her at the time; however, this may not necessarily predict one's career pathway or current interests. To exemplify this point, consider how many of your current academic colleagues have bachelor's degrees in fields other than social science. Also, consider potential learning disabilities. For example, a student with dyslexia may be working considerably harder to earn the same grades as his or her peers who do not have perceptual or learning disorders.

Employment

- Recent employment history
- Type(s) of work
- Start and end dates
- Reason(s) for leaving job(s)
- Satisfaction with job(s)
- Job stressors: workload, supervisor, coworkers, nature of work, and so on
- If unemployed, approximate length of unemployment
- Career goals

The client's employment history may be revealing. Take note of the types of positions that the client has had. Is there a seemingly random shift from one type of work to another? Is there a steady progression, advancing forward in a given field? Also notice the duration of each job: Would the client's duration at each job best be measured in months or years? Rapid job shifting may suggest a socialization problem, possibly with authority figures or peers. Alternatively, this may suggest a problem that may be central to the client (e.g., chronic lateness; difficulty focusing, following directions, or meeting deadlines; poor social skills). Details regarding the client's experience with coworkers and supervisors may provide useful insights regarding his or her propensity to deal effectively with peers, authority figures, and rules.

Family Structure

- Raised with: parent(s), siblings, others, pets, and so on
- Top three family or household rules or values (may be explicit or implicit)
- Tone of household: stressful, loving, strict, cheerful, cold, and so on
- Parents' work: jobs and hours
- Parents' level of education
- Parents' relationship: with each other and with children
- Sibling relations and rank (by age)
- Family problems: social, legal, medical, mental health, and so on
- Relationships with family members: past and present
- Current type of contact with family members: in person, telephone, e-mail, holiday visits only, none, and so on
- Current family structure with spouse, significant other, children, and so on

The environment in which one was raised can provide valuable information with respect to understanding the client's values and beliefs that were instilled into him or her during his or her early years. Additionally, understanding the nature of the client's relationship with his or her parents, siblings, and other family members, both past and present, may reveal valuable information regarding the nature of the client's support system and the type of relationships that the client engages in outside of his or her family. Knowing the client's sibling rank (e.g., oldest, middle, youngest) can also be relevant in terms of comprehending the client's social perspective and learned roles. Information regarding family problems may also be useful in understanding the client's adaptations in the present. For example, a client who was raised with a chronically ill family member may have served as a caretaker at that time. This role may resonate forward to other situations in the present (e.g., socially, within one's family setting, professionally).

Culture/Ethnicity

- Self-identification: cultural or ethnic group
- Positive and negative aspects
- Level of acculturation and identity with culture
- Spirituality: religious affiliations, practices, beliefs, ethical principles

One's culture or ethnicity may be represented in any number of ways. Clues may be expressed overtly as in one's attire, grooming, demeanor, dialect, or mannerisms. Alternatively, evidence of one's culture or ethnicity may be less observable, taking the form of selected practices, personally held philosophies, ethical principles, and life perspectives.

As with all aspects of the client, with respect to the client's identity as a member of a cultural or ethnic group, avoid the risk of stereotyping. Be open to understanding the client's unique adaptation to, indifference toward, or perhaps outright rejection of his or her heritage.

Make an effort to understand the strengths that the client may draw from his or her cultural or ethnic identity, as well as potential disadvantages (e.g., strict rules or principles, being a member of a minority group).

When considering a client's spirituality, keep in mind that the client may consider him- or herself a spiritual person without necessarily engaging in formal, organized religious practices, such as attending services, engaging in traditional rituals, or subscribing to a particular religion.

It may also be useful to understand the intergenerational aspects of the client's cultural or ethnic identity: Is the client's adaptation similar to or different from that of his or her parents or ancestry? To what extent might such generational variations or departures be associated with family cohesion or conflicts?

Social

- Friendships: number of friends, closeness
- Social activities: solo, couple, or group; type; frequency
- Social stressors
- Feelings toward others, in general

The manner in which one engages socially can suggest useful information in terms of understanding the client's propensity to involve others in his or her life. Although there is no simple formula for evaluating the client's socialization, understanding the cast of characters in the client's life and his or her perceived level of closeness with each can be useful. It can also be helpful to know how the client conceives each friend (e.g., deeply supportive, hang-out buddy). Also, knowing the client's propensity for social engagement can be helpful in terms of assembling intervention strategies: Is this a person who is willing to do things alone, or does he or she prefer to engage in activities that involve a friend or familiar cohort?

An assessment of functional social contacts along with an idea of social stressors and strained relationships can provide insight as to relational trends and problem-solving capabilities. Make an effort to understand the nature of the client's contacts with others. Is this someone whose social contacts are riddled with conflicts? Is this a person who is dedicated to proactively identifying and resolving conflicts as they arise in a relationship? Is this someone who (quietly) allows resentments to build cumulatively? Is this someone who is prompt to "fire" a friend upon a first offense? Does the client have a tendency to be a leader, a follower, or an even-handed participant when dealing with others?

Leisure

- Current activities: arts, hobbies, movies, music, reading, sports, television, theater, traveling, working out, writing, and so on
- Amount of time spent at each
- Level of enjoyment (1–5) [1 = low, 5 = high]
- Solo, partner, or group
- Past activities
- Activities that the client would like to try

Though it may sound trivial, make a point to gather information as to what leisure activities the client currently participates in. Ask about activities the client would like to try and what has delayed them. Some such activities may suggest otherwise missed talents, passions, or personality traits that the client may possess. Other such activities may suggest potentially problematic areas (e.g., illegal activities, alcohol or substance abuse, dangerous endeavors).

Leisure activities may suggest meaningful goals. For example, when working with a client who is looking for a (change in) vocation, it may be useful to review some of the activities that provide him or her with genuine pleasure and a sense of satisfaction. Leisure activities may offer clues as to the client's natural talents or passions. It can be equally useful to know if the client's leisure activities are typically solo (e.g., reading, video games) or partner or group activities (e.g., team sports, dance, playing cards).

In addition to inquiries about the client's present leisure activities, it can be useful to ask the client what activities he or she used to enjoy. Changes in the client's engagement in leisure activities may point to a significant life change (e.g., substantial loss or hurt, onset of depression, debilitating physical condition, embarking on a new relationship, close of a relationship, relocation, returning to school, job change).

Legal

- Past legal history
- Prison: reason, dates, durations
- Probation or parole
- Civil (e.g., divorce, custody, traffic violations)
- Criminal (e.g., theft, drug-related)
- Current legal status

Details regarding the client's legal history can suggest the level of stress that the client is experiencing—it can be emotionally taxing to be involved in legal proceedings. One's legal history may also suggest relevant goals (e.g., to abstain from stealing, anger management, to curb one's drinking or substance use). A singular offense may also suggest a better prognosis compared with clients presenting with multiple or repeat offenses.

Mental Status Exam

In addition to effectively engaging with clients to express themselves, a mental status exam (MSE) may provide a useful assessment tool for exploring and documenting the client's functioning. The MSE can help you build a more comprehensive impression of the client, identify key biopsychosocial factors pertinent to the client's condition, and assess the client's ability to function (Silver & Herrmann, 1991). An MSE can be thought of as a high-resolution snapshot of the client's life condition at a particular point in time (Wiger & Huntley, 2002). A sample of a completed MSE is presented in Appendix A (p. 261).

An MSE is an instrument for systematically assessing and documenting the quality of the client's mental functioning at the time of the interview. Occasionally, you may find an MSE as a preexisting part of the client's chart. Other times, you may be expected to conduct and document an MSE.

Unlike the fixed structure of the five-axis *DSM* mental health diagnoses, the content, structure, and thoroughness of an MSE can vary. The template that is presented in this chapter is fairly comprehensive in order to demonstrate the depth and breadth of characteristics that can be captured using an MSE. You or your agency may use some variation of this model.

The MSE, in its more comprehensive form, should include details of the condition under which the MSE was conducted, description of the person/appearance, state of consciousness, orientation, motor behavior, affect, speech, thought process, thought content, perceptions, judgment, memory, intellectual functioning, mental health diagnosis, and treatment recommendations. Each of these topics is covered in this section. When it comes to reading or assembling an MSE, it may be useful to refer to Appendix B, Diagnostic Terminology (p. 264), and Appendix C, Documentation, Symbols, and Abbreviations (p. 266).

The following section provides details as to the types of information within each area of the proposed MSE template, along with some applicable terminology.

Condition Under Which the MSE Is Conducted

- **Setting**—inpatient or outpatient clinic, office, hospital room, emergency room, prison, client's dwelling, street, shelter, and so on
- **Circumstances**—assessment of new client, suicide attempt, homeless walk-in, recently regained consciousness, and so on

Understanding the context in which an MSE is administered can be useful in interpreting the overall finding of the MSE. One might reasonably expect that assessing a homeless client on the street may present differently than a client who is seen in a hospital or clinic office. Also, describe the circumstances—the reason for administering the MSE. This can range from a routine assessment of a new client to profiling a client who was involved in a traumatic attack.

Description of Person/Appearance

- **Observable characteristics**—gender, age, race, attire (appropriateness), personal hygiene, piercings, tattoos, scars, attractiveness, femininity or masculinity, physical stature, grooming (appropriate or disheveled), and so on

Within reason, document your observations so that a colleague who may refer to this MSE will be able to build an approximate image of the client without actually seeing a photograph of the person. Consider writing your description so that the client could be identified in a crowd. You may include both objective and subjective impressions as in this sample excerpt:

Clothing appears casual—jeans, long-sleeve shirt, denim jacket, hiking boots, somewhat worn but well-mended and clean. Client appears comfortable despite layers of heavy clothing worn in warm weather.

State of Consciousness

- **Unconscious**—unable to wake, wakes to voice, wakes to loud verbal stimuli, wakes to touch, wakes promptly or slowly
- **Awareness**—alert, dazed, clouded, lethargic, intoxicated
- **Attention**—pays attention, ignores interviewer, ability to recall three to six digits
- **Concentration**—focuses on subject matter, ability to recall two to four letters

Describe the client's level of consciousness in terms of how awake or drowsy the client appeared and how attentive the client was. If the client is able to achieve a better focus upon your request (e.g., "I need you to pay closer attention"), this is worth documenting.

When using digit recall, consider using the same number sequence each time (e.g., the first five digits of an old phone number) so that when you ask the client to play back the number, you will have no trouble evaluating his or her accuracy. Similarly, when asking a client to recall letters, consider consistently using a sequence of letters that do not spell a word. You may wish to invent a sequence that is meaningful to you, thereby making it easy to validate the client's playback (e.g., **M D L B**—My Dad Likes Bagels).

Orientation (x 3)

- **Person**—What is your name?
- **Place**—Where are we now?
- **Time**—What is today's date?

Orientation has three dimensions:

1. *Person*—Does the client know *who* he or she is (simply ask the client, "What is your name?")?

2. *Place*—Does the client know *where* he or she is (city, state, facility, hospital, home, and so on)?

3. *Time*—Does the client know *when* he or she is (day, date, month, year)?

A client who is not confident in his or her response may hesitate or resist answering. You can gently prompt the client (once) to "just guess." If the client's response to a question is wrong, you need not correct him or her unless he or she asks. In instances where the client provides no answer, you may consider asking a related follow-up question. For example, if a client is hesitant regarding your *time* question, you might ask, "Who is the president of the United States?" The client's response may suggest the time frame that he or she believes he or she is in—replying "Reagan" would suggest that the client believes he or she is in the 1980s, whereas "Kennedy" would suggest the 1960s. Shorthand notation for a client being alert (judging from the "State of Consciousness" criteria) and properly oriented to person, place, and time is traditionally written as *A/Ox3* (alert and oriented times 3 [to person, place, and time]). Variations in the client's orientation can also be notated (e.g., "A/Ox1; knows name, disoriented to time and place").

Motor Behavior (Frequency and Magnitude of Movements)

- **Agitation**—small movements
- **Hyperactivity**—larger movements (nonsitting, pacing)
- **Psychomotor retardation**—reduction or absence of overall movements
- **Posturing**—odd positions
- **Echopraxia**—mirrors your standing position, seated posture, and movements
- **Stereotypical movement**—repetitive, non-goal-directed movements (hands, legs)
- **Waxy flexibility**—maintains any position that the client is physically molded into

Apart from socially appropriate movements (e.g., expressive hand gestures synchronous to dialogue, nodding, crossed legs, periodically shifting weight from one foot to another while standing), note the client's anomalous movements. Consider noting if such movements seem to be steady in presentation or correlated with the discussion of specific subject matter.

Affect (Displayed Emotional Signals—Facial and Voice Tone)

- **Range**—flat, blunted, restricted, limited, expansive, ultradramatic
- **Stability**—labile (rapid changes in affect, within minutes)
- **Appropriateness**—affect consistent or inconsistent with story or setting (voluntary or compulsory interview)
- **Reported mood**—based on the client's self-report

Affect pertains to the client's observable emotional presentation, whereas mood is about the client's inner experience of an emotion. For instance, a client may be smiling, thus projecting a joyous affect, whereas his or her (internal) mood may be fear. Note the client's predominate affect (e.g., depressed, subdued, bright) and also indicate the extent to which the client's affect seems to match the content of his or her discussion (e.g., "Affect varies appropriately per story content," "Presents with jubilant affect when discussing sibling's misfortunes").

Speech (Quality, Not Content)

- **Rate**—tempo
- **Quality**—volume
- **Amount**—low quantity = "poverty of speech," high quantity = "logorrhea"
- **Pressured speech**—intense, talks fast, high volume, difficult or impossible to interrupt

Describe *how* the client communicates in terms of speed, loudness, wordiness, and intensity. You may also note flexibility in the client's speech characteristics (e.g., "Initially, the client was speaking too fast to fully understand. Upon request, the client was able to slow down and articulate clearer"). Details regarding the *content* of the speech should be documented under "Thought Process."

Thought Process

- **Cogency**—organization and relevancy
- **Speech**—goal-directed or rambling
- **Linkages**—logical or illogical flow of ideas and concepts
- **Coherent**—strength of concept links or loose association (weak links)
- **Tangential**—fails to get to the point or address your question
- **Circumstantial**—includes extensive nonessential details
- **Flight of ideas**—rapidly moving from one idea to another with some discernible thread through ideas
- **Preservation**—needless repetition of same word or idea
- **Blocking**—abruptly stops speaking (may be midsentence) and unable to resume at derailed point
- **Clanging**—reciting rhyming words that do not make sense together
- **Word salad**—random words (may be spoken with conversational inflections)

Thought process describes the flow of the client's conversation. A thought process characterized by consistently cogent dialogue should be noted. Also, note exceptions. As in other aspects of the MSE, if the client's dialogue presents as atypical, you may make a specific request that the client adjust and then note the client's thought process after you make such a request. For instance, suppose a client's initial expression is a word salad (e.g., "The cap of the street and of not to the cloud for the pencil?"). If upon telling the client, "I'm sorry. I'm not understanding what you're saying. Can you tell me that in another way?" the client is able to provide a clearer sentence, this is worth documenting. Alternatively, if the client reiterates the same text or utters another equally confusing sentence, this is also noteworthy.

Thought Content

- **Preoccupation**—stuck on a single idea with strong affect
- **Delusions**—inflexibly adheres to a false belief system despite reasonable evidence to the contrary
- **Ideas of reference**—thinking that other things or people are in some way related to the client (e.g., believing that a stranger across the street is thinking about the client)
- **Thought broadcasting**—thinking that others can perceive the client's thoughts
- **Ideas of influence**—thinking that others are controlling the client's thoughts
- **Thought insertion**—thinking that someone or something put a thought into the client's head or forced him or her to act
- **Dangerousness**—probability of harm to self or others (suicidal or homicidal)

Thought content involves describing what the client thinks about, how the client processes his or her thoughts, and possible thought disorders. This section also provides you with the opportunity to document evidence of potential dangerous thinking that may put the client at risk of harming him- or herself or others and then to take appropriate protective steps.

In states that honor the Tarasoff law, if a client expresses an intent to harm an identified victim, you would be required to breach confidentiality to notify the appropriate authorities and make an effort to warn the specified victim.

In instances wherein you believe the client is at risk of harming him- or herself, you would be working along the lines of voluntary hospitalization. Should that fail, you would move toward arranging for the client to be assessed by a professional who has the training and authority to assess the client and, if necessary, facilitating an involuntary hospitalization.

Perceptions

- **Hallucinations**—sensory experiences in the absence of external sensory stimuli
- **Illusions**—sensory input with altered interpretation

Perceptual disturbances involve distortions in the way that the client experiences the environment.

Hallucinations involve the client sensing (hearing, seeing, feeling, tasting, or smelling) something in the absence of real-world or external stimuli (e.g., seeing a table that is not actually present).

Illusions begin with an actual sensory stimulation (e.g., seeing a table that is indeed present), but it is experienced in an erroneous manner (e.g., the table appears to be bending, moving, walking, or changing colors, size, shape, or composition).

Judgment

- **Soundness**—the quality of the client's ability to make reasonable decisions or plans
- **Appropriateness**—the extent to which the client's decisions or plans address the circumstance

Assessing the client's sense of judgment is not necessarily about the client's response to a single determining question. You should be gathering a sense of the quality of the client's judgment throughout the course of the interview. If you are unclear regarding the client's judgment, ask a question or two that require the client to derive an appropriate course of action given a relatively commonplace situation (e.g., "What would you do if you were in a theater and you smelled smoke?" "What would you do if you found a stamped, addressed envelope on the sidewalk?" "If you wanted to eat a bowl of soup, what would you need?").

Memory

- **Immediate**—5- to 10-minute recall
- **Recent**—24-hour recall
- **Remote**—more than 24-hour recall

Three realms of memory can easily be assessed:

Immediate memory involves recalling the last 5 to 10 minutes. To check for immediate recall, ask the client to remember three simple words (e.g., *dog, car,* and *hat*) and tell the client that you will ask him or her to repeat those words in a few minutes. Then continue the interview. After about 5 minutes, ask the client to recall the words. Consider using the same words each time so that you will reliably know if the client is correct.

Recent memory involves events that took place in the last 24 hours. The client should be able to answer questions about where he or she was and what he or she did yesterday.

Remote memory entails remembering more distant information (e.g., where the client grew up, his or her favorite elementary school teacher, his or her date of birth).

Intellectual Functioning

- Significantly above average
- Above average
- Average
- Below average
- Significantly below average

Although the subject of the client's highest level of education may not necessarily emerge, based on the course of your conversation, you may make a point to ask. You should also be able to make a reasonable estimate regarding the client's general level of intelligence.

Mental Health Diagnosis

The client's (five-axis) *DSM* mental health diagnosis, as detailed earlier in this chapter, should be included. This may consist of a preexisting diagnosis, input from members of a multidisciplinary team, or, once you are trained, your own diagnostic determination.

Treatment Recommendations

Based on your overall impression of the client, you should have a feel for who this person is in terms of his or her cognitive, emotional, and social functioning. Additional relevant elements, such as the client's wishes, needs, desires, preferences, and belief systems, may also emerge.

It is appropriate to include a brief statement regarding your ideas as to what you think the next step(s) should be for this client. This may involve the need for further assessment (e.g., mental health evaluation, risk to self or others, medical referral), or you may have a provisional treatment plan in mind. Naturally, prior to implementing any treatment plan, you would need to submit this proposed plan to the client, as it is subject to his or her approval and modifications.

Regardless of the evaluation instrument that you use, whether formal quantitative metrics or qualitative impressions, as with all determinations made when working with clients, consider the information that you gather as a valuable image of the client's condition up to that point in time. Bear in mind that people are dynamic. As such, periodic reevaluation should be an integral component in any treatment regime.

CHAPTER 3 EXERCISES

CONCEPT REVIEWS

Explain each concept in your own words. Where applicable, provide a case example without disclosing identifying information.

3.1 Case review (p. 124)

When such material is legitimately available, describe the rationale for conducting a case review prior to meeting a new client.

3.2 Mental health diagnosis (A) (p. 126)

Describe the structure and type of information contained on a five-axis *DSM* mental health diagnosis.

3.3 Mental health diagnosis (B) (p. 126)

What are some of the advantages that a mental health diagnosis affords?

3.4   **Mental health diagnosis (C) (p. 126)**

What are some of the potential drawbacks associated with mental health diagnoses?

3.5   **After meeting the client (p. 134)**

Describe some of the fundamental things that should occur during your initial contact with a client.

3.6   **Learning about the client (A) (p. 135)**

What are some of the factors that may inhibit the client from readily disclosing his or her problem or story?

3.7   **Learning about the client (B) (p. 135)**

If a client presents as uncertain where to begin, what are some techniques that may help the client embark on his or her storytelling?

3.8   **Written assessment (A) (p.138)**

What is the rationale for conducting and documenting a written assessment?

3.9   **Written assessment (B) (p. 138)**

What sort of information is included in a written assessment?

3.10   **Mental status exam (A) (p. 144)**

What is the rationale for conducting and documenting an MSE?

3.11   **Mental status exam (B) (p. 144)**

What sort of information is included in an MSE?

3.12   Written assessment versus mental status exam (pp. 138, 144)

Describe the difference between the type of information that is gathered on a written assessment and the type of information that is gathered on an MSE.

DISCUSSION POINTS

Discuss among your peers how you might handle these circumstances. Document the opinions expressed using a "+" or a "−" to indicate whether you agree or disagree with each opinion.

3.1 File frenzy

Due to a last-minute staffing change, your supervisor has assigned you to see a new client who has been approved for service. You have been handed an 80-page case file from the client's prior social worker, and the client's appointment is in 20 minutes.

3.2 Diagnostic dilemma

Your new client's behavior and coping seem to depart substantially from the diagnostic profile contained in his or her prior chart.

3.3 Diagnostic disclosure

Midsession, your client discloses a mental health diagnosis that is unfamiliar to you.

3.4 Say what I mean

The client persistently refers to his or her indecisive supervisor as "schizophrenic" and members of a particular political group as "retarded."

3.5 Quick start

Prior to reading or signing the treatment consent detailing the agency's policies and fee structure, the client embarks on disclosing a deeply emotional story.

3.6 Hard start

At the beginning of the initial appointment, the client sits silently for a few minutes. When you (gently) prompt the client to begin, the client starts crying.

3.7 Fresh start?

A client states: "I know my other doctor sent you my file—I had to sign for it, but she was totally incompetent and unprofessional—she really hated me. You can't believe anything that comes out of her."

3.8   MSE, past and present

You are noticing substantial differences between the client's conduct now and the client's conduct as documented on an MSE written over a year ago by another social worker.

3.9   All of me?

The client refers to the written assessment and asks why you need to know all of this information.

3.10   Mission improbable

Having conducted what you consider a reasonably thorough assessment, the client strongly disagrees with selected parts of your provisional treatment recommendations.

WRITTEN ASSESSMENT

1. Complete a written assessment using a client or a peer. If it is feasible to base this written assessment on an actual client, write your assessment in a manner that protects the client's identity. If you are assessing a peer, he or she may wish to provide genuine information, selectively fabricate a story, or portray a character from a role-play scenario detailed in a prior chapter.

- Self-concept

- Prior mental healthcare

- Physical

- Education

- Employment

- Family structure (family of origin and client's current family [spouse, children])

- Culture or ethnicity

- Social

- Leisure

- Legal

2. Acme Mental Health Center, a general service agency, has commissioned you to design the written assessment form that will become part of the intake questionnaire that all potential clients must complete prior to their first session. Each client will complete the survey at home, so be sure to include adequate instructions (e.g., rationale for completing a written assessment, information that should be included for each category and subcategory). You may wish to include some or all of the categories listed above, add some other categories, rearrange the order of the categories, and so on.

MENTAL STATUS EXAM AND ROLE-PLAY

Conduct an interview and assemble the corresponding MSE. Refer to the categories below to guide your inquiries and observations. Use form 1 in this section (p. 163) to document your initial findings. Form 2 (p. 166) may be used for a future MSE.

This exercise is flexible in terms of your subject selection: You may be able to interview an actual client in order to complete this exercise, in which case you should document your findings in a way that protects the client's identity.

If it is not feasible to involve a client in this exercise, you may engage in a peer role-play. This role-play should run about 15 minutes in order to provide you with a sufficient body of information to assemble the MSE. Alternatively, you may choose to execute one of the three role-play scenarios presented on p. 162, or if your partner is so inclined, he or she may wish to create and portray a plausible character with a corresponding story line for this exercise. It may be helpful to take some notes during this interview.

MSE Content Areas

- Condition under which the MSE was conducted
- Description of person/appearance
- State of consciousness
- Orientation
- Motor behavior
- Affect
- Speech
- Thought process
- Thought content
- Perceptions
- Judgment
- Memory
- Intellectual functioning
- Mental health diagnosis (Note: If you are inexperienced at making specific mental health diagnoses, document the signs and symptoms that you consider significant. For practice, you may wish to list the *DSM* five-axis array, stating the type of diagnostic information that is contained on each axis.)
- Treatment recommendations

MSE Role-Plays

3.1 Home of the Homeless

Jackie has entered a homeless shelter, seeking a place to spend the night. Jackie initially became homeless due to an unfortunate sequence of events (e.g., loss of job, inability to find work, illness, failure to keep up with rent, family issues, depression, hospitalization). Jackie would like to get off the streets but feels trapped due to the homeless conundrum: You cannot get a job without an address, and you cannot get an address without money for rent. Jackie has found some sources for food and places to sleep at night but longs for returning to a more stable, meaningful existence. Jackie occasionally resorts to alcohol as a means of temporary relief.

3.2 To Leave and Honor . . .

Dana has been in a close relationship with Ray for about 5 years. Through the accidental disclosure of a common friend, last week Dana learned that throughout the course of their relationship, Ray has engaged in numerous intimate encounters outside their relationship. Dana has confirmed parts of this and has not yet confronted Ray. Three days ago, Dana arranged to take some time off work and temporarily moved into a local hotel. Dana is not accepting calls and has not disclosed this location to anyone, including Ray. Dana is flooded with numerous strong feelings—anger, confusion, betrayal, indecision, and disbelief—and is uncertain as to how to proceed.

3.3 Lots of Losses

While on vacation, Jody's house was robbed. The loss was substantial, involving things of monetary and sentimental value. Since the robbery, Jody has experienced sleep disturbances (e.g., difficulty falling asleep, nightmares, repeatedly waking up to slight sounds, waking early). Jody is unable to feel relaxed or comfortable at home, startles easily, and is having problems concentrating at work. Jody has been experiencing a variety of emotions, including numbness, outrage, emptiness, and vulnerability.

MSE 1—Dᴀᴛᴇ ___/___/___

Condition under which the MSE was conducted:

Description of person/appearance:

State of consciousness:

Orientation:

Motor behavior:

Affect:

Speech:

Thought process:

Thought content:

Perceptions:

Judgment:

Memory:

Intellectual functioning:

Mental health diagnosis (or significant signs and symptoms):

Treatment recommendations:

MSE 2—Date ___/___/___

Condition under which the MSE was conducted:

Description of person/appearance:

State of consciousness:

Orientation:

Motor behavior:

Affect:

Speech:

Thought process:

Thought content:

Perceptions:

Judgment:

Memory:

Intellectual functioning:

Mental health diagnosis (or significant signs and symptoms):

Treatment recommendations:

4

Step II—Goal

Where Does the Client Want to Be?

I	II	III	IV	V
Assessment	**Goal**	**Objectives**	**Activation**	**Termination**

Rationale for Setting a Goal

There is an old joke:

Joe: *Where are you going?*

Moe: *I don't know.*

Joe: *How do you know when you're there?*

This silly exchange makes a valuable point: Without a destination in mind, one's life is likely to meander aimlessly. One's fate is essentially left to the random winds of chance. The indiscriminate, unguided happenstances to follow are unlikely to fulfill one's unique needs or desires in a specific or timely manner. This passive approach is unsuitable when it comes to working proficiently with clients. Since the client–social worker relationship is typically time-limited, well-selected goals are needed. Basically, clients seek out the services of a social worker when circumstances are not to their liking and they are seeking improvement; there is an unmet want or need with a solution that is currently unexecuted or unidentified (D'Zurilla & Godfried, 1971).

Without minimizing the client's problem, it can be helpful to inform the client that problems are a natural part of existence. Nobody leads a flawless life. In keeping with the principle of client empowerment (National Association of Social Workers, 1996), without implying guilt or blame, it can be useful to help clients identify the extent to which they are (at least partly) responsible for the problem at hand. The more a client can realistically claim responsibility for the existence of a problem, the more the problem is within his or her reach with respect to resolving it. Admittedly, this can take some courage on the client's behalf.

Conversely, the client who persistently perceives him- or herself as the helpless victim of powerful malevolent forces (e.g., bad luck, unfairness, mean people, disabilities) may momentarily enjoy the luxury of delegating blame to such awful entities. Unfortunately, the cost of conceiving the cause of the problem as exclusively out of his or her reach places the solution to the problem equally out of reach.

Recognizing one's role in the evolution of a problem essentially acknowledges that one's actions or inactions *do* count when it comes to influencing the shape of one's own circumstances. As such, the client may be able to take strategic actions in solving the problem (Bedell & Lennox, 1997).

A goal can be thought of as the future state that an individual strives to achieve. Goals reflect the individual's motives. Some goals may be conceived as efforts to adapt to one's environment (Schmuck & Sheldon, 2001).

Meaningfully selected goals can serve multiple purposes:

1. The goal can provide direction and guidance toward the desired change or achievement.

2. The goal can facilitate planning in terms of identifying the objectives (steps and resources) needed to achieve the goal.

3. Conceptualizing how things will be upon the completion of a goal can serve to motivate efforts directed toward the completion of a goal.

4. A goal can provide a "yardstick" for measuring the difference between the client's preintervention state and his or her state upon the completion of the goal. (Barney & Griffin, 1992)

An appropriate goal also serves to help the client focus his or her attention toward a potential solution. The client can direct his or her time, efforts, and resources in a direction that supports actions aimed at advancing the accomplishment of the goal. Since the prospect of actually achieving a goal is correlated with a desire for positive change, articulating meaningful goals can serve to energize the client, knowing that he or she is taking active steps toward improving his or her circumstances. As the client sees that such efforts are effective, this is likely to enhance the client's sense of empowerment, thereby motivating the client to proceed further. Essentially, success breeds success (Locke & Latham, 2002).

Problems Versus Goals

The presenting problem may suggest a corresponding goal. For instance, a client who reports that he or she smokes may reasonably wish to quit smoking. That would be an appropriate goal; however, it would be naive to think that the stated *problem* always points to an obvious *goal*. Consider a client who mentions that he or she smokes two packs of cigarettes per day. As a well-intended social worker, there are a number of seemingly reasonable assumptions that could take you down the wrong road:

1. It would be wrong to immediately assume that the client considers his or her smoking a problem—he or she may merely be mentioning it as a way of orienting you to his or her normal conduct.

2. You may erroneously assume that, since the client mentioned that he or she smokes, he or she wants to quit entirely. This may not necessarily be the case. The client may be seeking to alter his or her smoking in some other ways (e.g., reduce his or her smoking from two packs to one pack per day, stop smoking in the car).

3. Without having explored the client's history, smoking two packs per day may be something that the client is proud of—having cut down from three packs per day.

This simple example demonstrates that, while it is important to tend to the client's problems, characteristics, and overall story content, you should recap your understanding of the client's condition(s) and explicitly inquire about the client's goals. As important as it is for you to understand the client's problem(s), it is equally essential for the client to articulate specifically what he or she hopes to accomplish in the form of goals.

Intrinsic Versus Extrinsic Goals

One framework for conceptualizing goals involves differentiating between *intrinsic* and *extrinsic* goals (Kasser & Ryan, 1996). Intrinsic goals can be thought of as self-developmental in nature, aimed at evolving one's self, personal identity, or lifestyle. These goals involve such things as self-acceptance and sense of affiliation with one's community (Higgins, 1987; Little, 1993). Extrinsic goals are characterized by efforts to gain positive evaluation from others. This can take the form of competitively working toward financial success, popularity, or appearing (more) attractive.

Counterintuitive to the recent historical societal trends characterized by individuals striving for wealth and the accumulation of material possessions, those who focus on intrinsic goals tend to report higher levels of well-being than those who focus on extrinsic goals (Austin, 1998). It is hypothesized that intrinsic goals may be more satisfying in that they address innate psychological needs, such as autonomy, relatedness, competency, and growth (Deci & Ryan, 1985; Fromm, 1976; Maslow, 1954), and facilitate better focus with respect to one's awareness of his or her internal states (Gibbons et al., 1985), whereas extrinsic goals do not (Kasser & Ryan, 1993). In instances where the client identifies goals that are predominately extrinsic in nature, it may be helpful to summarize these findings and encourage the client either to reform or reprioritize his or her goals or to consider including some intrinsic goals as well.

Though potentially more fulfilling, efforts directed at pursuing intrinsic goals can be rigorous, as such goals involve altering the structure of how one thinks, behaves, and feels. As one might expect, working toward such goals, though worthwhile, can be the source of considerable stress (Salmela-Aro, 1992; Salmela-Aro & Nurmi, 1997).

As your assessment of the client advances, be cognizant of his or her personality traits. Clients who are extroverts are likely to be drawn toward social goals, whereas more introverted clients tend to focus on goals that facilitate safety (Emmons, 1989).

Fundamental Attributes of a Goal: SMART

Social work is about working with the client to achieve actual changes to improve the quality of his or her life. Since goals are about real-life changes, real parameters must be taken into account when considering meaningful goals. A common model for forming and assessing the suitability of a goal is the SMART model, which suggests that a goal should consist of five attributes: **S**pecific, **M**easurable, **A**ttainable, **R**ealistic, and **T**imely.

Specific

Goals must be indicated in specific terms. Vague goals lead to vague outcomes. For example, consider the potential of achieving a fairly simple goal: a meeting. Suppose the stated goal is "We should get together sometime." The vagueness of this well-intended goal confounds one's ability to carry it out in real life: We do not know precisely what the nature of this "get-together" will be, we do not know when it will happen, and we do not know where it will happen. As this goal stands, it is highly unlikely that it can actually be accomplished. Now consider this more specific alternative: "Let's have lunch this Saturday at noon. Meet me at Ponty's at Pico and Sepulveda." This more specific statement includes the precise information necessary to actually carry out the goal: We now know that this get-together is going to be a lunch, and we know exactly where and when this lunch will take place. Specificity makes this an achievable goal.

Clients may initially express goals in vague terms (e.g., "I've got to lose some weight," "I want things to be more peaceful at home," "My sleep is all messed up," "I really should go back to school"). Such statements provide valuable clues as to the nature of the client's dissatisfaction. As such, work with the client to re-form such phrases into more specific language. For instance, the statement "I've got to lose some weight" fails to express how much weight. There is a substantial difference between the efforts involved in working to lose 10 pounds (about 4.5 kilograms) and those involved in working to lose 100 pounds (about 45 kilograms). Collaborate with the client to state goals in terms that are as specific as possible (e.g., "I want to be 10 pounds lighter"). Think of a goal as a destination: You cannot get *there* if you do not know where *there* is. Specificity is essential.

You will need to be prepared for incidents wherein the client may feel overwhelmed by one or more significant problems. In such cases, the client may not articulate the problem(s) in a discrete, identifiable form. When this occurs, gently but firmly coach the client to break out the specific elements that make up their troublesome circumstances as in the following example:

Cl: *My life is a complete mess.*

Sw: *What are some of the things that are making your life so messy these days?*

The client's statement is useful in that it expresses the client's general sense of dissatisfaction. The social worker prompts the client to elaborate on the specific element(s) that are causing the client to see his or her life as a mess.

> *Cl: I'm not sure where to begin. OK, my daughter's grades are dropping like a stone, my blood pressure's up again, and I feel like my work is going nowhere. I just don't know where to go with all of this.*

The brief inquiry helped the client elucidate the specific elements that are the sources of his or her stress: (a) daughter's poor academic performance, (b) elevated blood pressure, and (c) dissatisfaction with work.

Referring to the above dialogue, the next step would be to gather further details regarding each of the (three) stated problems in order to comprehend the weight and possible relationships among them. For example, it may be found that the client's daughter's poor performance is correlated with the client's rise in blood pressure. With respect to the client's working conditions, it would be useful to know if this is a new problem associated with a change in the client's personal or professional life or if this problem has been festering for some time.

The exploration of such problems moves you closer to helping the client identify which issues will be addressed and in which order, as well as to helping the client derive the corresponding goals.

Another possibility is that the client is unable to identify the problem, even in vague terms. Instead, the client may report a symptom, a set of symptoms, or an incident. In such instances, you would still be working with the client to identify the goal(s), but first you must locate the specific problem(s). One strategy for gaining more specific information in such cases is to prompt the client to discuss the onset of the symptoms. Essentially, something, at some point, changed. The big question is "What's the something?" This "something" that changed may involve feelings, actions, events, or thoughts:

Feelings—Look for recent changes in feelings (e.g., loss, hurt, fear, anger, anxiety, concern, uncertainty, confusion, guilt, loneliness, vulnerability). Be curious as to alterations in the intensity, frequency, and duration of the client's feelings, as well as emotional reactions that are atypical for the client (e.g., no longer laughs, listless, cries often, startles easily).

Actions—Take note of uncharacteristic, (seemingly) irrational, or socially inappropriate behaviors (e.g., sleeping more or less than usual, eating more or less than usual, changes in socialization or leisure activities).

Events—Seek out any exceptional occurrences, new circumstances, changes, or losses in the client's life (e.g., relocation, losses or deaths, changes in health).

Thoughts—Be aware of changes in the client's thought content and topics of discussion. Recent obsessive thoughts or concerns may be relevant (e.g., fixation on a thought or belief, hopelessness, confusion, inability to focus or concentrate, easily distracted).

In any case, ask the client to discuss when the symptoms began and what was going on at that time. Also, engage the client to talk about what life was like *before* the symptoms began and what life has been like *since* then.

Cl: *I just don't know what's wrong with me. I'm exhausted all the time, and all I want to do is go to sleep.*

Sw: *What's your sleeping like these days?*

The social worker begins by gathering information regarding the client's current state based on the symptoms mentioned.

Cl: *It's odd. As soon as I get home, I lie down for a nap in my clothes, in broad daylight, and then wake up about 4 or 5 hours later. Then I get something for dinner, brush my teeth, and go to bed for the night. I sleep straight through the night . . . no dreams. And that's it. Even when I'm awake, all I can think about is how sweet it will be to just go to sleep. Now that's just not like me.*

Sw: *It's not like you? What was your sleeping like before?*

Gather baseline information: What was the client's sleeping like before the onset of the problem?

Cl: *Just regular—like anyone else: 7 or 8 hours a night, and that's it. I've never needed to nap before.*

Sw: *When did you start feeling so tired?*

Identify the time frame of the onset.

Cl: *About 4 months ago.*

Sw: *What was going on 4 months ago?*

Identify the events of the critical time frame.

Cl: *Well, I moved.*

Sw: *You moved. From where to where?*

The social worker continues gathering details.

Cl: *From my apartment to my parents' house.*

The social worker would proceed by asking the client to discuss such things as the client's mood, level of activity, and sleep prior to this move. Also, the social worker would pursue details regarding the life event(s) that propagated this change in living conditions and the nature of the client's new living conditions. Once specific problems have been identified, appropriate goals may emerge. Parenthetically, whenever a client presents with symptoms that are physical in nature—such as, in this case, the symptoms of a sleep disorder—you cannot assume that the cause is social or emotional. A medical referral is in order.

Measurable

Measurability enables you and the client to assess the client's progress toward accomplishing the goal and, for that matter, completion. In the prior example involving a goal of losing 10 pounds (about 4.5 kilograms), one can easily measure progress. A loss of 1 pound (about 0.5 kilogram) indicates 10% completion, a 2-pound (almost 1-kilogram) loss is 20% completion, and so on. When the measurement indicates a 10-pound loss, one can consider the goal complete.

Measurability enables monitoring. Measurements that show an unanticipated direction may suggest the need to reevaluate the goal or the means being used to accomplish that goal. For example, suppose that instead of the client losing weight, he or she begins gaining weight. Another possibility is that the measurement indicates no change over time. Again, this suggests that something about the intervention may require tuning. Through measurement, progress or lack of progress toward accomplishing a goal can be assessed.

Weight loss is a fairly simple metric to capture: Just step onto the scale and read the number; however, not all such phenomena are measured as easily. There are numerous prepared rapid assessment instruments (RAIs) designed to measure a variety of specific conditions. Typically, these instruments are administered in a pre- and posttest fashion: Prior to embarking on a selected intervention, the client would complete the instrument. This establishes a baseline score, which represents the client's starting point. At some point(s) during the intervention or upon the conclusion of the intervention, the same instrument would be readministered, providing a quantitative or graphical representation of the client's progress by comparing the scores (baseline vs. now).

Most RAIs are simple for all involved: Clients are typically asked to respond to a short list of objective yes-or-no, circle-the-number, or check-the-box questions that can be answered in a few minutes. Most such instruments do not require statistical expertise or access to computing software. Often the scoring is simply a matter of adding up the client's (numerical) responses and applying that total to a simple scaled key for interpretation (e.g., 0–3 = low, 4–7 = medium, 8–10 = high).

Alternatively, you may wish to collaborate with the client to design a concise, straightforward instrument consisting of questions that pertain specifically to the client's symptoms or goals. For example, suppose a client describes frequently getting into verbal confrontations. You may work with the client to assemble a customized self-reporting tool that captures the key behaviors that are unique to the client's circumstances as shown in Figure 4.1.

For simplicity, only the *daily totals* have been plotted. It may be valuable to plot the other three lines on this chart using different colors or separate graphs in order to track the client's confrontational engagements in each of the three domains: work, home, and elsewhere. Clearly, this simple measurement technique and graph can serve to inform both you and the client as to where he or she stands in terms of progress toward achieving the specified goal(s).

Attainable

A goal needs to be something that, with the right resources and efforts, the client can actually achieve. For example, consider an adult client who is 5 foot, 5 inches (about 1.7 meters) tall and weighs 200 pounds (about 91 kilograms). The client's desire to lose 30 pounds (about 13.6 kilograms) is an attainable goal, whereas wanting to grow another foot taller is unattainable.

Confrontation log for week of 9/18

Day:	Mon	Tue	Wed	Thu	Fri	Sat	Sun
Confrontations at work:	4	3	2	1	1	–	–
Confrontations at home:	2	3	3	3	1	2	1
Confrontations elsewhere:	1	2	1	1	0	2	1
Daily total:	7	8	6	5	2	4	2

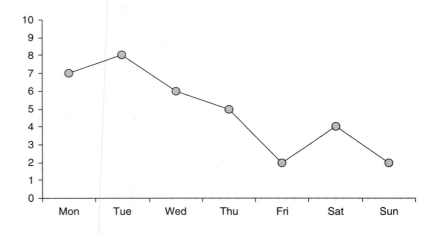

Figure 4.1   Daily Journal of Verbal Confrontations

Realistic

Although the notion of a goal may be rooted in a wish, a fantasy, or an abstract desire, in order to be achievable, a goal must be realistic. Continuing with the weight-loss example, it is realistic to expect that with proper diet and exercise, the client could lose 30 pounds (about 13.6 kilograms); however, it is unrealistic to think that this can be accomplished within 1 week.

As a social worker, even for goals that are realistic, it may be useful to delve deeper. Assuming that the goal to lose 30 pounds were accomplished, reflect on the client's *expectations*—do they seem realistic? For example, upon further exploration, you may discover that the client believes that losing 30 pounds will benefit his or her overall health. This is a reasonable expectation, whereas believing that the weight loss will immediately double the number of his or her friends is less plausible. You might consider including this as a point worthy of discussion.

Timely

Each goal requires a time frame that specifies a start time and a (provisional) end time. Continuing with the above example, the goal to lose 30 pounds (about 13.6 kilograms) is a useful notion; however, in order to actually bring this goal to fruition, one must know precisely when the diet and exercise regimen is set to begin. Further, a reasonable end date should be indicated. This can help mediate such things as caloric intake and the amount and type of exercise that the client should consider in order to achieve the goal by the specified date.

As important as it is to specify an end date, it is equally important to be flexible. As the client embarks on the mission to accomplish the goal, the actual implementation may prove to be easier or more complex than anticipated. Real life can hold surprises that cannot be anticipated on paper; hence, as implementation advances, there may need to be some appropriate adjustments to the end date.

Supplemental Attributes of a Goal

Legal

As a social worker, you are committed to working with clients on goals that are legal. You should not partake in planning, encouraging, or otherwise advocating that the client embark on goals that are dishonest, fraudulent, or deceptive in nature (National Association of Social Workers, 1996). If a client expresses dissatisfaction with a social condition or a law that seems unfair, it would be appropriate to work with the client to achieve the desired changes using legitimate means.

Concurrence With the Client's Values

Goals are about the change(s) that the client wants to see in his or her life. The client's self-determination is essential when it comes to setting goals. In your role as a social worker, you are certainly in the position to help clients focus their thinking and address their feelings as they pertain to identifying goals, but the ultimate determination as to what a client decides to do (or not do) is up to him or her. Self-determination must remain at the forefront of each step of the process, persistently honoring the client's right to choose and empowering clients to make decisions on their own behalf (National Association of Social Workers, 1996).

Ownership

As a client begins to develop and articulate goals, it can be helpful to explore the origin of the goal—who *owns* this goal? Specifically, it can be useful to know if the goal that the client is proposing is something that he or she genuinely wishes to achieve or if some perceived authority figure (e.g., parent, sibling, spouse, peer) may be manipulating, exerting pressure, or otherwise attempting to impose his or her will on the client. Clues that the client may not "own" the goal include a lack of enthusiasm when discussing the goal, vague or poorly detailed plans, and a marked inconsistency with the client's personality, history, or choice of leisure activities. If you begin to sense that the client may not really own the goal, it would be appropriate to ask about this. Pursuit of goals for which one has no passion can be a rough, dreary, and time-consuming process, which can potentially erode the client's self-esteem and ultimately may not take the client to a gratifying or fulfilling place.

In the context of a real-time encounter with a client, it may be difficult to reliably recall all of these parameters. The main notion to keep in mind when working with clients is that the goal needs to be *specific* and *fit* the client.

Additional Techniques for Identifying a Goal

Clients who seek your services may have put considerable thought and effort into conceptualizing their problem(s) prior to your initial encounter with them. It is entirely possible that a client will enter his or her first session with a plausible goal (or set of goals) already in mind. Sometimes, relevant goals may emerge throughout the course of the early interviews. In instances where goals are not forthcoming, consider using some imaginative techniques to help clients elucidate their goals.

Recap Problems

In early sessions, since so much new information may be revealed, you may find it helpful to take some notes. Toward the end of the session, if no specific goals have emerged, consider briefly reviewing your notes and flagging problems or concerns that the client has expressed. Work with the client to prioritize these problems, identifying which problem(s) he or she would like to work on first. Ultimately, this should lead to the formation of the initial goals.

Magical Goals

A client who is not yet fully comfortable with you may be fearful of making a mistake or revealing too much; hence, he or she may restrain or filter thoughts or feelings before speaking. The client may feel constrained, expressing only (safe) rational notions. Encouraging the client to deliberately depart from strictly logical thinking can permit him or her to engage in some fantasy solving, which may include valuable emotions and desires when articulating goals. This is where *magical goals* can come into play: One way to do this is to ask the client, "If anything were possible, how do you wish things could be?" or "If you could just snap your fingers (or push a button) and have things suddenly change, what would your life look like?" You could also hand the client your pen and say, "Imagine this is a magic wand. I want you to think about what's going on in your life, wave the wand, and then make three wishes." Although some of the client's expressions may seem to be rooted in fantasy, each warrants discussion. Further exploring the client's *magical wishes* could lead to the articulation of relevant real-life problems and corresponding goals.

Brainstorming

A more formal variation of *magical goals* involves brainstorming, which has been used to cultivate ideas in a variety of realms ranging from artistic to industrial problem solving. The brainstorming method, as described by Roger von Oech (1998), can easily be adapted as a tool for helping clients identify and prioritize relevant goals.

Step 1: Generate Ideas

Brainstorming begins by explaining to the client that it is time to express all of the ideas about what he or she would like to see in his or her life. These ideas can include wishes, desires, dreams, ideal living conditions, things or people that the client wishes could vanish from his or her life, things or people that the client wishes would suddenly emerge in his or her life, and so on. During this process, there are no wrong or bad ideas. Wild and even impossible ideas are welcome. As ideas are being generated, write each one on a card (one idea per card). If you do not have cards, use slips of paper.

The principle of this step is to keep the idea valve open—just let all of the ideas come out in an unregulated, nonjudgmental fashion, regardless of feasibility. At times, a usable idea may be in line just behind a silly idea. Sometimes a crazy-sounding idea can be effectively combined with one or several other ideas to build a solution. It is also possible that an implausible idea may trigger some valuable alternate ways of thinking about a problem and potentially point the way to an unanticipated solution or way of conceptualizing the problem. Hence, you do not want to inhibit the flow of ideas with real-world constraints (e.g., "That's too expensive," "That's illegal," "I could never do that," "That would never work"). Avoid the temptation to judge the ideas as they emerge. Negative evaluations at this point could shut down the process or result in filtering—just write everything down. During this step, you may contribute or suggest ideas to include on this list. Actively demonstrating this process at the beginning may help get the ball rolling.

Step 2: Sort

When you and the client run out of ideas, it is time to assess the ideas that have been gathered. Each idea needs to be evaluated in terms of feasibility. The SMART model presented earlier in this chapter may provide guidance in helping the client determine which ideas should stay and which should go. One way to do this is to ask the client to sort the cards into three piles: 1 = good idea, 2 = possibly usable, 3 = absolutely not usable.

Step 3: Select

Eliminate the #3 ideas. Keep the #1 and #2 ideas in their groups, and arrange them on the tabletop so that all of the cards are visible. Encourage the client to take some time to look over the ideas. Suggest that the client look for patterns or trends—is there a theme to the ideas indicating a possible life direction? Look for groupings—the cards may be logically clustered together, suggesting one or more (bigger) goal. Provide the client the opportunity to move the cards around on the tabletop to cluster related goals together or prioritize the goals.

A graphical demonstration of the entire brainstorming method is presented in Chapter 5 (p. 199).

Serial and Parallel Goals

As you embark on helping the client identify and rank goals, it will become clear that some goals are *serial,* meaning that one goal must be completed before embarking on the next goal, and other goals are *parallel,* implying that such goals can be pursued simultaneously.

Serial goals may consist of a series of two or more goals that need to be pursued in order. For example:

1. Earn a bachelor's degree.

2. Earn a master's degree.

In the foregoing example, clearly, the first goal must be accomplished *before* the second goal.

Parallel goals may involve two or more goals pursued during the same time frame. For example:

1. Get a dog.

2. Buy a new vacuum.

3. Register to vote.

The notion of serial and parallel goals will be discussed further in future chapters.

Simplification

The many parameters associated with identifying and setting meaningful goals may be too cumbersome to bring to mind in the real-time realm of working with clients. Much of what has been discussed in this chapter may be reduced to a couple of simple questions: "Specifically, what does the client want to accomplish?" and "Does this goal seem reasonable?" You can consider these straightforward questions silently or engage the client to address them with you. In cases wherein a goal seems unreasonable, based on the points discussed in this chapter, it may be helpful to cite the specific attribute(s) of the goal that seems implausible to you and work with the client to either better understand or reform the goal into something that could actually be executed and achieved in real life.

CHAPTER 4 EXERCISES

CONCEPT REVIEWS

Explain each concept in your own words. Where applicable, provide a case example without disclosing identifying information.

4.1 **Rationale for setting a goal (A) (p. 169)**

Describe how identifying and setting goals facilitates the process.

4.2 **Rationale for setting a goal (B) (p. 169)**

What difficulties may be encountered in the process should actual goals not be specified?

4.3 **Problems versus goals (p. 170)**

What is the difference between a problem and a goal?

4.4   Intrinsic versus extrinsic goals (p. 171)

Describe the difference between intrinsic and extrinsic goals in terms of their characteristics and potential outcomes.

4.5   Fundamental attributes of a goal (p. 172)

Explain the rationale for setting SMART goals.

4.6   Supplemental attributes of goals (p. 177)

Aside from the SMART criteria, what considerations are relevant when considering goals?

4.7   Identifying goals (p. 178)

Describe some techniques for identifying goals.

4.8   **Brainstorming (A) (p. 178)**

What is the rationale for brainstorming?

4.9   **Brainstorming (B) (p. 178)**

Explain the brainstorming process.

4.10   **Serial versus parallel goals (p. 179)**

Describe what is meant by *serial* and *parallel* goals and provide examples of each.

DISCUSSION POINTS

Discuss among your peers how you might handle these circumstances. Document the opinions expressed using a "+" or a "−" to indicate whether you agree or disagree with each opinion.

4.1   Hear me out?

In a client's first session, he or she is conveying a lengthy and complex story that seems to be relevant. The session is drawing to an end, and goals have not yet been discussed.

4.2   The problem with problems

After some storytelling, the client pauses and expresses feeling bad that he or she cannot solve the problem (or problems) on his or her own.

4.3   Sleepy symptoms

The client tells you that recently he or she has been sleeping a lot, isolating, and feeling blue but is unclear as to what the problem might be.

4.4 Gold goals

The client is physically disabled and aspires to be an Olympic gold medalist.

4.5 Payback time?

The client is extremely angry at an ex-partner. The issues involve emotional betrayal, stolen money, and unreturned property. The client seems focused on crafting a vengeful plan.

4.6 Everything goes

The client has articulated multiple ambitious goals, each of which seems suitable. The client has not expressed an implementation plan yet, but considering what is involved with each goal, it does not seem plausible that all of the goals can be pursued at the same time.

4.7 Go for the goal

The client has verbalized several problems but no specific goals.

4.8 Pi or pie?

The client is a proficient mathematician who seems excited when discussing his or her skills with computers. When discussing goals, the client listlessly mentions that he or she is going to be enrolling in a culinary academy.

4.9 Calling all friends! Calling all friends!

The client reports that instead of doing what really needs to be done, he or she tends to spend a lot of time chatting with friends on the phone. The client does not understand why you are recommending that he or she keep a call log for a week, detailing the start and stop time of each call.

4.10   Detail deficiency

The client describes his or her life as "really screwed up."

ROLE-PLAY 4.1 PLETHORA O' PROBLEMS

Note: Guidelines for role-play implementation, feedback, and documentation can be found in the "Overview of Exercises" section (p. xiii).

Conner has tolerated a number of problems that have been persisting for a long time (e.g., overbearing family member, unstable close relationship, shifting work hours, substance abuse); however, the recent onset of a new problem (e.g., health issue, death of a family member or pet) has made things feel unmanageable. Conner has not yet specified any goals.

Client

- Discuss some of the long-term problems and how you have managed to live with them (e.g., steadily increasing workload, living in a noisy neighborhood, difficult family).
- Discuss the emergence of several new problems (e.g., coping with an allergy, living with a friend whose relationship recently ended) and the impact that these have had on your life.
- Present as uncertain how to proceed: Should the old or new problems be addressed, and in what order?

Social Worker

- **Recap problems** (p. 178)—Reiterate the problems that Conner has mentioned along with the estimated duration of each problem. Consider asking Conner to rate how bothersome each problem feels (e.g., 1 = slightly annoying, 5 = extremely intolerable).
- **Problems versus goals** (p. 170)—For each problem that Conner wishes to see resolved or reduced, collaborate with Conner to derive suitable corresponding goals.
- **SMART goals** (p. 172)—Use appropriate criteria to evaluate each goal. As necessary, collaborate with Conner to refine or rephrase goals.

Role-Play 4.1 Self-Evaluation

(1 = needs further work, 5 = excellent)

1	2	3	4	5	Recap problems
1	2	3	4	5	Problems versus goals
1	2	3	4	5	SMART goals
1	2	3	4	5	_____
1	2	3	4	5	_____

Role-Play 4.1 Case Notes

_____

_____

_____

_____

_____

_____

_____

_____

_____

_____

_____

_____

_____

_____

_____

_____

_____

_____

_____

_____

_____

_____

_____

ROLE-PLAY 4.2   GOBS O' GOALS

Lou presents as excited and ambitious to achieve a number of diverse goals (e.g., resolving a long-standing family conflict, considering a career change, possibly ending a relationship, learning a foreign language). At this point, Lou is uncertain where to begin.

Client

- Mention some goals that are Attainable (e.g., learning a foreign language, becoming a great musician), with time frames or methods that are not Realistic (e.g., achieving linguistic fluency in 1 month, learning to play an instrument just by listening to music).
- State some virtuous goals that lack Specificity (e.g., getting really smart, getting on top of things, getting your life on track, having a happy family).
- Discuss that, ultimately, you would like to get a luxury car and possibly cosmetic surgery.

Social Worker

- **SMART goals** (p. 172)—One by one, discuss the extent to which each goal meets the SMART criteria and the rationale for adjusting the goals accordingly.
- **Serial and parallel goals** (p. 170)—If Lou is uncertain as to what order the goals should be executed in, guide Lou in prioritizing goals (from most to least important). Discuss which goals should be performed before others (serial goals) and which goals might be pursued simultaneously (parallel goals).
- **Intrinsic versus extrinsic goals** (p. 171)—Encourage Lou to talk about the expectations associated with each goal. Engage Lou in discussion regarding the intrinsic and extrinsic nature of each goal.

Role-Play 4.2 Self-Evaluation

(1 = needs further work, 5 = excellent)

1	2	3	4	5	SMART goals
1	2	3	4	5	Serial and parallel goals
1	2	3	4	5	Intrinsic versus extrinsic goals
1	2	3	4	5	_____
1	2	3	4	5	_____

Role-Play 4.2 Case Notes

ROLE-PLAY 4.3 A LITTLE TOO QUIET

Austin's life used to involve a variety of fulfilling activities (e.g., engaging employment, playing sports regularly, traveling, dining and socializing with friends). Recently, Austin has been reduced to feeling unenthusiastic about work and isolating during most nonworking hours. Austin has not answered the phone or read e-mail or postal mail in more than 2 weeks. When there is a knock at the door, Austin pretends not to be home.

Client

- Mention how you used to be pleased to wake up and take on the day, but now, you really just would rather not do much.
- If asked, hint at the fact that these changes came on fairly recently, coinciding with a significant loss (e.g., death of a family member or another loved one, financial loss, staffing or policy change at work, rejection letter, end of a significant relationship, change in health).
- Present as motivated to return to your prior level of functioning but uncertain how to do that.

Social Worker

- **Specificity** (p. 172)—Recap the difference between Austin's life now and how, until recently, it used to be. Prompt Austin to indicate when things began to change, and try to gather some details as to what was going on around that time (e.g., losses, hurts, changes).
- **Magical goals** (p. 178)—If Austin is unable to articulate how things got so bad, consider using one of the magical goal techniques to gain insight as to what the root problem (and corresponding goal) might be.
- **Attainable** (p. 175)—If Austin indicates a wish that is unattainable (e.g., reuniting with a spouse who has remarried, restoring someone who died), empathetically acknowledge the wish but also help Austin select an associated goal that is (more) attainable (e.g., grieving and accepting the loss).

Role-Play 4.3 Self-Evaluation

(1 = needs further work, 5 = excellent)

1	2	3	4	5	Specificity	
1	2	3	4	5	Magical goals	
1	2	3	4	5	Attainable	
1	2	3	4	5	_____	
1	2	3	4	5	_____	

Role-Play 4.3 Case Notes

_____

_____

_____

_____

_____

_____

_____

_____

_____

_____

_____

_____

_____

_____

_____

_____

_____

_____

_____

_____

_____

_____

_____

_____

_____

_____

5

Step III—Objectives

How Does the Client Get From Here to There?

I	II	III	IV	V
Assessment	**Goal**	**Objectives**	**Activation**	**Termination**

Objectives plot the map detailing how the client will advance from the initial starting point to achieving the specified goal. The strategic plan includes a sequenced list of the objectives detailing the actions, resources, time frames, and incentives for each step (McClam & Woodside, 1994).

Definitions

Before demonstrating how to construct objectives, it is necessary to define the following concepts, which are involved in creating the strategic (implementation) plan: goal, objective, action, resource, time frame, incentive, and strategy.

Goal

The desired destination—what the client wishes to accomplish

As discussed in Chapter 4, the goal indicates the client's destination. The goal can also be thought of as the desired change. Everything in the action plan should, in some way, contribute to accomplishing the client's goal.

Objective

A set of actions and/or resources

Objectives can be thought of as subgoals, indicating precisely what is to be done (next) at each point along the route. Objectives can be represented graphically as in Figure 5.1.

Figure 5.1   Sequential Objectives Lead to the Goal

Action

Something that needs to be done to accomplish the objective

Grammatically, actions are verbs. Actions are essentially the "legs" of the plan, indicating what the client is to do at each point. Actions are typically something that the client does directly (e.g., exercises for 30 minutes three times per week, writes two pages per day). Alternatively, an action may be indirect— something that the client delegates to someone else (e.g., accountant to prepare his or her tax return, Dr. Jones to write him or her a letter of recommendation). Occasionally, actions may be a combination of direct and indirect. This would involve the client taking an action with someone else (e.g., meeting with a study group, rehearsing with performance partner[s]).

Resource

Anything or anyone useful in accomplishing the objective

Grammatically, resources are nouns: A resource is any person, place, or thing that is useful in accomplishing the objective. A resource may be a person (e.g., a significant other, a mentor, an instructor). Resources may take the shape of a place (e.g., somewhere to study, a place to rehearse, a sports field). Resourceful things may be tangible (e.g., money, transportation, office supplies, appropriate attire, tools, software), a service (e.g., child care, a housekeeper, a tutor), or abstract (e.g., time, information, emotional support, quiet).

Time Frame

Specifies the due date of each objective

Consider Parkinson's law, which states that work expands so as to fill the amount of time available for its completion (Binder, 2004). It is easiest to think of this in terms of deadlines or the absence thereof. For example, a person who is given *4 hours* to clean out a closet will have the job done in *4 hours,* whereas a person who is given *4 weeks* to clean out the same closet will take *4 weeks* to accomplish the job. It follows that a person who has *forever* (no deadline) to clean out the closet will virtually take *forever* to do the job.

The phenomenon of Parkinson's law has also been observed in professional settings. Clinically, treatment plans that specify a total number of sessions at the onset of therapy have been shown to motivate clients to advance accordingly to meet the specified deadline (Reynolds, et al., 1996). Collaboratively working with the client to specify realistic time frames to accomplish tasks (objectives or goals) can put a positive spin on the intervention, suggesting that such tasks *can* be completed within the time allotted (Mann, 1973).

Incentive

Reward for completing each objective

As each objective is accomplished, incentives can serve both to celebrate the accomplishment of the task at hand and to motivate the client to embark on the next objective or goal. Incentives may be *explicit* or *implicit.* An explicit incentive involves some form of external reward, such as indulging in a treat or gratifying activity for accomplishing an objective or a goal (e.g., a special dinner out for getting admitted to a master of social work program). Alternatively, an incentive may be implicit, meaning that the accomplishment of the objective or goal is reward enough (e.g., getting admitted to an MSW program acknowledges your qualifications and can open the door to multiple new opportunities).

Strategy

A series of objectives aimed at accomplishing the goal

The strategy, or "strategic plan," can be thought of as a comprehensive "to-do" list, wherein the accomplishment of each successive objective advances the client toward achieving the specified goal.

Objectives in Detail: The Strategic Plan

In order to better conceptualize this system of objectives comprising actions, resources, time frames, and incentives, all leading toward the accomplishment of a specified goal, consider the graphical template of a strategic plan as presented in Figure 5.2.

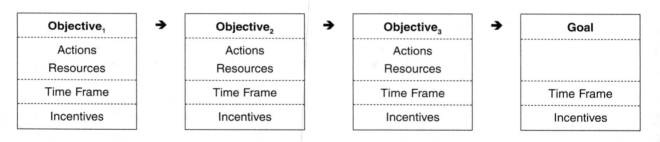

Figure 5.2   Strategic Plan Template

At this point, Figure 5.2 may seem somewhat confusing or abstract. Just as it can be helpful to study the picture on the cover of a jigsaw puzzle box before starting, it may be useful for you to take a moment to refer to Figure 5.6 (p. 199) to see what a sample completed strategic plan looks like. This will provide you with a concrete image of the sample strategic plan that will be assembled, one row at a time, throughout the course of this chapter.

In order to demonstrate how to build a strategic plan, consider a goal that you should be familiar with: getting admitted to an MSW program. Using the template presented in Figure 5.2, begin by filling in the goal—"Get admitted to MSW program"—and then identify the sequence of objectives that will be used to advance toward the goal as shown in Figure 5.3.

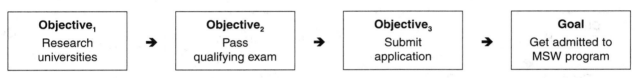

Figure 5.3   Strategic Plan: Goal and Objectives Loaded

Next, beginning with Objective$_1$, load in the *actions* and *resources* needed in order to accomplish each objective as shown in Figure 5.4.

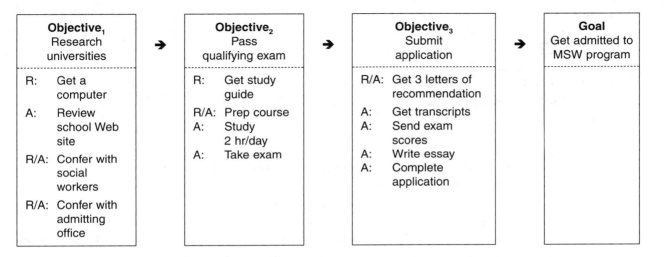

Figure 5.4   Strategic Plan: Actions and Resources Loaded Into Each Objective

NOTE: A = Action, R = Resource.

The next step involves specifying the time frame (due date) for the goal and each objective as shown in Figure 5.5. In this case, the application deadline (February 1) is fixed, so that should be loaded into the goal first. The objectives can then be back-timed using February 1 as the anchor point.

To explain: Since the goal is to submit the application by February 1, Objective$_3$ ("Submit application") is assigned the due date: January 20. This leaves some time to verify that all of the materials have arrived properly, allowing for about a week to (re)send any material that may have been misplaced.

Knowing that it can take several weeks for the testing service to deliver official scores, Objective$_2$ ("Pass qualifying exam") indicates a testing (due) date of December 10. Another consideration in setting this date involves allowing the client sufficient time to prepare for the test.

The time frame for Objective$_1$ ("Research universities") is then derived.

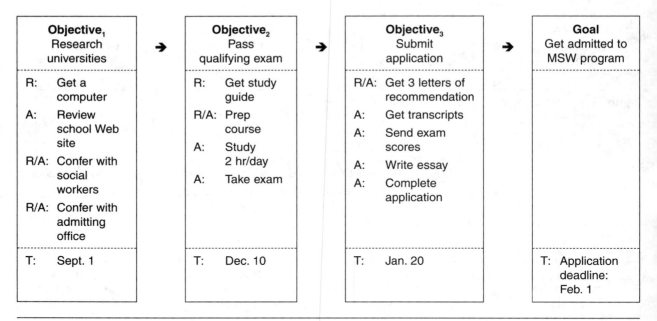

Figure 5.5   Strategic Plan: Time Frames Included

NOTE: A = Action, R = Resource, T = Time frame (due date).

In this particular case, back-timing was used in order to meet the fixed due date set by the university for submitting the application. Alternatively, the client may choose to build the timing forward starting from Objective$_1$.

As important as it is to specify realistic time frame estimates, it is equally important to be flexible. It is one thing to plot a plan on paper, and it is another thing to actually implement the plan in real life. It may be difficult to accurately predict precisely how long it can take to accomplish an objective, particularly when it is a new endeavor. Over- or underestimating time frames is not uncommon.

As each objective is carried out, essential substeps commonly emerge. Work with the client to anticipate the possibility that it may be necessary to adapt the plan accordingly.

Finally, offer the client the opportunity to specify incentives in order to reward the accomplishment of each objective as shown in Figure 5.6. As mentioned earlier, incentives may be explicit (e.g., buying or doing something special). Alternatively, the client may come to discover that the accomplishment of an objective carries powerful implicit rewards (e.g., enhanced motivation, sense of accomplishment or mastery, relief, excitement that the completion of the goal is now nearer than ever).

For readability, the objectives and their corresponding actions, resources, time frames, and incentives have been presented in a side-by-side fashion on a single page. When working with clients, it may be more feasible to use a separate sheet of paper or index cards to document each objective. Also, feel free to create a (possibly simpler) customized format of your own. As you work with this model or some variation of it, you will likely find adaptations that work better for you and your client.

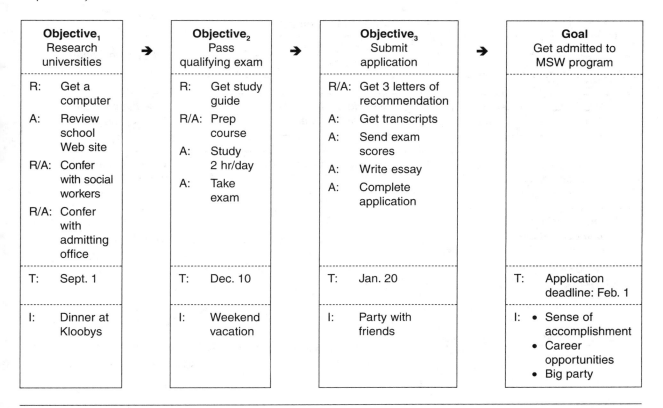

Figure 5.6   Strategic Plan: Appropriate Incentives Included

NOTE: A = Action, R = Resource, T = Time frame (due date), I = Incentive.

Specifying Resources: Brainstorming Demonstrated

Each action detailed under the objectives must be carried out. For example, using the actions under Objective$_1$, some actions, such as "Review school Web site," could be considered fairly straightforward as most schools post relevant information on easily accessible Web sites. Other actions, such as "Get a computer," could be approached in any number of ways. The brainstorming technique for deriving meaningful goals as mentioned in Chapter 4 can also be applied to any (sub)part of this process, as in the following example: Brainstorm alternatives for achieving the action "Get a computer."

Step I: Generate Ideas

Begin by encouraging the client to come up with as many ideas as possible without judging them, no matter how implausible the ideas might seem. Just write down every idea that emerges on cards or slips of paper as shown in Figure 5.7. In order to get things going, you may wish to submit a few ideas—some reasonable, some intentionally ridiculous just to demonstrate this step in the brainstorming process and engage the client. Resist the temptation to judge the ideas during this phase of brainstorming, no matter how crazy they may sound, as this will only serve to shut down the flow of the more meaningful ideas that will follow.

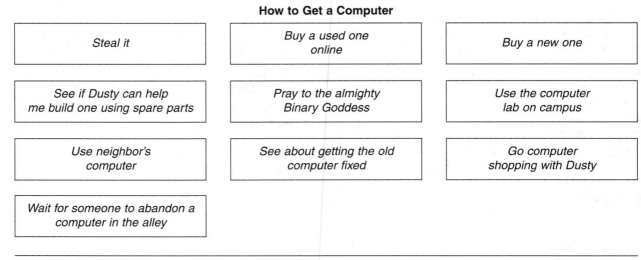

Figure 5.7   Brainstorming Step I: Generate Ideas

Step II: Sort

Once you and the client have run out of ideas, have the client sort them using a three-point system: 1 = good idea, 2 = possibly usable, 3 = not usable, as shown in Figure 5.8.

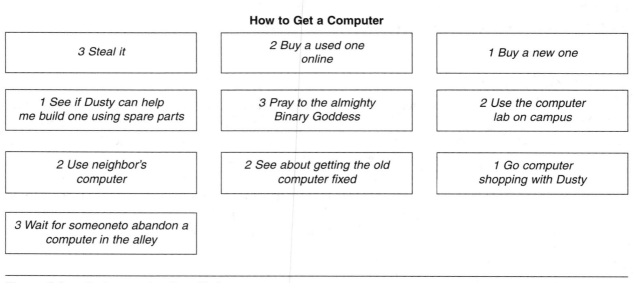

Figure 5.8   Brainstorming Step II: Sort

Step III: Select

At this step, the client will select the action items. Have the client arrange the #1 items, placing the best #1 item at the top. In this example, the client has selected "See if Dusty can help me build one using spare parts" as the best course of action. "Buy a new one" and "Go computer shopping with Dusty" are tied as the next best alternatives. Next, do the same for the #2 items. At this point, an ordered set of viable options should emerge as shown in Figure 5.9, thus suggesting the path toward potential solutions.

How to Get a Computer
#1 options

1 See if Dusty can help *me build one using spare parts*

1 Buy a new one	*1 Go computer* *shopping with Dusty*

#2 options

2 See about getting the old *computer fixed*

2 Buy a used one *online*

2 Use neighbor's *computer*	*2 Use the computer* *lab on campus*

Figure 5.9   Brainstorming Step III: Select

The brainstorming problem-solving method can be applied broadly. This process can be used to derive goals, objectives, and alternative work-around plans as (unanticipated) confounds or substeps emerge throughout the process.

Alternate Sources for Assembling Strategies

For instructive purposes, the strategy for earning an MSW degree was derived in a stepwise fashion from the ground up; however, not all such plans must necessarily be conjured up starting from a blank page. Some goals are relatively commonplace. As such, an appropriate prepared strategy may already be available. For example, starting up a small business may be new to the client, but it is not at all a new endeavor. There may already exist applicable "how-to" books, reputable Web sites, seminars, courses, or organizations that offer access to necessary information and resources (e.g., business license forms, small-business loan instructions, advertising/marketing strategies, consultants). Although each individual plan may require some customization, identifying and modifying a prepared plan may likely be more efficient and thorough than attempting to build the strategic plan starting from a blank slate.

Consider gathering information from existing resources to guide the assembly of your strategies:

Individuals—Confer with supportive or knowledgeable people.

Models and exemplars—Can someone who has already accomplished the goal provide guidance?

Places—Are there places that attract people whose talents or goals concur with the client's (e.g., communities dedicated to the arts, technology, culinary delights)? Alternatively, the client may need a place that is conducive to advancing his or her mission (e.g., a quiet library, an office away from home, a sports field, a rehearsal space).

Organizations—Existing organizations may be available that focus on the achievement of the specified goal (e.g., a small-business association, a nursing school, a police academy).

Programs—Prepared programs may exist that can help the client achieve the goal (e.g., internships, apprenticeships, volunteer opportunities, trade schools, seminars) (Egan, 1994).

Serial and Parallel Planning

As mentioned in Chapter 4, some goals are serial, meaning that $Goal_1$ (earn a bachelor's degree) must be completed before efforts toward $Goal_2$ (earn a master's degree) can begin. Other goals are parallel, meaning that $Goal_1$ (learn a musical instrument) and $Goal_2$ (plant a garden) can be pursued during the same time frame.

For purposes of clarity, the strategic plan demonstrated in this chapter (getting admitted to an MSW program) was presented as a serial model with one objective leading to the next, until the goal is achieved. Realistically, this strategic plan could be proposed as a mixed model, using both parallel and serial processes as shown in Figure 5.10.

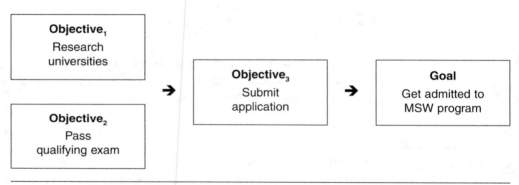

Figure 5.10   Strategic Plan Mixed Model With Parallel (O_1 & O_2) and Serial (O_1 & O_2 ➔ O_3 ➔ G) Processes

Figure 5.10 depicts $Objective_1$ ("Research universities") and $Objective_2$ ("Pass qualifying exam") being pursued in parallel (during the same time frame). After completing both of those steps, the client would proceed in a serial fashion, advancing to $Objective_3$ ("Submit application") and ultimately reaching the goal ("Get admitted to MSW program"). Try to think openly. Many such variations are possible.

Client Perspective

Fleshing out the objectives involved in accomplishing a goal enables the client to see the map of the steps (work) that will be involved. Seeing this path laid out, the client has the opportunity to contemplate the goal from a variety of realistic angles: Does this look easier or harder than initially anticipated? What does the time frame look like? Might there be alternative goals, strategies, or objectives worth pursuing? Is this feasible? Does this (still) look worthwhile or appealing? Is the client (still) willing to do this? Does the goal now look more compelling than ever?

Reviewing the strategic plan on paper provides the client a valuable opportunity to make essential determinations to embrace, modify, abandon, or consider viable alternatives prior to and while embarking on the mission.

CHAPTER 5 EXERCISES

CONCEPT REVIEWS

Explain each concept in your own words. Where applicable, provide a case example without disclosing identifying information.

5.1   Goal (p. 194)

Describe what a goal is.

5.2   Objectives (A) (p. 194)

Describe what an objective is and the rationale for setting objectives.

5.3   Objectives (B) (p. 194)

Describe the components of an objective: actions and resources.

5.4   Time frame (A) (p. 195)

What is the rationale for specifying time frames (deadlines) for each objective and goal?

5.5   Time frame (B) (p. 195)

Describe the notion of "back-timing."

5.6   Incentives (A) (p. 195)

What role(s) do incentives play in advancing from one objective to the next?

5.7   Incentives (B) (p. 195)

What is the difference between *implicit* and *explicit* incentives?

5.8 Strategy/strategic plan (p. 196)

Explain what a strategy/strategic plan is in terms of the goal.

5.9 Brainstorming (p. 199)

Describe the three-step brainstorming process and the rationale of each step (I—Generate Ideas, II—Sort, III—Select).

5.10 Alternate sources for strategies (p. 201)

Strategic plans and the associated objectives need not always be constructed from the ground up. Describe some alternate ways of arriving at a strategic plan.

DISCUSSION POINTS

Discuss among your peers how you might handle these circumstances. Document the opinions expressed using a "+" or a "−" to indicate whether you agree or disagree with each opinion.

5.1 Let's go, let's go!

The client has expressed a meaningful goal and wants to begin working on it right away. The client presents as fairly impatient and does not understand why you are recommending that objectives be specified.

5.2 Kick-back client

While reviewing the client's objectives, you notice that nearly all of the actions are *indirect*—things that *other* people are to do.

5.3 No time at all

The client has designated a reasonable goal and set of objectives; however, the time frame cells are either blank or have a "?" in them.

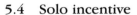

5.4 Solo incentive

The client has included one incentive associated with the goal but none for the objectives.

5.5 Alone in the brainstorm

The client is hesitant to partake in the brainstorming process and has asked you to do it for him or her.

5.6 All good things

During Step II of the brainstorming process (Sort), the client assigns all of the ideas to category #1—*good ideas*.

5.7 Red light

After assembling the objectives, the client is hesitant to commit to the project as it stands.

5.8   Liking the unlikely

One of the objectives that the client has specified involves a person whom the client has, in past sessions, characterized as chronically undependable.

5.9   Death of a deadline

The client has been making decent progress at achieving objectives; however, it is beginning to look like he or she may not be able to meet the time frame that was specified for the goal. The client expresses feeling like a failure.

5.10   Easy street?

The client is in the midst of pursuing two different goals using two separate strategic plans. Through your discussions, you have noticed that whenever the client encounters a difficulty when pursuing one goal, he or she immediately switches to working toward the other goal.

ROLE-PLAY 5.1 A DARK AND BRAINSTORMY NIGHT

Note: Guidelines for role-play implementation, feedback, and documentation can be found in the "Overview of Exercises" section (p. xiii).

About 3 months ago, Bobby started waking up nearly every night, fearful that someone or something has entered the bedroom. Bobby is unable to return to sleep until thoroughly searching the bedroom, closet, and surrounding area. This is starting to feel like age-inappropriate behavior, which is leading to a sense of guilt and exhaustion.

Client

- Discuss how the nightly room searches require getting up and turning on the lights to anxiously check doors, windows, the closet, under the bed, and the bathroom. This lengthy and stressful interruption in your sleep leaves you drowsy the next day.
- Express how silly you feel—that each time, you find nothing, but you cannot seem to stop checking.
- Present as unfamiliar with the brainstorming process, but be willing to partake.

Social Worker

- **Goal** (p. 194)—Work collaboratively with the client to derive an appropriate goal (e.g., to sleep through the night, to make night security checking more efficient).
- **Brainstorming** (p. 199)—Guide the client through the brainstorming process. Consider focusing on alternatives to switching on the light and getting out of bed to perform the security checks.
- **Objectives** (p. 194)—Based on the top findings of the brainstorming process, collaborate with the client to build objectives that lead toward the goal.

Role-Play 5.1 Self-Evaluation

(1 = needs further work, 5 = excellent)

1	2	3	4	5	Goal
1	2	3	4	5	Brainstorming
1	2	3	4	5	Objectives
1	2	3	4	5	_____
1	2	3	4	5	_____

Role-Play 5.1 Case Notes

ROLE-PLAY 5.2 OBJECTION TO OBJECTIVES

Reece lists multiple seemingly unrelated problems (e.g., with work, family, partner, health, and socialization). When you propose specifying corresponding goals, Reece is relatively cooperative; however, there is resistance when it comes to assembling objectives for each goal.

Client

- Explain that you have always been a free spirit and that things eventually just tend to work out.
- Mention that this is the first time that you have been faced with so many different problems at once (e.g., with work, family, significant other, health, and school) and that it feels overwhelming.
- Present as agreeable to setting goals but moderately resistant to setting objectives, which seems like micromanagement.

Social Worker

- **Resources** (p. 195)—Per Reece's positive experience and attitude regarding prior problem solving, inquire about the resources (people, places, and things) that have been helpful in the past. Some of these resources may be useful in assembling (informal) objectives.
- **Serial and parallel goals** (p. 202)—Help Reece define which goals are serial and which are parallel. For serial goals, coordinate with Reece to identify the best order for the goals. For parallel goals, discuss the rationale for prioritizing.
- **Objectives** (p. 194)—If Reece resists writing down specific objectives, engage him or her in conversation that helps you understand how he or she conceives the solving process. Curiously ask Reece to (informally) discuss how he or she might accomplish various steps in the process.

Role-Play 5.2 Self-Evaluation

(1 = needs further work, 5 = excellent)

1	2	3	4	5	Resources
1	2	3	4	5	Serial and parallel goals
1	2	3	4	5	Objectives
1	2	3	4	5	_____
1	2	3	4	5	_____

Role-Play 5.2 Case Notes

ROLE-PLAY 5.3 LIGHTS, CAMERA, INACTION

According to Mason's spiritual belief system, it is not appropriate to force things to happen—essentially, if something is supposed to happen, it will just happen. Faced with some persistent problems (e.g., substantial weight change, deepening depression, academic slippage, decaying close relationship, financial hardship), Mason is haltingly considering taking some action.

Client

- Insist on including a ritual known as "tutsling," which consists of a unique set of practices (e.g., lighting candles, a dance, a chant, wearing something, eating something) as an action within each objective.
- When setting the time frame for each objective, ask the social worker to offer a recommendation and then propose substantially extending the deadline.
- Despite the presence of multiple problems, explain that you would not be comfortable trying to change more than one thing (at a time).

Social Worker

- **Actions** (p. 195)—If Mason describes something that is unfamiliar to you (e.g., a ritual, a belief system), consider making some appropriate inquiries.

- **Time frame** (p. 195)—Prompt Mason to set a time frame for the objectives or for the accomplishment of the goal. If Mason proposes lengthy time frames, you may inquire about the rationale. Consider pointing out some potential consequences related to prolonged time frames (e.g. resolution of the problem delayed, may extend beyond termination date).

- **Brainstorming** (p. 199)—Encourage Mason to partake in a separate brainstorming exercise for each problem. The principle behind this is that if Mason is willing to work on one problem only, the brainstorming may provide guidance in making a selection (e.g., identifying the easiest problem, identifying the problem that, once resolved, will provide the most relief).

Role-Play 5.3 Self-Evaluation

(1 = needs further work, 5 = excellent)

1	2	3	4	5	Actions
1	2	3	4	5	Time frame
1	2	3	4	5	Brainstorming
1	2	3	4	5	_____
1	2	3	4	5	_____

Role-Play 5.3 Case Notes

_____

_____

_____

_____

_____

_____

_____

_____

_____

_____

_____

_____

_____

_____

_____

_____

_____

_____

_____

_____

_____

_____

6

Step IV—Activation

Moving From Intention to Implementation

I	II	III	IV	V
Assessment	**Goal**	**Objectives**	**Activation**	**Termination**

The strategic plan that has been built thus far is fundamentally a blueprint for progressing toward a goal; however, metaphorically speaking: *A blueprint is an essential step in building a house, but you can't live in a blueprint.* Therefore, it is time to put the strategic plan into action.

Five Stages of Change

In order to comprehend how clients make the leap from *planning* actions to *taking* actions, it may be helpful to consider a model detailing five stages of change (Prochaska, DiClemente, & Norcross, 1992):

I. *Precontemplation*: The client is not even considering change. The client may be unaware of the need to change, the client may not want to change, or the client may not "own" the problem—conceiving the problem as something that someone else should resolve.

II. *Contemplation*: The client recognizes the need to change and now begins to "own" the problem. The client sees that the problem, and ultimately the solution, is in his or her hands.

III. *Preparation*: The client has made a decision to take some meaningful problem-solving action in the near future. The client may be considering prior (failed) efforts at attempting to solve this problem. Reflecting on past failed attempts may be discouraging. Alternatively, reviewing what has worked, what has not worked, and what has not yet been tried may affirmatively suggest a potential action pathway.

IV. *Action*: The client has begun actual efforts toward achieving the change (which is what this chapter is about).

V. *Maintenance*: The final stage of change begins when the goal is achieved. From there forward, the client will focus on consolidating the gains made and direct his or her efforts toward relapse prevention (as covered in Chapter 7—Termination).

Laying the Groundwork for Change

Positive Mindset

Coping with change involves planning, purpose, and a mental image of the goal in order to select, assemble, and carry out meaningful actions (Bandura, 2001). The steps taken thus far—specifically, identifying goals and assembling the strategic plan—serve to build a meaningful pathway for the implementation steps that follow.

Self-confidence, defined as the client's belief that he or she is capable of succeeding at the goal (Geen, 1995), has been identified as a key predictor in terms of goal accomplishment (or failure). Negative belief systems may inhibit meaningful actions (Beck, 2005). For example, if the client believes that only an especially agile chef is qualified enough to bake something as delicate as a soufflé, the client may simply turn away from this challenge, reasoning, "It's just going to fall and turn to mush, so why even try?" In choosing not to try, the client forfeits any chance for success, which would inherently challenge his or her sense of ineptitude. As such, you may find yourself appropriately discussing self-esteem issues with the client at some point in the process.

Clients with a more robust sense of self-confidence and optimism tend to have stronger support systems, which are more readily accessible in times of stress (Taylor & Brown, 1994). This suggests that clients whose support systems are absent or negative may have a better chance at achieving goals if more positive social associations are built.

Social Support

The functional support model suggests that people involved in close relationships cope better during challenging times. Having one or more people with whom they can vent and process problems facilitates a sense of support, encouragement, and practical assistance and an alternate point of view for problem-solving efforts (Greenglass, 1993; Wills, 1990). Depending on the circumstances and the individuals involved, social support can provide reassurance, direction, and advice when needed.

Social support can provide two levels of benefit:

1. The *general effect* is the day-to-day benefit that one derives from being involved in a supportive social network.

2. The *buffering effect* is associated with the supplemental help that one derives from a supportive social network in times of need (Cohen & Wills, 1985).

Robust social systems can also be useful with respect to enhancing the client's commitment to the goal during the activation phase. Commitment can be characterized as one's propensity to stick with the pursuit of a goal. Clients who choose to disclose a goal to members of their support system can enhance the likelihood of accomplishing the goal in terms of relational mutuality: The client, having disclosed this goal to a friend, feels more compelled to fulfill this (implicit) commitment. Additionally, members of the client's support system can help remind the client of how important the goal is, help the client focus, and help reenergize the client at moments of difficulty (Hollenbeck, Williams, & Klein, 1989).

In instances wherein a supportive social network is absent, neutral, or negative (naysayers), having even one person who provides understanding or encouragement can serve as a motivator to the client. Certainly, as the client's social worker, you can fulfill this role to some extent on a temporary basis, but continue to work with the client to identify at least one person who can fulfill this position. If such a person does not appear to be present in the client's life, explore beyond the boundaries of the client's current social realm. Consider: Who might serve as a qualified mentor? Are there others who might serve as potential peers in the form of individuals or communities with similar interests (e.g., schools, organizations, support groups, Web sites, online newsgroups)?

Homework

As valuable as it is for clients to gain direction, support, and insights through the process of your contact with them, it is insufficient for clients to merely talk about how to solve problems during sessions. Clients need to focus on actually carrying out the plans that will advance them toward the specified goal(s) *between* sessions as well.

In order to help motivate clients to engage in such efforts outside of sessions, it may be useful to point out that the session time, typically about an hour once a week, constitutes less than 1% of the client's week. To further exemplify the power of this point, consider a musical analogy: Playing the piano only during the weekly lesson is not the way to become proficient. A serious music student must take action (practice) throughout the course of the week if any significant progress is to be made.

Beck (2005) proposes a comprehensive homework program for clients, aimed at carrying out the actions specified in the corresponding objectives. The term *homework* may carry negative connotations to the client, as homework is often thought of as tedious work that teachers make people do. Hence, consider using a different label for the activities that the client is to carry out between sessions. Such proactive terms as *action plan* or *care plan* may be more appealing. (Note: For sake of consistency, the term *homework* will be used throughout the rest of this section.)

The homework should be based on the objectives specified in the strategic plan. Homework may be incorporated into the session structure—opening with a review of activities accomplished since the last session. Sessions can conclude with you and the client collaboratively plotting the activities that the client will embark on during the course of the next week. Each homework activity should be derived from the objectives and include the specified actions, resources, time frame, and incentive(s).

As each homework component is assembled, be consistently aware of the content (load) of the homework and the client's attitude toward it. If the content seems too heavy, too light, or unrealistic, consider discussing this with the client in order to adjust the load. Also, consider the balance of the collaborative process in deriving homework. If the client's contribution to the homework process seems low, this may suggest a lack of engagement, disinterest, or an evolving dependency on you. Such observations bear discussion and possibly adjustment.

When homework is being derived, it may be helpful to ask the client, "Using a 0–100% scale, what would you honestly say is the likelihood that you'll be able to do this [by next week]?" If the client's answer is low (e.g., less than 70%), negotiate with the client to modify the plan into something more doable (e.g., "How could this be changed to boost that likelihood?"). This is also a useful tool when reviewing the client's progress, particularly when the client falls substantially short of accomplishing the targeted objective.

If progress stalls or slows during the activation phase, motivation may be a problem. Typically, one thinks of motivation as the precursor to action (e.g., "I'll start working on XYZ when I feel more motivated"). Consider proposing to the client a converse proposition—that sometimes action leads to motivation. For example, you might suggest that the client, whether or not he or she feels motivated, just begin working on XYZ uninterrupted for a specified time frame (e.g., Wednesday from 6:00 to 7:00) and then evaluate the progress. The client may discover that the task is not as laborious as imagined. Additionally, at the end of that hour, the client should be encouraged to evaluate the work that he or she has accomplished. This could provide a timely sense of motivation that was initially missing. Also, when entering unfamiliar territory, it can be difficult to make accurate estimates as to how long it will take to accomplish a particular task. This 1-hour trial method can help you and the client tune time estimates accordingly.

As motivated and well-intended as you may be, it is important to consistently recognize that clients and their circumstances are unique. As such, there really is no typical time frame or single best method for starting and sustaining progress toward goals. Clients implement change at different paces depending on a multitude of factors, including the nature of their personality, cultural norms, capabilities, feelings, thoughts, social conditions, support systems, problems, available resources, and other elements competing for the client's time and attention. As with all aspects of client care, you must not only start where the client is but also respectfully move at the client's pace.

Evaluation

As the client embarks on actually carrying out the objectives, ongoing evaluation enables both you and the client to assess and objectively document the effectiveness of the client's progress or lack thereof (Berlin & Marsh, 1993; Bloom, Fischer, & Orme, 2003). Positive evaluation outcomes suggest the effectiveness of the intervention, whereas flat or negative evaluations may suggest the need to tune the implementation or possibly the goal.

In addition to providing information regarding the client's performance, evaluation can also serve to motivate clients, thereby promoting further progress (Poulin, 2000). When advancement or improvement is seen, this can fuel further efforts—success breeds success. When progress is stagnant or negative, consider (re)framing such findings as an opportunity to take a fresh look at the problem or approach used to address it (e.g., "Is there something that we missed?" "Did something get in the way?" "Is there something else going on here?" "Did something unexpected happen?" "What parts of this need to be reworked?").

Clients may derive a supplemental benefit from engaging in the evaluation process in the form of *reactivity.* Reactivity occurs when, regardless of the intervention, the very process of (self-)observation or recording data brings about a change. One form of reactivity is the "Hawthorne effect" whereby the client's awareness of the fact that his or her conduct is being (self-)monitored has the power to bring about a measurable improvement in performance (Cook, 1967).

As mentioned in Chapter 4, there are numerous rapid assessment instruments (RAIs) that can be used to objectively evaluate the client's progress. Each of these instruments is designed to focus on a specific clinical issue. RAIs are appealing for both you and the client in terms of simplicity and convenience. From the client's standpoint, most of these instruments consist of a brief set of questions with either check-the-box– or circle-the-number–type responses. Statistical skills or computers are unnecessary when interpreting these ready-to-use instruments—most of which are scored merely by adding up the numbers associated with each response and then applying the total to some sort of evaluation scale (e.g., 1–7 poor functioning, 8–11 moderate functioning, 12–15 good functioning, 16–20 excellent functioning).

The following texts may be useful in selecting evaluation instruments to track the client's performance:

- Corcoran, K., & Fischer, J. (2000). *Measures for clinical practice: A sourcebook* (3rd ed., Vol. 1: Couples, families, and children, Vol. 2: Adults). New York: Free Press.
- Hudson, W. W. (1982). *The clinical measurement package: A field manual.* Homewood, IL: Dorsey Press.
- Tripodi, T. (1994). *A primer on single-subject design for clinical social workers.* Washington, DC: NASW Press.

In cases where there does not seem to be a prepared instrument that is appropriate to the client's condition, objectives, or goal, it may be appropriate to compose a brief customized survey instrument. Familiarity with the format of existing RAIs will help guide you in the process of collaboratively constructing a relevant instrument with your client.

Identifying and Resolving Problems in Activation

As the client carries the plans from paper into real life, it is reasonable to expect that there may be some challenges in the client's adaptation both internally (cognitively and emotionally) and externally (reactions of others, access to resources, etc.). Naturally, part of the activation process involves recognizing and effectively dealing with such challenges as a normal part of the change process.

Addressing Dysfunctional Beliefs

Negative belief systems can severely confound the activation process. Three such aspects that should trigger red flags to process with clients are self-defeating beliefs, biological determination, and diagnoses and trait labels (Bedell & Lennox, 1997).

> *Self-Defeating Beliefs*—If the client presupposes that he or she will gain little or nothing from partaking in the change process, this will virtually eliminate the client's motivation to carry out the strategic plan.

> *Biological Determination*—Clients who are predisposed to a mental health diagnosis that is considered physiologically based, such as schizophrenia and certain forms of anxiety disorder or depression, may presume that their condition blocks their ability to achieve the desired changes.

> *Diagnoses and Trait Labels*—Individuals who have been assigned a mental health diagnosis or diagnoses may be led to embrace the label, using the diagnosis as a means of delineating what they *cannot* do, hence bringing about the corresponding expected negative outcome.

From your standpoint, it can be valuable to recognize and acknowledge these potential confounds and provide a new layer of hope with respect to each. It is appropriate to respectfully challenge self-defeating beliefs. For example, while recognizing a client's history of low self-confidence, consider framing his or her efforts as a fresh start—a new opportunity to achieve meaningful change, independent of the past.

For clients presenting with biological determination, while you should acknowledge that such conditions present some extra challenges that may not be present for others, this does not necessarily mean that the potential for meaningful change is out of reach. Try to understand how the client conceptualizes his or her disorder and collaboratively build customized strategies that enable the client to move forward using a style and pace that uniquely fits him or her.

In instances where the client cites an inherent flaw within him- or herself that will impede progress toward the goal, respectfully discuss the plausibility of the client's assertion and then work from a reasonably optimistic standpoint (e.g., "I get that you're faced with some obstacles that just aren't there for most people. But I also know how resilient you can be. I'm thinking that, if this is really important to you, we should be able to find some alternative—some way of adjusting things so that you can move forward with this").

Watch for other potential roadblocks that may take the form of cognitive distortions, which can lead to either passive (avoidant) or anxious implementation. Such distortions may take the form of *arbitrary inference*—overestimating the likelihood of a negative event—or *magnification*—characterizing a potentially negative outcome as catastrophic (Beck & Freeman, 1990; Michelson & Ascher, 1987). In such instances, it is appropriate to respectfully challenge such thinking or behaviors via cognitive restructuring (Beck, 1976), also referred to as cognitive modification (Meichenbaum, 1977).

Stress

During the activation phase, the client's level of stress should be taken into consideration. Stress, like other emotional elements, can come from a variety of sources. Some stresses may be related to the change at hand, whereas other stresses may be associated with issues independent of the client's change efforts. It is neither necessary nor realistic to eliminate all stress prior to embarking on change efforts. A certain amount of stress can actually facilitate change.

When stress is too low, this suggests that the client does not perceive his or her circumstances as particularly unsatisfactory or uncomfortable. As such, the client feels less motivated to execute a plan to change his or her circumstances—essentially, low stress can be correlated with the attitude that things are acceptable as they are, so why go to the effort of changing anything?

Conversely, when stress is too high, one is unable to function effectively, much less take on the extra chore of attempting to alter his or her situation. These two extremes exemplify the heart of the Yerkes-Dodson law, which states that there is an optimal level of anxiety (stress) for effective performance; performance improves as anxiety increases up to a point, beyond which performance deteriorates (Yerkes & Dodson, 1908).

If it is found that the client's anxiety level is too high to facilitate effective performance, consider teaching the client a simple progressive muscle relaxation technique (Jacobson, 1938) that can be used in moments of stress, wherein the client is instructed to deliberately tense selected muscle groups to about 75% of his or her capacity, hold it for a short time, and then release the tension all at once (Goldfried & Davidson, 1976).

A common source of stress may involve goal conflicts or overcommitment to multiple possibly diverse activities, which may confound the accomplishment of the selected goal (McBride, 1990). You may encounter instances where multiple activities are competing for the client's attention or when the pursuit of one goal is in contention with another goal (e.g., scheduling conflicts, financial constraints). In such cases, engage the client to consider each goal in terms of feasibility, priority, and outcome potential. In the real world of activation, it is essential to recognize that not everything can necessarily be accomplished simultaneously. Work with the client to identify and prioritize these activities. Propose that some items, perhaps those near the bottom of the list, might be delayed, delegated to someone else, or (temporarily or permanently) dropped.

Motivation

As goals become more challenging, people tend to use better strategies, perform better, and show better performance than when embarking on less challenging goals. If the objective or goal bar is set too low, the client may sense that there is no significant difference between the way things are now and how things would be if the objective or goal were accomplished. This sort of low-bar perception can make change efforts seem unwarranted (Chesney & Locke, 1991). If the client's execution seems sluggish and the goal appears to be relatively insubstantial, this may be an opportunity to have the client "upgrade" his or her goal and reattempt its achievement.

Ownership

Goal setting is highly personal. The client must be involved in the establishment of goals that are important to him or her (Cormier & Hackney,

2005). If the client's progress is slow, feels laborious, or has stalled entirely, consider challenging the client to honestly (re)consider the origin of the goal. Try to determine if this goal is something that the client truly believes in or if perhaps the client was pressured into pursuing a goal by an outside source or internalized expectation (e.g., parent, peer, another perceived authority figure). If the source of the goal turns out to be external in nature, it may be difficult for the client to find the motivation to rigorously pursue the steps necessary to propel him- or herself closer to a future in the shape of *someone else's* dream.

This is a vital point: Even when pursuing a genuinely desirable goal, there are going to be difficult points encountered along the way. When working toward a goal for which one has no passion, there is no joy or satisfaction on the journey to the goal. *All* of the points feel difficult and uninteresting. Often, goals are successive in nature (e.g., "Once I get X done, I'll be set to work on Y"), so in the broader sense, accomplishing a goal for which one has no passion leads nowhere worthwhile.

For example, consider a student who has no interest in numbers or business but blindly complies with his or her parents' wishes for him or her to become an accountant. Even when pursuing a field of genuine interest, there will be good and bad classes. For this student, who has no interest in the field of accountancy, there would be no good classes. One might expect that his or her grades would be poor and the work would be painstakingly dull. Finally, graduation would come, and the client would now be poised for an entry-level accounting position that would bore him or her.

When you sense that a client is in pursuit of a goal for which he or she has no passion, this warrants discussion. Consider asking the client if his or her goal selection might be coming from an external influence. This may be an opportunity to discuss the characters in the client's life along with the corresponding emotional or power structure. It may also be valuable to (re)visit some of the client's actual talents, dreams, interests, desires, passions, wishes, and so on. Such discussions may suggest modifying the existing goal or deriving more personally suitable (desirable) goals that could provide for a more powerful sense of motivation, driven by the potential for a more fulfilling future.

Review Objectives/Goals

If progress toward a goal seems halted or otherwise impeded, there are a number of techniques that may be used to help spur further action (Kanfer & Schefft, 1988) in the form of guidance, tuning, and tracking progress.

Guidance—Clients may benefit from the real-world experience of having mentors or models who have actually achieved the objective or goal that the client is pursuing.

Tuning—The client may need to modify his or her environment in order to make it more conducive to taking the necessary actions. Identify and build strategies for effectively reducing the effects of habits, people, and circumstances that inhibit progress.

Be open to adjusting the strategic plan as needed. As mentioned earlier, the strategic plan can be a useful map for proceeding toward a goal, but ultimately, all such plans must be carried out in real life. When indicated, work with the client to modify the objective or goal as needed (e.g., simplify, reorganize, include supplemental actions or resources, break complex actions into substeps).

As discussed earlier, it can be difficult to derive realistic time frames prior to implementation. Over- and underestimations are common. Be open to adjusting the time frames as needed.

Tracking Progress—Work with the client to collaboratively build and include some form of self-monitoring into his or her implementation, or review the progress upon the completion of each objective. Even if RAIs are not being used, consider the utility of using simple informal estimates to discuss the client's progress toward an objective or a goal (e.g., "At this point, it looks like you're about halfway to achieving your goal. Let's take a moment to talk about what's working and what, if anything, might help this work better").

In cases where the client has not specified explicit incentives, he or she may derive motivation from your genuine words of encouragement. Such encouragement need not be reserved solely for the final accomplishment of an objective. Progressive acknowledgement of the client's forward motion is always worth mentioning.

CHAPTER 6 EXERCISES

CONCEPT REVIEWS

Explain each concept in your own words. Where applicable, provide a case example without disclosing identifying information.

6.1 **Stages of change (p. 215)**

Describe the five stages of change and your potential role at each stage.

6.2 **Positive mindset (p. 216)**

What are the advantages to having a positive mindset?

6.3 **Social support (p. 216)**

How can the presence of a supportive social system aid in the client's activation?

6.4 **Homework (p. 217)**

Discuss the rationale for homework.

6.5 **Evaluation (A) (p. 218)**

Briefly describe what is meant by "evaluation."

6.6 **Evaluation (B) (p. 218)**

How might evaluation serve the client during the activation phase?

6.7 **Addressing dysfunctional beliefs (A) (p. 219)**

Give some examples of dysfunctional beliefs that may confound the client's activation.

6.8   **Addressing dysfunctional beliefs (B) (p. 219)**

How might you address the client's dysfunctional beliefs?

6.9   **Stress (p. 220)**

What is meant by an "optimum level of stress"?

6.10 **Ownership (p. 221)**

Describe what is meant by "ownership of the goal" and discuss how the source of the ownership may affect the client's performance.

DISCUSSION POINTS

Discuss among your peers how you might handle these circumstances. Document the opinions expressed using a "+" or a "−" to indicate whether you agree or disagree with each opinion.

6.1 **Waiting room**

For the past several weeks, the client has been reporting that he or she is having trouble getting started on carrying out the second objective.

6.2 **The finish line?**

The client enters with the strategic plan in hand and proclaims, "Well, I'm not going to do this."

6.3 **I hate homework!**

When you initially propose collaboratively specifying a homework assignment, the client cringes. The client reports that he or she thought that all of the work was supposed to happen during appointment hours.

6.4 Measure me not

The client feels that it is wrong to measure people and resists the idea of including an evaluation piece in his or her work.

6.5 Something special

After making some progress, the client reports that due to his or her special characteristics or disabilities, progress will likely be slower.

6.6 Good enough?

Citing an accomplished sibling, the client feels that, as an "average person," he or she does not have what it takes to move forward with the activation plan.

6.7   **Larger than life?**

You have noticed that the client has a propensity to exaggerate at times. The client feels intimidated by the goal, fearing that it is just too unwieldy to start and that it will take a very long time to accomplish.

6.8   **Why change?**

The client has not yet taken action toward what appears to be a fairly simple goal.

6.9   **Whose goal?**

The client has processed through the initial objectives with few hesitations; however, progress has recently slowed to a crawl. As you come to know the client better, the goal begins to appear out of synch with his or her interests. When you ask the client where the idea for this goal came from, the client listlessly replies, "Oh, I don't know."

6.10 Half-empty?

Each week, the client returns feeling disappointed that his or her homework is only about half-done.

Role-Play 6.1 Blue Is for Girls, Pink Is for Boys?

Note: Guidelines for role-play implementation, feedback, and documentation can be found in the "Overview of Exercises" section (p. xiii).

Angel is in the early steps of activation and is excited about the prospect of ultimately achieving the specified goal. Angel has been very selective about confiding in others regarding this goal, which involves taking on a role usually fulfilled by the other gender (e.g., female truck driver, male nurse). At times, Angel reports feeling guilty about this.

Client

- You come from a traditional family. You expect that your family might disapprove of your goal, but you know that you cannot keep this secret forever.
- Discuss your concern with timing: If you disclose your news too early, this may (emotionally or socially) derail your efforts. If you disclose too late, you risk being perceived as deceptive.
- Mention that your family means well and only wants to protect you from (imminent) failure due to some characteristics that your family feels you lack.

Social Worker

- **Social support** (p. 216)—Ask about the individuals that Angel has already confided in, and discuss the nature of those relationships.
- **Addressing dysfunctional beliefs** (p. 219)—Angel's family has labeled him or her as limited in some way (physically, emotionally, or mentally), but according to your observations, these labels seem invalid, irrelevant, or exaggerated.
- **Stress** (p. 220)—Ask Angel about his or her level of stress (e.g., "How high is your level of stress? Is it rising, stable, or dropping?") and the extent to which this stress might be affecting his or her performance.

Role-Play 6.1 Self-Evaluation

(1 = needs further work, 5 = excellent)

1	2	3	4	5	Social support
1	2	3	4	5	Addressing dysfunctional beliefs
1	2	3	4	5	Stress
1	2	3	4	5	_____
1	2	3	4	5	_____

Role-Play 6.1 Case Notes

ROLE-PLAY 6.2 SOMEONE ELSE'S IDEA?

Gale is a college junior majoring in economics. Gale has been earning mostly Cs in these courses and seldom elaborates on the content of the courses or his or her future life in the business sector. Gale's father is a successful economist, and Gale has one sibling with an MBA. Gale's noneconomic GPA is around 3.7.

Client

- Mention, matter-of-factly, that you have accomplished about 60% of the required economics courses and how bored you are with the subject.
- As you discuss some noneconomic courses or interests (e.g., working with children, computers, travel), show (much) greater enthusiasm.
- When asked about your future after graduating with an economics degree, express vagueness as to what the next step might be.

Social Worker

- **Ownership** (p. 221)—If it seems that pursuing economics is out of character, ask if Gale might be attempting to fulfill someone else's wishes (e.g., a parent's, an academic advisor's, another authority figure's). Consider asking what Gale wishes he or she could be pursuing (instead).

- **Homework** (p. 217)—Discuss the nature of the (academic) homework: What is it like, and how long does it take to accomplish (e.g., "Are there delays in getting started or keeping going? Are there any interesting or fun parts? Are there [noneconomic] courses where the homework flows better?").

- **Social support** (p. 216)—Discuss the nature of Gale's social support system: Who has Gale discussed his or her concerns with (e.g., family, social friends, other students, instructors)? Is there someone that Gale is trying to please or avoid disappointing?

Role-Play 6.2 Self-Evaluation

(1 = needs further work, 5 = excellent)

1	2	3	4	5	Ownership
1	2	3	4	5	Homework
1	2	3	4	5	Social support
1	2	3	4	5	_____
1	2	3	4	5	_____

Role-Play 6.2 Case Notes

_____

_____

_____

_____

_____

_____

_____

_____

_____

_____

_____

_____

_____

_____

_____

_____

_____

_____

_____

_____

_____

_____

_____

ROLE-PLAY 6.3 THE CHECKERED FLAG . . . ALMOST

After several years of effort, Mickie has completed a writing project (e.g., a novel, an autobiography, a book of poetry). Upon reaching the final objective, which involves seeking a literary agent, Mickie has halted. Mickie has not discussed this project with anyone.

Client

- Express concerns of not knowing what you will do after this goal is completed.
- Discuss your fears: If your work is rejected, you will feel hurt, and if it is published, your work will be out there for others to judge.
- Talk about how much you have enjoyed pursuing this goal and that when it is over, you are concerned that the joy will end.

Social Worker

- **Social support** (p. 216)—Ask Mickie to discuss who has been supportive throughout this (and other) projects. Such individuals may be particularly useful during this emotionally challenging phase.
- **Addressing dysfunctional beliefs** (p. 219)—Having reviewed a sample of Mickie's writing, you believe that the work is good. Consider discussing Mickie's concerns about being too emotionally fragile to handle potentially negative feedback or constructive criticism.
- **Review objectives/goals** (p. 222)—Encourage Mickie to seek consult from a potential mentor—someone has likely faced these issues and may be able to provide useful guidance (e.g., an author that Mickie admires, an English professor, a published peer).

Role-Play 6.3 Self-Evaluation

(1 = needs further work, 5 = excellent)

1	2	3	4	5	Social support
1	2	3	4	5	Addressing dysfunctional beliefs
1	2	3	4	5	Review objectives/goals
1	2	3	4	5	_____
1	2	3	4	5	_____

Role-Play 6.3 Case Notes

_____

_____

_____

_____

_____

_____

_____

_____

_____

_____

_____

_____

_____

_____

_____

_____

_____

_____

_____

_____

_____

_____

_____

7

Step V—Termination

Continuing the Mission Independently

I	II	III	IV	V
Assessment	**G**oal	**O**bjectives	**A**ctivation	**Termination**

What Is Termination?

In a social work setting, *termination* refers to the process of ending contact with the client. In most other settings, termination is typically conceived of as the *moment* of separation, whereas ideally, in a social work setting, termination is a *process* that involves actively and deliberately dealing with the feelings and thoughts that you and the client experience as the close of the professional relationship draws near. Termination is a key step in the process, enabling the client the opportunity to consolidate acquisitions, generalize skills learned, and form plans for continuing efforts toward achieving goals that are (still) in progress. In cases wherein the goal was successfully accomplished, termination would focus on means for the client to maintain the achieved goal. Such discussion may also include plans for the client to embark on the next goal(s) independent of you.

Effective termination or referral to another social worker or professional can maximize and help maintain the treatment gains, whereas a poorly handled termination or referral can undo or weaken such gains (O'Donohue & Ferguson, 2003).

When Does Termination Happen?

There are a number of cues that can signal the time for appropriate termination. The *Code of Ethics of the National Association of Social Workers* provides relatively pragmatic guidelines regarding termination: "Social workers should terminate services to clients and professional relationships with them when such services and relationships are no longer required or no longer serve the clients' needs or interests" (National Association of Social Workers, 1996, section 1.16).

Others build on this recommendation, suggesting that termination should be cued when (a) the clinical relationship is no longer helpful, (b) the goal is accomplished, or (c) progress toward the goal suggests an appropriate ending time (e.g., the start of the activation process or when activation is well underway) (Hackney & Cormier, 2001). Termination may also be indicated in instances when the goal is only partially complete and it is recognized that the residual portion is unattainable (McClam & Woodside, 1994). Another potential indicator for termination can be when the client's new behavior is sufficiently integrated into the client's repertoire and is reinforced by naturally occurring consequences in his or her environment (Nelson & Politano, 1993).

How Does Termination Happen?

Ideally, the process of termination should begin when both you and the client mutually agree that the professional relationship is due to close—that it is time for the client to resume functioning independently (Weddington & Cavenar, 1979). More often, it is the social worker, endowed with a relatively more objective point of view, who usually suggests termination, expecting that the client will agree (Nelson & Politano, 1993; Wetchler & Ofte-Atha, 1993).

When proposing the notion of termination to the client, consider framing it as an appropriate transition—a step toward furthering the client's independence, wherein the client is endowed with a new level of functioning, as opposed to packaging the termination solely as a separation event (Hackney & Cormier, 1996).

Termination Need Not Be Forever

While termination marks the end of regular contact, it does not necessarily imply a permanent departure. Under certain conditions, the client may choose to return for further services at some point in the future (Binder, 2004; Shulman, 1999).

The social worker–client realm can be thought of as an environment wherein the client can identify meaningful goals and get things moving in an appropriate direction. As such, should insurmountable confounds emerge after termination, a return to the social worker for further assistance may be warranted.

The steps toward termination may begin during the activation phase and may take several forms depending on the needs of the client: (a) The client may continue seeing the social worker throughout the course of activation, (b) the client may see the social worker intermittently (e.g., every other week, prior to embarking on the next objective, as complications are encountered), or (c) the client may terminate contact with the social worker at the start of the activation phase and carry out the objectives independently (Egan, 1994).

Regardless of which of these options is executed, the end of regular (weekly) sessions is an opportunity to wean the client from the process of meeting with you on a regular basis, instilling a sense of accomplishment, independence, and empowerment.

Types of Termination

Unscheduled

Despite your best efforts, there will be times when the client terminates prior to what you might consider an optimum breaking point. A client may terminate prematurely due to external factors (e.g., a move, a physical illness or disability, financial constraints). Alternatively, the client may simply feel that he or she has attained as much help as is needed at this time and therefore suspend sessions (Smith, 1983). There will also be times when the client terminates therapy abruptly and provides no reason (Hackney & Cormier, 2005).

Scheduled

As discussed earlier, termination may be scheduled to coincide with the identification of the goal (and possibly objectives), the launch of the activation, or the resolution of the goal. Alternatively, termination may involve a pre-designated date as indicated by the agency's policy or the client's benefits, wherein the maximum number of sessions is specified. In some cases, terminations are scheduled to coincide with the conclusion of a student's internship. Other forms of scheduled termination involve transfers, referrals, and time-limited interventions.

Transfers

A transfer consists of terminating your contact with a client and the client beginning contact with a different social worker or another healthcare professional (e.g., psychologist, psychiatrist). Transfers may be necessitated for any number of reasons: You may be leaving the agency or changing roles, or it may be the case that the professional relationship is no longer beneficial to the client (Wood & Wood, 1990).

Transferring involves telling the client about the proposed change within a time frame that allows for discussion and planning. It is recommended that you involve the client in the decision to transfer, honoring the client's right to self-determination. Consider working with the client to make the transition. Ideally, it can be facilitative for the client to meet his or her new social worker (or other healthcare professional) during the process of concluding sessions with you (Bostic, Shadid, & Blotcky, 1996; O'Reilly, 1987).

Due diligence should be made by all parties involved in order to facilitate the best continuity of care as possible. This involves not only you and the client but also the receiving social worker (or other healthcare professional) working together to arrange for a smooth, well-informed transition: "The [receiving] social worker should carefully consider the client's needs before agreeing to provide services" (National Association of Social Workers, 1996, section 3.06).

Considering the nature of the (professional) relationship that exists between you and the client, transfers are more than mere administrative operations. Feelings and a sense of relationship can also be relevant elements that must be recognized and dealt with. Naturally, the client may experience any number of feelings (e.g., abandonment, anger, gratitude, indifference). Despite your professional perspective, it is expected that at times you may experience your own set of feelings pertaining to such transfers. Some social workers may experience a sense of guilt for deserting the client or failing to (fully) cure the client (O'Reilly, 1987). As a result, it is important to remember that any such efforts are collaborative in nature. Neither member is 100% liable for the client's outcomes, be they negative or positive.

Referrals

Referrals differ from transfers in that transfers involve you stopping service to the client entirely as another professional begins, whereas referrals involve you continuing to work with the client to some degree while including a *supplemental* provider in the client's care plan.

You may consider offering the client a referral when "other professionals' specialized knowledge or expertise is needed to serve clients fully or when social workers believe that they are not being effective or making reasonable progress with clients and that additional service is required" (National Association of Social Workers, 1996, section 2.06). In order to reduce the likelihood that the client could perceive the referral negatively (e.g., rejection, too damaged for any one provider to handle), openly share your rationale for offering each referral. Be clear that your intention is to put the client in front of someone who can provide a supplemental, specialized service that could be a valuable component in his or her care plan. It may be helpful to normalize the referral process by pointing out that this is common practice among medical professionals: Depending on the patient's condition, physicians regularly make referrals to specialists (e.g., neurologists, nephrologists, orthopedists) in order to deliver the best possible package of care to patients.

Time-Limited Interventions

Short-term intervention models may specify a limited number of sessions. Preknowledge of the termination date can actually serve as a catalyst in motivating the process (Weddington & Cavenar, 1979).

In time-limited settings, it is possible that not all of the client's issues will be fully resolved during the allotted time (Binder, 2004). In such cases, it can be beneficial to track the client's progress, skills, and positive adaptations throughout the process in the event that the client needs to complete the residual treatment plan without the benefit of your contact.

Depending on the nature of the facility and your role, the termination may include "booster sessions," which are scheduled after termination with decreasing frequency (progressively longer periods between sessions). Ultimately, the goal of booster sessions is to help keep the client on track, employing the skills learned in sessions to continue advancement toward the goal or prevent relapse (Sudak, 2006).

While there may be follow-up or booster sessions upon the (initial) termination, it is important that you do not engage in personal contact with clients during any part of the process, including posttermination. Such contact would constitute a dual or multiple relationship, which is ethically inappropriate (National Association of Social Workers, 1996).

Depending on the setting and the characteristics of the case, you may have the opportunity to implement variations in the termination process. This might involve tapering the frequency of the sessions as termination approaches. This gradual technique, wherein there are progressively longer periods between sessions, helps provide the client with a less abrupt adaptation to termination. It also affords you and the client the opportunity to observe and appropriately tune the client's functioning as the duration between appointments increases, thereby facilitating a progressive sense of functional independence (Stadter, 1996).

Progressive Termination

In most instances, a progressive approach to termination is considered the preferred method. Through the course of contacts, make a point to regularly allocate some time for discussing the client's progress to date. Such dialogues can include feelings and thoughts regarding the client's goals, work accomplished, lessons learned, work left to be done, and termination.

At the Start of the Process

Under ideal circumstances, termination should not be reserved for the last few minutes of the final meeting. It is recommended that the topic of termination be introduced at the onset of the process, even if you are in a position to let the client decide when termination is to happen (Kramer, 1986), realistically framing the client–social worker affiliation as a stable but *temporary* professional relationship. When feasible, it is preferred that termination be planned and implemented in a manner that is appropriate and meaningful to the client. In assembling the specifics of the termination, consider the influences of the client's past experiences with respect to how he or she has dealt with separation and loss. Effectively working through the termination process can provide the client with valuable skills that can be generalized to coping effectively with the many losses and endings endemic throughout the normal course of the client's life cycle (McRoy, Freeman, & Logan, 1986).

During the Process

During the course of your contact with clients, it can be useful to periodically devote some time to the topic of termination. Tend to the client's thoughts, feelings, and concerns when discussing the nature of this temporary relationship and the impending termination (Sudak, 2006). This progressive approach serves to help clients comprehend where they stand both chronologically and progress-wise, thereby better preparing them for the foreseeable separation (Safran & Muran, 2000). Depending on their history, current circumstances, and personality, some clients will find termination quite challenging. In such cases, appropriately preparing such clients for termination becomes even more essential (Quintana, 1993; Safran & Muran, 2000).

One technique for effectively preparing clients for termination in a progressive and comprehensive manner involves concluding each session with some brief discussion covering three relatively intuitive points: (1) Summarize the main points of this session, (2) generalize what has been learned from one experience and apply it to other instances, and (3) identify the next steps (Shulman, 1999). These concluding discussions should also include voicing and processing the corresponding emotional aspects: (a) the client's feelings regarding today's session, (b) how the client feels about his or her progress to date, and (c) feelings regarding the next steps and his or her overall outlook regarding termination.

As termination approaches, you may wish to allocate progressively more time per session to addressing the pending closure of this professional relationship. If a specific termination date is known, mentioning this date and the number of contacts remaining may help reify and focus these discussions.

At the Close of the Process

Independent of how much discussion has been directed toward termination throughout the course of the process, the final session affords an appropriate opportunity to consolidate gains that the client has accumulated, citing progress, new skills, adaptations, techniques, and information learned, as well as the potential for carrying such experiences and proficiencies forward, beyond termination (Quintana, 1993).

Mutual Emotional Aspects of Termination

As the client steps closer toward terminating the supportive relationship with newly acquired skills, this provides a unique opportunity to help the client identify his or her new level of proficiency, thereby serving to enhance his or her sense of self-reliance and confidence. It is also a time to address the emotional impact that this closure has on you and the client as the professional relationship draws to a close (Bostic, Shadid, & Blotcky, 1996; Hayes, Follette, & Follette, 1995).

As the professional relationship is built, both you and the client typically develop some sense of the other person. This may consist of feelings, such as admiration, pride, or enjoyment of the other person. Hence, the impending closure of the professional relationship can represent a mutual loss for both participants (Leigh, 1998). Considering the personal issues processed in such a setting, you and the client may, over time, develop a genuine rich (professional) relationship. Part of the termination process involves acknowledging the depth of this contact along with the necessity to relinquish it while retaining the gains derived from it (Sudak, 2006).

Termination, which involves letting go, can present a challenge to the client, who may have become accustomed to having your support and guidance. Additionally, you may experience your own sense of loss and uncertainty regarding the fate of your client (Murdin, 2000). Despite how cognitively aware you and the client are of the approaching termination, the separation process can evoke powerful mutual feelings as the closure of a meaningful relationship in which both members are invested nears. Having worked closely with the client toward identifying and pursuing meaningful goals, it can be emotionally challenging to sever this collaborative relationship (Shulman, 1999). Any number of feelings, such as sadness, denial, anger, relief, resentment, anxiety, rejection, fear, or guilt, may be present for you and the client (Goodyear, 1981; McRoy, Freeman, & Logan, 1986).

Emotional Aspects of the Social Worker

Despite efforts to provide your services in a professional and objective manner, even the most experienced social worker is prone to valid emotional reactions when it comes time for termination. It has been noted that some professionals believe that once they are out of the picture, the client will have a significant unfulfillable void in his or her life, and these professionals use this presumption as an implicit justification for unnecessarily prolonging the duration of their contact with clients (Kupers, 1988). Positive countertransference, wherein you develop feelings of liking or fondness toward a client, may also tempt you to resist termination, thereby inappropriately prolonging the process (Weddington & Cavenar, 1979). This is not to imply that you should be unfeeling. Quite the contrary. Throughout the course of the professional relationship, particularly with respect to termination, it is vital to recognize and effectively cope with your feelings in the interest of providing the best possible service to your clients.

Ideally, as you observe the client achieve objectives and advance closer to the accomplishment of the specified goal(s), your attitude may appropriately be one of pride—that the client can (now) function relatively self-reliably and independently. In some ways, this is akin to the bittersweet pride that a parent feels as a child develops and aptly outgrows the need for that parent's day-to-day guidance, thereby marking a transition (not a termination) in the parent-child relationship. Conversely, the type of termination that you will face with clients presents a different type of challenge in that it signifies the close of the relationship (Weddington & Cavenar, 1979). As such, it can be valuable to reflect on the preamble of the *Code of Ethics of the National Association of Social Workers*: "The primary mission of the social work profession is to enhance human well-being and help meet the basic human needs of all people, with particular attention to the needs and empowerment of people . . ." (National Association of Social Workers, 1996).

Just as there is no such thing as a "typical client," there is no *single* appropriate feeling or set of feelings when it comes to termination. In instances where the sessions were fraught with conflict, nonperformance, counterproductive conduct, negative attitudes, poor rapport, or other challenging aspects, it is reasonable that your feelings regarding termination may lean toward indifference or even relief (Shulman, 1999).

Emotional Aspects of the Client

The ending of regular sessions marks the beginning of a new phase for the client, involving new skills and new or ongoing demands. The client may initially experience some anxiety regarding his or her ability to function effectively without your help. It can be useful to acknowledge this and to point out that part of the growth process is learning to deal effectively with some level of uncertainty (Shulman, 1999). You may find that even suggesting the time frame for termination may be met with a variety of reactions depending on the unique characteristics of the client and his or her circumstances: Some clients may feel good about their progress and motivated to continue their efforts independently. Other clients may feel nervous about the prospect of being on their own. Either way, clients may experience a genuine sense of sadness as the end of a meaningful relationship draws near (Murdin, 2000).

The process of termination can be particularly challenging for patients whose circumstances or diagnoses are characterized by separation, dependency, or attachment issues. The client's reaction to termination may reflect his or her past adaptations to losses, which may involve guilt, denial, acting out, self-defeating behaviors (or thoughts), symptom increase, reemergence of old symptoms (regression), or an inability to generalize learned behaviors. Such clients may react with any number of adverse emotions, particularly feelings of abandonment and depression (Bostic, Shadid, & Blotcky, 1996; Wetchler & Ofte-Atha, 1993).

Cognitive and emotional techniques can be used to address such issues as they arise in the termination process. From a cognitive standpoint, guide the client to review his or her growth and advancement toward meaningful goal(s), pointing the way to more independent functioning and continued focused growth (Murdin, 2000). From an emotional perspective, consider empathetically acknowledging and openly addressing the feelings as they emerge (e.g., sadness, resentment, regret, gratitude, grief, anger, guilt). Anger is a common feeling among clients as termination approaches. Effectively processing the client's emotions can serve the client well both now and in the future. According to Mann (1973), "A setting of warmth, support, encouragement, and strength serves well the patient's desire and need to incorporate the therapist as a good, nonambivalent object and to leave treatment with the kind of internalized object that promotes growth and the capacity to move away independently" (p. 60).

Consolidating Gains

Overall, the termination process serves as a vehicle for you and the client to achieve a sense of closure, wherein the mutual expression of feelings and thoughts pertaining to the ending phase can be aired and dealt with.

Approach the termination process in a way that helps the client feel good about the work accomplished. Based on the client's performance throughout your contact with him or her, express your confidence that the client has demonstrated the capacity to function effectively (between sessions). Hence, it follows that he or she has what it takes to independently complete the current goal and to identify and effectively undertake other meaningful goals (Kottler, 1991).

Termination is a time for both you and the client to sum up what has been learned, what has been accomplished, and what each of you will take away from this experience. If discussion regarding what the client has learned and accomplished throughout the course of care is vague, solicit the client to provide specific examples of lessons learned and objectives or milestones achieved. Consolidating the ending process can help the client generalize his or her learning to (better) cope with new experiences (Shulman, 1999).

Due to the gradual nature of the change process, the client may not readily be able to articulate specific aspects of his or her growth. In such cases, it may be helpful to review the early pages of the client's file—realistically contrasting the status of the client's life at the beginning of the process with how it is now.

Termination is an opportunity to place the client's recent work within the overall context of the client's life cycle. This involves actively acknowledging that, despite the end of the professional relationship between you and the client, the challenge of advancing one's life is never really done. For many people, the completion of one goal naturally suggests the next goal as one advances throughout the course of a meaningful and fulfilling life.

Consolidating gains is not reserved exclusively for positive terminations. In cases wherein the client is dissatisfied with the progress or lack thereof, it can be valuable to engage the client to discuss, as specifically as possible, what his or her expectations were and what might have made things work better. The client may cite specific criticisms directed at you (e.g., not supportive enough, not bold enough, not directive enough, not attentive enough, not sensitive enough).

Though it can be challenging to hear such feedback, such venting is useful in that it enables the client the opportunity to voice and process his or her feelings and to discuss the feasibility of making such adjustments.

Next, without assigning blame, encourage the client to discuss what he or she may have done (or not done) that may have confounded his or her mission (e.g., procrastinating, blaming others, being unfocused, feeling anxious, feeling uncommitted, waiting for you or someone else to do or say something, skipping or canceling appointments). Depending on the client's response, you might want to take a moment to commend his or her courage to respond candidly.

Finally, work with the client to combine these two topics: What does the client wish you had done differently, and what does the client wish he or she had done differently? Encourage the client to provide specific details. You may point out elements that you consider feasible and those that seem inappropriate. Be clear about the purpose of this conversation: Often we learn more from mistakes than we do from easy successes. The point of this review is to shed light on an alternate approach to the problem-solving process. This review may suggest a better approach for when the client is prepared to try again, either independently, with you, or with a different social worker or healthcare provider.

Posttermination Planning

It is worth explicitly pointing out that while the process of working with clients may be used to identify and achieve goals as well as shore up the client's resourcefulness, the end of sessions does not mark the end of the client's mission; nor does termination imply the end of problems or the problem-solving process (McClam & Woodside, 1994). Just because termination is afoot, this does not necessarily mean that the client has gone as far as he or she can go in terms of psychological (or life) development (Wachtel, 2002). Further growth may involve the completion of the goal that is in progress, the identification and completion of the next goal, or a series of future goals.

Based on the client's character and projected path, work with the client to identify and normalize the challenges and potential setbacks that may likely be encountered. Such discussions may suggest applicable tools, techniques, and adaptations that the client has learned and employed throughout the process, both during and between sessions (Sudak, 2006).

Identifying the client's needs and availability of socially supportive resources can serve to supplement the client's posttermination functionality (Strupp & Binder, 1984). Such supportive resources may include self-help groups or personal support systems (e.g., family, friends, significant other) to advance the mission (Egan, 1994). Additional posttermination resources may include peer groups, literature, community resources for vocational counseling or education, supplemental educational services, and, in the case of transfers or future professional contact, the client's next social worker (Shulman, 1999).

Goal Still in Progress

In instances wherein the completion of the specified goal does not coincide with the termination date, consider framing this type of termination positively, as a work in progress as opposed to failure to meet a deadline. It is appropriate to point out that all progress counts as valuable movement forward—the client is closer to accomplishing the goal than he or she was before.

Work with the client to evaluate the degree to which he or she has achieved the goal. Consider reviewing each objective on the client's strategic plan, detailing the extent to which each action and resource worked, what roadblocks were encountered, and how each was resolved. Also, take some time to review the nature of the relationship that you and the client had with each other. Such discussions may provide insights to the client that may be generalizable to other relationships in his or her life (Evans, Hearn, Uhlemann, & Ivey, 1998). If the client seems anxious about his or her ability to follow through on the mission without your help, consider discussing the efforts that he or she has put forth *between* appointments—wherein the client functioned competently in your absence. This can help facilitate an essential sense of self-confidence and autonomy.

Goal Accomplished

There will be times when the client's accomplishment of the goal matches the termination date. An accomplished goal can be thought of as a *finite* goal or a *maintenance* goal.

A *finite* goal has a discrete, objective ending (e.g., graduating from college, taking a trip, writing a story, finding a job). For forward-looking clients, the completion of a finite goal may suggest the next desired goal(s); after earning a bachelor's degree, the goal may be to earn a master's, find related work, relocate, begin an exercise program, and so on.

A *maintenance* goal involves achieving a specified threshold and consistently taking steps to maintain the gains achieved. Maintenance goals include conditions that are considered chronic in nature (e.g., achieving and *maintaining* sobriety, building and *continuing to practice* positive work habits, learning and *persistently applying* anger management techniques), wherein the overarching goal is relapse prevention.

With respect to maintenance goals, some form of homework should continue beyond termination, as a key component in the ongoing intervention. Clients with chronic conditions can benefit by identifying relapse triggers and strategies to avoid or better cope with the emergence of such triggers. In the event of relapses or slips, work realistically with the client to cope with the emotional challenges of such events. Use this as a learning opportunity for the client by having him or her discuss and document the conditions that led to this relapse. Based on this review, it may be possible to creatively consider what can be done to recognize or control for future such incidents and form corresponding adaptations (Sudak, 2006).

Next Goal

As stated previously, termination may be characterized by full or partial completion of finite or maintenance goals. As the process draws to a close, regardless of the client's status, discussion regarding the continuity of the client's life is warranted. The next step(s), which will take place outside, independent of you, may involve continued movement toward the specified goal, maintaining gains, or identifying and advancing toward different goals. Normalize the notion that with some meaningful work, life can get better, but it never gets perfect. Throughout life, it is appropriate to be faced with some unresolved problems—nobody has all the answers on hand at any given time. You may wish to point out that not all problems can be 100% solved; however, many problematic situations can be reduced or managed in some way.

Take some time to specifically cite the successful coping skills and work-around solutions that the client has demonstrated, both during and between sessions. Realistically express your genuine confidence that he or she will have further opportunities to continue to grow and to use what has been learned to independently address and effectively handle life's challenges as they naturally emerge (Shulman, 1999).

CHAPTER 7 EXERCISES

CONCEPT REVIEWS

Explain each concept in your own words. Where applicable, provide a case example without disclosing identifying information.

7.1   What is termination? (p. 237)

Describe what is meant by "termination" in a social work setting.

7.2   When does termination happen? (p. 237)

List some cues that suggest it may be time to terminate.

7.3   How does termination happen? (p. 238)

Termination does not always mean ending contact abruptly. Describe some variations in termination style.

7.4   **Unscheduled termination (p. 238)**

What are some conditions wherein the client may spontaneously end his or her contact with you?

7.5   **Scheduled termination (p. 239)**

Discuss the conditions related to scheduled termination: (a) goal accomplished, (b) transfers, (c) referrals, (d) time-limited interventions.

7.6   **Progressive termination (A) (p. 241)**

What is meant by "progressive termination"?

7.7   **Progressive termination (B) (p. 241)**

What are the advantages of implementing a "progressive termination"?

7.8   **Mutual emotional aspects of termination (p. 242)**

Describe some of the emotional issues that both you and the client may face when embarking on termination.

7.9   **Emotional aspects of the social worker (p. 242)**

What are some of the emotional issues that you, as a social worker, may face with respect to termination?

7.10   **Emotional aspects of the client (p. 243)**

What are some of the emotional issues that your clients may face with respect to termination?

7.11   **Posttermination planning (p. 245)**

Describe the elements that can make up posttermination planning.

7.12   **Goal still in progress (p. 245)**

Discuss some techniques for helping clients continue working toward unfinished goals upon termination.

7.13   **Goal accomplished—finite goals (p. 246)**

Describe what is meant by a "finite goal" and corresponding posttermination planning.

7.14   **Goal accomplished—maintenance goals (p. 246)**

Describe what is meant by a "maintenance goal" and corresponding posttermination planning.

DISCUSSION POINTS

Discuss among your peers how you might handle these circumstances. Document the opinions expressed using a "+" or a "−" to indicate whether you agree or disagree with each opinion.

7.1   Done . . . or are we?

The client has worked hard and accomplished his or her goal in 7 weeks and has three more sessions allotted.

7.2   "So long" is not "goodbye"

As termination approaches, the client is concerned that he or she may encounter difficulties maintaining the gains achieved while working with you and also doubts if he or she can effectively identify and carry out the next goal.

7.3   Pomp and circumstances

During your internship, you mention your departure date to each client periodically, starting from your first appointment. As your graduation date approaches, one client seems surprised and hurt that you will actually be leaving him or her.

7.4   The biz

The client has made some substantial progress toward fulfilling the specified goal, and at this time, he or she needs to embark on a lengthy business trip.

7.5   Something special

The client has revealed a condition or diagnosis that you feel would be best treated by a specialist at a reputable facility. Upon offering the client the referral, the client responds by telling you that he or she feels comfortable with you and prefers to get all of his or her care from you (only).

7.6   Missing inaction

You have a client who has not made much progress over considerable time. After conferring with your supervisor, it is decided that termination is in the client's best interest. The client has missed the appointment wherein you were going to discuss this with him or her.

7.7   Second movement: duet or solo?

The client has accomplished the specified goal and feels prepared to cope independently; however, as termination approaches, the client has alluded to a different issue that suggests the need for further sessions.

7.8   Keeping gains

The client has achieved the initial steps in resolving a chronic problem (e.g., sobriety, controlling rage, punctuality) and is appropriately concerned about relapse upon termination.

7.9   Resent . . . the end is near!

Your client has made substantial progress toward accomplishing the specified goal. During the final session, despite your efforts to facilitate progressive termination, the client expresses anger at you for abandoning him or her.

7.10   Gone but not forgotten

Shortly after an appropriate termination, you find yourself thinking a lot about a particular client.

Role-Play 7.1 I'll Drink to That . . . Not!

Note: Guidelines for role-play implementation, feedback, and documentation can be found in the "Overview of Exercises" section (p. xiii).

After a long bout with drinking, Lonnie has benefited from working with you and regularly engaging in AA (Alcoholics Anonymous) meetings. Lonnie has achieved stable sobriety and resolved some meaningful issues. It is mutually decided that it is time to terminate.

Client

- As termination nears, you are considering ending your contact with AA as well.
- Express satisfaction with the care that you received for the identified (drinking) problem but dissatisfaction in that you thought that most of your other problems would be resolved also.
- Discuss your concerns about losing access to care.

Social Worker

- **Maintenance** (p. 246)—Discuss the nature of chronic conditions, such as alcoholism, and the value of having a posttermination relapse prevention plan in place, which includes support systems (e.g., AA).
- **Next goal** (p. 246)—Normalize the notion that life is a successive process, wherein the accomplishment of one goal can free up (emotional and cognitive) resources, providing the opportunity to identify and address other problems in the form of the next goal(s).
- **Termination need not be forever** (p. 238)—If Lonnie expresses concerns about losing contact with you, discuss some options for possible posttermination sessions (e.g., scheduled booster sessions, identifying cues that may suggest the need to return for further sessions).

Role-Play 7.1 Self-Evaluation

(1 = needs further work, 5 = excellent)

1	2	3	4	5	Maintenance
1	2	3	4	5	Next goal
1	2	3	4	5	Termination need not be forever
1	2	3	4	5	_____
1	2	3	4	5	_____

Role-Play 7.1 Case Notes

ROLE-PLAY 7.2 FAMILY AND BEYOND

Kris initially sought help to cope with an unrealistically demanding family. Kris has developed a more robust sense of self and appropriate boundaries, enabling him or her to identify and accomplish some goals that are personally meaningful, but there is still some work to be done. At this point, you believe that Kris can and should pursue the remaining goals (e.g., smoking cessation, starting an exercise program, career advancement) independently—without further sessions.

Client

- Mention that you are concerned that without weekly contact and encouragement, you are likely to revert to giving in to your family's whims at the cost of derailing the pursuit of your own goals and personal and professional development.
- Explain that the social worker is the first person who has taken an interest in your wishes and helped you form your desires into doable goals and how you will miss that.
- Ask the social worker if, as a professional, he or she has any feelings regarding the pending termination.

Social Worker

- **Termination need not be forever** (p. 238)—Discuss alternate methods of termination (e.g., progressively longer gaps between appointments, periodic booster appointments).
- **Emotional aspects of the client** (p. 243)—Encourage Kris to discuss feelings and thoughts related to termination—how Kris perceives the loss of your contact as a supportive figure.
- **Emotional aspects of the social worker** (p. 242)—While maintaining your sense of comfort and boundaries, discuss how you feel about the end of regular weekly sessions with Kris. Consider including feelings that pertain to the progress that Kris has accomplished (e.g., pride, confidence).

Role-Play 7.2 Self-Evaluation

(1 = needs further work, 5 = excellent)

1	2	3	4	5	Termination need not be forever
1	2	3	4	5	Emotional aspects of the client
1	2	3	4	5	Emotional aspects of the social worker
1	2	3	4	5	_____
1	2	3	4	5	_____

Role-Play 7.2 Case Notes

_____

_____

_____

_____

_____

_____

_____

_____

_____

_____

_____

_____

_____

_____

_____

_____

_____

_____

_____

_____

_____

_____

_____

_____

ROLE-PLAY 7.3 DISSATISFACTION GUARANTEED

After sufficient time, it has become clear that Terry has not made much progress toward achieving the specified goal(s) (e.g., anger management, controlling substance abuse, losing weight, resolving depression). Terry has presented as unmotivated or unwilling to take any serious actions regardless of the multiple strategies that have been mutually assembled. Ethically, termination is indicated.

Client

- Express your disappointment that the social worker did not fix you or resolve your problem(s).
- Propose that the process was a complete waste of time and money.
- When appropriate, take some responsibility for the outcome.

Social Worker

- **Emotional aspects of the client** (p. 243)—Allow Terry to voice his or her feelings about having not accomplished the goal(s) set forth. Solicit what his or her expectations were for you and for him- or herself throughout the process.
- **Consolidating gains** (p. 244)—While acknowledging the validity of Terry's disappointment, discuss the lessons learned from this experience. Prompt Terry to identify what specific conditions may have precluded a better outcome (e.g., Might Terry have taken more or different actions? Should other life factors have been tended to first?). Realistically engender hope that, having identified these factors, this may better inform Terry's next attempt.
- **Emotional aspects of the social worker** (p. 242)—To the extent that you feel comfortable, tactfully discuss your feelings with respect to this termination (e.g., frustration, disappointment in yourself and/or Terry, hope that Terry may reattempt independently or with a different social worker).

Role-Play 7.3 Self-Evaluation

(1 = needs further work, 5 = excellent)

1	2	3	4	5	Emotional aspects of the client
1	2	3	4	5	Consolidating gains
1	2	3	4	5	Emotional aspects of the social worker
1	2	3	4	5	_____
1	2	3	4	5	_____

Role-Play 7.3 Case Notes

_____

_____

_____

_____

_____

_____

_____

_____

_____

_____

_____

_____

_____

_____

_____

_____

_____

_____

_____

_____

_____

_____

_____

Appendix A

Sample Mental Status Exam (MSE)

As stated earlier in the text, there is no universal format for a mental status exam (MSE). The content may vary depending on such things as setting, agency practices, forms, client population, level of detail available, and the time allotted to carry out an MSE. The following are some of the topics commonly covered in an MSE:

- Condition under which the MSE is conducted
- Description of person/appearance
- State of consciousness
- Orientation
- Motor behavior
- Affect
- Speech quality
- Thought process
- Thought content
- Perceptions
- Judgment
- Memory
- Intellectual functioning
- Mental health diagnosis
- Treatment recommendations

The following is a sample of a fairly typical MSE. For clarity, each section begins as a new paragraph beginning with the section header. Alternatively, this could have been written in a more narrative fashion, without explicit section breaks.

MSE for Adrian

Condition under which the MSE is conducted—*Adrian was interviewed in a private one-on-one office at Acme Mental Health Center during her first appointment on July 16 at 4:00 p.m. Adrian is a new client brought in by her parents who are concerned, describing her as "so depressed and dark." Adrian confirms that there have been persistent (verbal) confrontations with her parents and academic problems, both of which have grown progressively worse over the past 6 months.*

Description of person/appearance—*Adrian is a 16-year-old Caucasian female, approximately 5 ft, 10 in. (about 1.8 m), of appropriate weight, with fair skin; long, straight, light-brown hair; blue eyes; and no glasses. She presents as moderately attractive and well groomed, with good personal hygiene, age-appropriate clothing and use of cosmetics (skillfully applied facial makeup and elaborate multicolored nail polish), pierced ears (one pierce in each earlobe), and no observable tattoos or scars, and she is wearing seven rings (costume jewelry)—two on some fingers. She carries a simple, average-sized purse.*

State of consciousness—Adrian presents as alert and oriented x3. She is attentive and provides prompt and reasonable responses to most questions.

Motor behavior—Adrian's stride is somewhat slow—once seated, she sat fairly still with her arms crossed most of the time.

Affect—Adrian presents with a good range of emotion that is context appropriate. Initially, she presented as fairly blunted with limited facial expression and negative eye contact. She describes her overall mood as "terrible . . . just bad," which is consistent with her discussion of circumstances at home and school. She exhibits some elevation in her affect when discussing her boyfriend and hopes for an enduring and loving future with him.

Speech quality—Verbalizations are articulate and tend to be consistent with her depressive affect: slow, low in volume, occasionally to the level of a whisper. When her voice becomes inaudible, she belligerently repeats her words or phrases upon (courteous) request. Adrian tends to resist engaging in dialogue—her adaptation (in this setting) is to respond to questions in a relatively brief fashion. After warming up, her responses became somewhat more forthcoming and detailed.

Thought process—Adrian presents with cogent thinking. Her responses to questions, though occasionally briefly delayed, reflect attentiveness and logical/linear reasoning, appropriately addressing the questions as asked. She demonstrates the ability to reason concretely and abstractly in manners that are contextually appropriate.

Thought content—Adrian's thoughts seem to focus on her perception that her parents are unnecessarily rigid in their thinking, rules, punishments, and overprotective style. Adrian explains that this interferes with her ability to speak and act freely/spontaneously and restricts her interaction with friends (e.g., curfews, no sleepovers, no out-of-town travel with friends). There is no evidence of thought disorders or dangerousness to self or others.

Perceptions—Adrian does not exhibit signs of perceptual anomalies and denies any history of hallucinations or illusions but does report occasionally having exceptionally vivid dreams during nocturnal sleep about once a week over the last few months.

Judgment—Adrian presents with appropriate judgment, guided by a good sense of conscience, reasonably anticipating the consequences of her actions.

Memory—Memory appears to be intact: reliable and rapid recall of immediate, recent, and remote incidents.

Intellectual functioning—Adrian's conversational engagement demonstrates her ability to think effectively both concretely and abstractly. Adrian comfortably and appropriately demonstrates a sophisticated vocabulary and analogical thinking. Prior academic report cards indicate above-average academic performance despite comments detailing recurring disruptive/distracting socializing with peers during class time. More recent report cards show a substantial decline in marks, classroom conduct, and verbal confrontations with teachers.

Mental health diagnosis

I: 296.22—*Major Depressive Disorder, Single Episode, Moderate (provisional)*
    V61.20—*Parent-Child Relational Problem*

II: V71.09—*No Diagnosis on Axis II*

III: *Adrian reports no physical health problems or diagnoses and no history of major injuries or accidents.*

IV: *Persistent confrontations over multiple issues with parents, escalating over past 5–6 months. Low to moderate sibling and peer support. Academic problems appear to be secondary to family and social stressors.*

V: *GAF = 68 (current), 82 (highest in last year)*

Treatment recommendations—Recommend weekly individual sessions with Adrian along with weekly family sessions to assess general family history, structure, norms, functioning, and dynamics among parents and siblings. To provide referral to Dr. Ralston for mental health evaluation for possible short-term use of antidepressant medication. To coordinate treatment plan with Dr. Ralston and monitor progress. To reassess in 3 months.

Appendix B

Diagnostic Terminology

The following is a partial list of diagnostic terminology that you may encounter or use in case documentation.

Agitation—Small movements

Agnosia—Unable to recognize or identify objects

Alogia—Poverty of speech (brief, empty replies)

Anhedonia—Unable to experience any pleasure (prolonged)

Aphasia—Disorganized language

Apraxia—Inability to do motor tasks

Ataxia—Uncoordinated muscular movements

Avolition—Inability to initiate and persist in goal-directed activities

Bradycardia—Slow pulse

Catalepsy—See "Waxy flexibility"

Catatonic excitement—Unstimulated excessive motor activity

Catatonic negativism—Resistance to instruction or attempts to being physically moved

Catatonic posturing—Inappropriate or bizarre physical positioning

Catatonic rigidity—Rigid posture, resistance to being physically moved

Circumstantial speech—Includes excessive nonessential details in responses or storytelling

Delusion—False belief system

Dysarthria—Neurological speech impediment

Echolalia—Repeating the interviewer's word(s) verbatim

Echopraxia—Mirroring others' physical actions

Hyperactivity—Larger movements

Hyperacusis—Very sensitive to sound

Hypnagogic phenomenon—Hallucination occurring just prior to falling asleep

Ideas of influence—Believing that others control one's thoughts

Ideas of reference—Believing that other things, people, or events are related to oneself

Labile—Quickly cycling affect

Logorrhea—Too much speech

Macropsia—Perceiving objects as larger than they actually are

Micropsia—Perceiving objects as smaller than they actually are

Myocardial infarction (MI)—Heart attack

Nystagmus—Involuntary rapid eye oscillations

Orientation—(x3) person, place, time

Postpartum—After childbirth

Poverty of speech—Too little speech

Preservation—Needless repetition of same idea

Pressured speech—Speaks fast or in a high volume; may be difficult or impossible to interrupt

Psychomotor retardation—Movements too idle

Stereotypical movement—Repetitive non-goal-directed movements

Tachycardia—Elevated pulse

Thought broadcasting—Believing that others are hearing or receiving one's thoughts

Thought insertion—Believing that others put thoughts into one's head

Waxy flexibility—Able to pose client into unusual, sustained positions (with catatonic schizophrenics)

Appendix C

Documentation, Symbols, and Abbreviations

Some clinical settings accept selected symbols and abbreviations in case documentation; others do not. Be sure to find out what style of documentation is customary at each facility. The following is a list of some of the most commonly used symbols and abbreviations.

Notations often used in social work settings:

↓—Decrease

↑—Increase

ΨDx—Mental health diagnosis (*DSM*)

A/Ox3—Alert and fully oriented (to person, place, and time)

c̄—With

Cl—Client

D/C—Discharge or discontinue

Dx—Diagnosis

F/T—Follow-through

Hx—History

p̄—After

Px—Problem

R/T—Related to

S/O—Significant other

Sw—Social worker

Th—Therapist

Tx—Treatment

Supplemental notations often used in medical social work settings:

BID—Twice a day

NPO—Nothing by mouth

PRN—As needed

Pt—Patient

Q4H—Every 4 hours (can use any number)

QD—Once daily

QID—Four times a day

QOD—Every other day

Rx—Prescription

Sfx—Side effects

TID—Three times a day

References

Alarcon, R. D. (1995). Culture and psychiatric diagnosis: Impact on DSM-IV and ICD-10. *Psychiatric Clinics of North America, 18*(3), 449–465.

American Psychiatric Association. (2000). *Diagnostic and statistical manual of mental disorders* (4th ed., Text rev.). Washington, DC: Author.

Anderson, S. C., & Mandell, D. L. (1989). The use of self-disclosure by professional social workers. *Social Casework, 70*(6), 259–267.

Andreasen, N. C. (2007). DSM and the death of phenomenology in America: An example of unintended consequences. *Schizophrenia Bulletin, 33*(1), 108–112.

Austin, A. W. (1998). The changing American college student: Thirty-year trends, 1966–1996. *The Review of Higher Education, 21,* 115–135.

Baker, F. M. (1988). Afro-Americans. In L. Comas-Diaz & E. E. H. Griffith (Eds.), *Clinical guidelines in cross-cultural mental health* (pp. 151–181). New York: Wiley.

Baker, F. M., & Lightfoot, O. B. (1993). Mental health care of ethnic elders. In A. C. Gaw (Ed.), *Culture, ethnicity, and mental illness* (pp. 517–522). Washington, DC: American Mental Health Press.

Bandura, A. (1986). *Social foundations of thought and action: A social cognitive theory.* Englewood Cliffs, NJ: Prentice Hall.

Bandura, A. (2001). Social cognitive theory: An agentic perspective. *Annual Review of Psychology, 52,* 1–26.

Barcus, C. (2003). Recommendations for the treatment of American Indian populations. In Council of National Psychological Association for the Advancement of Ethnic Minority Interests (Ed.), *Psychological treatment of minority populations* (pp. 24–28). Washington, DC: Association of Black Psychologists.

Barkham, M. (1989). Brief prescriptive therapy in two-plus-one sessions: Initial cases from the clinic. *Behavioral Psychotherapy, 17,* 161–175.

Barney, J. B., & Griffin, R. W. (1992). *The management of organizations.* Boston: Houghton Mifflin.

Basch, F. M. (1980). *Doing psychotherapy.* New York: Basic Books.

Basch, F. M. (1988). *Understanding psychotherapy: The science behind the art.* New York: Basic Books.

Beck, A. T. (1976). *Cognitive therapy and emotional disorders.* New York: International Universities Press.

Beck, A. T., & Freeman, A. M. (1990). *Cognitive therapy of personality disorders.* New York: Guilford Press.

Beck, J. S. (2005). *Cognitive therapy for challenging problems: What to do when the basics don't work.* New York: Guilford Press.

Bedell, J. R., & Lennox, S. S. (1997). *Handbook for communication and problem-solving skills training: A cognitive-behavioral approach.* New York: Wiley.

Berkman, C. S., & Zinberg, G. (1997). Homophobia and heterosexism in social workers. *Social Work, 42*(4), 319–332.

Berlin, S. B., & Marsh, J. C. (1993). *Informing practice decisions.* New York: Macmillan.

Bernal, G., & Gutierrez, M. (1988). Cubans. In L. Comas-Diaz & E. E. H. Griffith (Eds.), *Clinical guidelines in cross-cultural mental health* (pp. 233–261). New York: Wiley.

Binder, J. L. (2004). *Key competencies in brief dynamic psychotherapy: Clinical practice beyond the manual.* New York: Guilford Press.

Blizinsky, M., & Reid, W. (1980). Problem focus and change in a brief treatment model. *Social Work, 25,* 89–93.

Bloom, B. L. (1997). *Planned short-term psychotherapy: A clinical handbook.* Needham Heights, MA: Allyn & Bacon.

Bloom, M., Fischer, J., & Orme, J. G. (2003). *Evaluating practice: Guidelines for the accountable professional.* Boston: Allyn & Bacon.

Bohart, A. C., Elliott, R., Greenberg, L., & Watson, J. (2002). Empathy. In J. C. Norcross (Ed.), *Psychotherapy relationships that work* (pp. 89–108). New York: Oxford University Press.

Bohart, A. C., & Greenberg, L. S. (1997). *Empathy reconsidered: New directions in psychotherapy.* Washington, DC: American Psychological Association.

Bordin, E. S. (1979). The generalizability of the psychoanalytic concept of the working alliance. *Psychotherapy: Theory, Research and Practice, 16*(3), 252–260.

Bostic, J. Q., Shadid, L. G., & Blotcky, M. J. (1996). Our time is up: Forced termination during psychotherapy training. *American Journal of Psychotherapy, 50*(3), 347–359.

Brammer, L. M. (1993). *The helping relationship* (5th ed.). Needham Heights, MA: Allyn & Bacon.

Breuer, J., & Freud, S. (1955). Studies on hysteria. In *The standard edition of the complete psychological works of Sigmund Freud* (Vol. 2). London: Hogarth Press. (Original work published 1895)

Brewer, M., & Brown, R. (1998). Intergroup relations. In D. T. Gilbert, S. T. Fiske, & G. Lindzey (Eds.), *The handbook of social psychology* (4th ed., pp. 554–594). New York: McGraw-Hill.

Cannell, C., Miller, P., & Oksenberg, L. (1981). Research on interviewing techniques. In S. Leinhardt (Ed.), *Social methodology* (pp. 389–437). San Francisco: Jossey-Bass.

Carkhuff, R., & Berenson, B. (1977). *Beyond counseling and therapy* (2nd ed.). New York: Holt, Rinehart & Winston.

Chesney, A. A., & Locke, E. A. (1991). Relationships among goal difficulty, business strategies, and performance on a complex management simulation task. *Academy of Management Journal, 34*, 400–424.

Cohen, S., & Wills, T. A. (1985). Stress, social support, and the buffering hypothesis. *Psychological Bulletin, 98*, 310–357.

Cook, D. I. (1967). *The impact of the Hawthorne effect in experimental designs in educational research.* Columbus: Ohio State University.

Cook, S. W. (1978). Interpersonal and attitudinal outcomes in cooperating interracial groups. *Journal of Research and Development in Education, 12*, 97–113.

Corcoran, K., & Fischer, J. (2000). *Measures for clinical practice: A sourcebook* (3rd ed., Vols. 1 & 2). New York: Free Press.

Cormier, S., & Hackney, H. (2005). *Counseling strategies and interventions* (6th ed.). Boston: Pearson Education.

Couper, M. P., Singer, E., & Kulka, R. A. (1998). Participation in the 1990 decennial census: Politics, privacy, pressure. *American Politics Quarterly, 26*, 59–80.

Crenshaw, W., Bartell, P., & Lichtenberg, J. (1994). Proposed revisions to mandatory reporting laws: An exploratory survey of child protection service agencies. *Child Welfare, 73*(1), 15–27.

Dana, R. H. (1993). *Multicultural assessment perspectives for professional psychology.* Boston: Allyn & Bacon.

Deci, E. L., & Ryan, R. M. (1985). *Intrinsic motivation and self-determination in human behavior.* New York: Plenum.

Doster, J., & Nesbitt, J. (1979). Psychotherapy and self-disclosure. In G. Chelune & associate (Eds.), *Self-disclosure* (pp. 177–224). San Francisco: Jossey-Bass.

D'Zurilla, T. J., & Godfried, M. R. (1971). Development and preliminary evaluation of the social problem solving inventory. *Psychological Assessment, 2*, 156–163.

Egan, G. (1994). *The skilled helper* (5th ed.). Pacific Grove, CA: Brooks/Cole.

Egan, G. (2006). *Essentials of skilled helping: Managing problems, developing opportunities.* Belmont, CA: Wadsworth.

Emmons, R. A. (1989). Personal strivings: An approach to personality and subjective well-being. *Journal of Personality and Social Psychology, 51,* 1058–1068.

Epstine, R. S. (1994). *Keeping boundaries: Maintaining safety and integrity in the psychotherapeutic process.* Washington, DC: American Mental Health Press.

Evans, D., Hearn, M., Uhlemann, M., & Ivey, A. (1993). *Essential interviewing* (4th ed.). Pacific Grove, CA: Brooks/Cole.

Evans, D. R., Hearn, M. T., Uhlemann, M. R., & Ivey, A. E. (1998). *Essential interviewing—A programmed approach to effective communication* (5th ed.). Pacific Grove, CA: Brooks/Cole.

Farber, B. A. (2003). Patient self-disclosure: A review of the research. *Journal of Clinical Psychology, 59*(5), 589–600.

Farber, B. A., & Hall, D. (2002). Disclosure to therapists: What is and is not discussed in psychotherapy. *Journal of Clinical Psychology, 58*, 359–370.

Fisher, J., & Corcoran, K. (1994). *Measures for clinical practice* (2nd ed.). New York: Macmillan.

Friedmann, A. (2005). Anthropological aspects of psychiatry. *WMW Wiener Medizinische Wochenschrift, 155*(23), 517–523.

Fromm, E. (1976). *To have or to be?* New York: Harper & Row.

Garfield, S. L. (1989). *The practice of brief psychotherapy.* New York: Pergamon.

Garland, A. F., Plemmons, D., & Koontz, L. (2006). Research–practice partnership in mental health: Lessons from participants. *Administration and Policy in Mental Health and Mental Health Services Research, 33*, 517–528.

Gaw, A. C. (1993). Mental health care of Chinese Americans. In A. C. Gaw (Ed.), *Culture, ethnicity, and mental illness* (pp. 245–280). Washington, DC: American Mental Health Press.

Geen, R. G. (1995). *Human motivation: A psychosocial approach.* Pacific Grove, CA: Brooks/Cole.

Gibbons, F., Smith, T., Ingram, R., Pearce, K., Brehm, S., & Schroeder, D. (1985). Self-awareness and self-confrontation: Effects of self-focused attention on members of clinical population. *Journal of Personality and Social Psychology, 48*, 662–675.

Goldfried, M., Burckell, L., & Eubanks-Carter, C. (2003). Therapist self-disclosure in cognitive-behavioral therapy. *Journal of Clinical Psychology, 59*(5), 555–568.

Goldfried, M. R., & Davidson, G. C. (1976). *Clinical behavior therapy.* New York: Holt, Rinehart & Winston.

Goldfried, M. R., & Davidson, G. C. (1994). *Clinical behavior therapy* (Expanded ed.). New York: Wiley.

Goodyear, R. K. (1981). Termination as a loss experience for the counselor. *Personal and Guidance Journal, 59*, 347–350.

Greenglass, E. R. (1993). The contribution of social support to coping strategies. *Applied Psychology International Review, 42*, 323–340.

Hackney, H., & Cormier, L. S. (1996). *The professional counselor* (3rd ed.). Boston: Allyn & Bacon.

Hackney, H., & Cormier, L. S. (2000). *The professional counselor: A process guide to helping* (4th ed.). Needham Heights, MA: Allyn & Bacon.

Hackney, H., & Cormier, L. S. (2001). *The professional counselor* (4th ed.). Boston: Allyn & Bacon.

Hackney, H., & Cormier, L. S. (2005). *Counseling strategies and interventions* (6th ed.). Boston: Allyn & Bacon.

Hayes, N., & Stratton, P. (2003). *A student's dictionary of psychology* (4th ed.). London: Hodder Arnold.

Hayes, S. C., Follette, W. C., & Follette, V. M. (1995). Behavior therapy: A contextual approach. In A. S. Gurman & S. B. Messer (Eds.), *Essential psychotherapies: Theory and practice.* New York: Guilford.

Hepworth, D. H., & Larsen, J. (1993). *Direct social work practice: Theory and skills* (4th ed.). Belmont, CA: Brooks/Cole.

Higgins, E. T. (1987). Self-discrepancy: A theory relating self and affect. *Psychological Review, 94*, 319–340.

Hill, C., Helms, J., Speigel, S., & Tichener, V. (1988). Development of a system for categorizing client reactions to therapist interventions. *Journal of Counseling Psychology, 35*, 27–36.

Ho, M. K. (1992). *Minority children and adolescents in therapy.* Newbury Park, CA: Sage.

Hollenbeck, J. R., Williams, C. R., & Klein, H. J. (1989). An empirical examination of the antecedents of commitment to difficult goals. *Journal of Applied Psychology, 74*, 18–23.

Horvath, A. O., & Symonds, B. D. (1991). Relation between working alliance and outcome in psychotherapy: A meta-analysis. *Journal of Counseling Psychology, 38*(2), 139–149.

Howard, K. I., Kopta, S. M., Krause, M. S., & Olinsky, D. E. (1986). The dose-effect relationship in psychotherapy. *American Psychologist, 41*, 159–164.

Hudson, W. W. (1982). *The clinical measurement package: A field manual.* Homewood, IL: Dorsey Press.

Ivey, A. (1983). *Intentional interviewing and counseling.* Monterey, CA: Brooks/Cole.

Jacobson, E. (1938). *Progressive relaxation* (Rev. ed.). Chicago: University of Chicago Press.

Kadushin, A. (1990). *The social work interview: A guide for human service professionals* (3rd ed.). New York: Columbia University Press.

Kagle, J., & Kopels, S. (1994). Confidentiality after Tarasoff. *Health and Social Work in Education, 19*(3), 217–222.

Kanfer, F. H., & Schefft, B. K. (1988). *Guiding therapeutic change.* Champaign, IL: Research Press.

Kasser, T., & Ryan, R. M. (1993). A dark side of the American dream: Correlates of financial success as a central life aspiration. *Journal of Personality and Social Psychology, 63,* 410–422.

Kasser, T., & Ryan, R. M. (1996). Further examining the American dream: Differential correlates of intrinsic and extrinsic goals. *Personality and Social Psychology Bulletin, 22,* 280–287.

Kettenbach, G. (2004). *Writing SOAP notes with patient/client management formats* (3rd ed.). Philadelphia: F. A. Davis.

Knapp, H. (2007). *Therapeutic communication: Developing professional skills.* Thousand Oaks, CA: Sage.

Kottler, J. (1991). *The complete therapist.* San Francisco: Jossey-Bass.

Kramer, S. A. (1986). The termination process in open-ended psychotherapy: Guidelines for clinical practice. *Psychotherapy, 23*(4), 526–531.

Kupers, T. A. (1988). *Ending therapy: The meaning of termination.* New York: New York University Press.

Lambert, M. J., & Ogles, B. M. (2004). The efficacy and effectiveness of psychotherapy. In M. J. Lambert (Ed.), *Bergin and Garfield's handbook of psychotherapy and behavior change* (5th ed., pp. 139–193). New York: Wiley.

Leigh, A. (1998). *Referral and termination issues for counsellors.* London: Sage.

Lindsey, D. (1994). Mandated reporting and child abuse fatalities: Requirements for a system to protect children. *Social Work Research, 18*(1), 41–54.

Little, B. (1993). Personal projects and the distributed self: Aspects of a cognitive psychology. In J. Suls (Ed.), *Psychological perspectives on the self* (Vol. 4). Hillsdale: NJ: Lawrence Erlbaum.

Locke, E. A., & Latham, G. P. (2002). Building a practically useful theory of goal setting and task motivation: A 35-year odyssey. *American Psychologist, 57*(9), 705–717.

Maholick, L. T., & Turner, D. W. (1979). Termination: That difficult farewell. *American Journal of Psychotherapy, 33,* 583–591.

Mahoney, M. (1991). *Human change processes: The scientific foundations of psychotherapy.* New York: Basic Books.

Maier, T. D. (2006). Evidence-based psychiatry: Understanding the limitations of a method. *Journal of Evaluation in Clinical Practice, 12*(3), 325–329.

Mann, B., & Murphy, K. (1975). Timing of self-disclosure, reciprocity of self-disclosure, and reactions to an initial interview. *Journal of Counseling Psychology, 22*(4), 303–308.

Mann, J. (1973). *Time-limited psychotherapy.* Cambridge, MA: Harvard University Press.

Martinez, C. (1986). Hispanic mental health issues. In C. B. Wilkerson (Ed.), *Ethnic psychiatry* (pp. 61–87). New York: Plenum.

Martinez, C. (1993). Mental health care of Mexican Americans. In A. C. Gaw (Ed.), *Culture, ethnicity, and mental illness* (pp. 431–466). Washington DC: American Mental Health Press.

Maslow, A. H. (1954). *Motivation and personality.* New York: Harper & Row.

McBride, A. B. (1990). Mental health effects of women's multiple roles. *American Psychologist, 45,* 381–384.

McClam, T., & Woodside, M. (1994). *Problem solving in the helping professions.* Pacific Grove, CA: Brooks/Cole.

McRoy, R. G., Freeman, E. M., & Logan, S. (1986). Strategies for teaching students about termination. *The Clinical Supervisor, 4*(4), 45–56.

Meichenbaum, D. H. (1977). *Cognitive-behavior modification: An integrative approach.* New York: Plenum.

Michelson, L., & Ascher, L. M. (1987). *Anxiety and stress disorders: Cognitive behavioral assessment and treatment.* New York: Guilford Press.

Murdin, L. (2000). *How much is enough: Endings in psychotherapy and counselling.* London: Routledge.

National Association of Social Workers. (1996). *Code of ethics of the National Association of Social Workers.* Washington, DC: Author. Available at http://www.socialworkers.org

Nelson, W. M., & Politano, P. M. (1993). The goal is to say "good-bye" and have the treatment effects generalize and maintain: A cognitive-behavioral view of termination. *Journal of Cognitive Psychotherapy: An International Quarterly, 7*(4), 251–263.

Neukrug, E. (2002). *Skills and techniques for human service professionals: Counseling environment, helping skills, treatment issues.* Pacific Grove, CA: Brooks/Cole.

Nicholas, R. A., & Berman, J. S. (1983). Is follow-up necessary in evaluating psychotherapy? *Psychological Bulletin, 93,* 261–278.

Nugent, W. (1992). The affective impact of a clinical social worker's interviewing styles: A series of single-case experiments. *Research on Social Work Practice, 2*(1), 6–27.

O'Donohue, W. T., & Ferguson, K. E. (2003). *Handbook of professional ethics for psychologists: Issues, questions, and controversies.* Thousand Oaks, CA: Sage.

O'Reilly, R. (1987). The transfer syndrome. *Canadian Journal of Psychiatry, 32,* 674–678.

Paniagua, F. A. (2005). *Assessing and treating culturally diverse clients: A practical guide* (3rd ed.). Thousand Oaks, CA: Sage.

Peck, M. S. (1998). *People of the lie.* New York: Simon & Schuster.

Pedersen, P., Draguns, J., Lonner, W., & Trimble, J. (1996). *Counseling across cultures* (4th ed.). Thousand Oaks, CA: Sage.

Perlis, R. H. (2005). Misdiagnosis of bipolar disorder. *The American Journal of Managed Care, 11*(9), S271–S274.

Poulin, J. (2000). *Collaborative social work: Strength-based generalist practice.* Itasca, IL: F. E. Peacock.

Prochaska, J., DiClemente, C., & Norcross, J. C. (1992). In search of how people change. *American Psychologist, 47,* 1102–1114.

Quintana, S. M. (1993). Toward an expanded and updated conceptualization of termination: Implications for short-term individual psychotherapy. *Professional Psychology: Research and Practice, 24,* 426–432.

Reynolds, S., Stiles, W. B., Barkham, M., Shapiro, D. A., Hardy, G. E., & Reeves, A. (1996). Acceleration of changes in session impact during contrasting time-limited psychotherapies. *Journal of Consulting and Clinical Psychology, 64,* 577–586.

Richardson, E. H. (1981). Cultural and historical perspectives in counseling American Indians. In D. W. Sue & D. Sue (Eds.), *Counseling the culturally different: Theory and practice* (pp. 216–255). New York: Wiley.

Rogers, C. (1957). The necessary and sufficient conditions of therapeutic personality change. *Journal of Consulting Psychology, 22,* 95–103.

Root, M., Ho, C., & Sue, S. (1986). Issues in the training of counselors for Asian Americans. In H. P. Lefley & P. B. Pedersen (Eds.), *Cross-cultural training for mental health professionals* (pp. 199–209). Springfield, IL: Charles C Thomas.

Rubin, A., & Babbie, E. (1993). *Research methods for social work* (2nd ed.). Pacific Grove, CA: Brooks/Cole.

Sackett, D. L., Rosenberg, W. M. C., Gray, J. A. M., Haynes, R. B., & Richardson, W. S. (1996). Evidence-based medicine: What it is and what it isn't [Electronic version]. *British Medical Journal, 312,* 71–72. Retrieved August 1, 2008, from http://www.bmj.com/cgi/content/full/312/7023/71

Safran, J. D., & Muran, J. C. (2000). *Negotiating the therapeutic alliance: A relational treatment guide.* New York: Guilford Press.

Salmela-Aro, K. (1992). Struggle with self: The personal projects of students seeking psychological counseling. *Scandinavian Journal of Psychology, 33,* 330–338.

Salmela-Aro, K., & Nurmi, J.-E. (1997). Positive and negative self-goals and subjective well-being: Prospective study. *Journal of Adult Development, 4,* 171–186.

Schmuck, P., & Sheldon, K. (2001). *Life goals and well-being: Towards a positive psychology of human striving* (pp. 149–150). Seattle, WA: Hogrefe & Huber.

Shulman, L. (1977). *A study of the helping process.* Vancouver, Canada: University of British Columbia.

Shulman, L. (1999). *The skills of helping individuals, families, groups, and communities* (4th ed.). Itasca, IL: F. E. Peacock.

Silver, I., & Herrmann, N. (1991). History and mental status examination. In J. Sadavoy, L. Lazarus, & L. Jarvik (Eds.), *Comprehensive review of geriatric psychiatry.* Washington, DC: American Mental Health Press.

Simon, J. (1988). Criteria for therapist self-disclosure. *American Journal of Psychotherapy, 52*(3), 404–415.

Simonson, N. (1976). The impact of therapist disclosure on patient disclosure. *Journal of Transpersonal Psychology, 23,* 3–6.

Singer, E., Mathiowetz, N., & Couper, M. (1993). The impact of privacy and confidentiality concerns on survey participation: The case of the 1990 U.S. census. *Public Opinion Quarterly, 57,* 465–482.

Smith, E. J. (1981). Cultural and historical perspectives in counseling blacks. In D. W. Sue & D. Sue (Eds.), *Counseling the culturally different: Theory and practice* (pp. 141–185). New York: Wiley.

Smith, S. (1983). Interrupted treatment and forced terminations. *International Journal of Psychoanalytic Psychotherapy, 9,* 337–352.

Stadter, M. (1996). *Object relations brief therapy.* Northvale, NJ: Aronson.

Stewart, R. E., & Chambless, D. L. (2007). Does psychotherapy research inform treatment decisions in private practice? *Journal of Clinical Psychology, 63*(3), 267–281.

Strupp, H. H., & Binder, J. L. (1984). *Psychotherapy in a new key: A guide to time-limited dynamic psychotherapy.* New York: Basic Books.

Sudak, D. M. (2006). *Cognitive behavioral therapy for clinicians.* Philadelphia: Lippincott Williams & Wilkins.

Sue, D. W. (1992). The challenge of multiculturalism: The road less traveled. *American Counselor, 1*(1), 6–14.

Sue, D. W., & Sue, D. (Eds.). (2003). *Counseling the culturally different: Theory and practice* (4th ed.). New York: Wiley.

Sullivan, G., Duan, N., Mukherjee, S., Kirchner, J., Perry, D., & Henderson, K. (2005). The role of services researchers in facilitating intervention research. *Mental Health Services, 56,* 537–542.

Sutherland, S. (1996). *The international dictionary of psychology* (2nd ed.). New York: Crossroads.

Swenson, S. L., Buell, S., Zettler, P., White, M., Ruston, D., & Lo, B. (2004). Patient-centered communication: Do patients really prefer it? *Journal of General Medicine, 19*(11), 1069–1079.

Taylor, S. E., & Brown, J. D. (1994). Positive illusions and well-being revisited: Separating fact from fiction. *Psychological Bulletin, 116,* 21–27.

Tharp, R. G. (1991). Cultural diversity and treatment of children. *Journal of Consulting and Clinical Psychology, 59,* 799–812.

Tourangeau, R., & Rasinski, K. (1988). Cognitive processes underlying context effects in attitude measurement. *Psychological Bulletin, 103,* 299–314.

Tourangeau, R., Rips, L. J., & Rasinski, K. (2000). *The psychology of survey response.* New York: Cambridge University Press.

Traux, C., & Mitchell, K. (1971). Research on certain therapist interpersonal skills in relation to process and outcome. In A. E. Bergin & S. L. Garfield (Eds.), *Handbook of psychotherapy and behavior change: An empirical analysis.* New York: Wiley.

Tripodi, T. (1994). *A primer on single-subject design for clinical social workers.* Washington, DC: National Association of Social Workers.

Ulman, K. H. (2001). Unwitting exposure of the therapist: Transferential and countertransferential dilemmas. *Journal of Psychotherapy Practice and Research, 10,* 14–22.

Viscott, D. (1976). *The language of feelings.* New York: Pocket Books.

Von Oech, R. (1998). *A whack on the side of the head* (3rd ed.). New York: Warner Books.

Wachtel, P. L. (2002). Termination of therapy: An effort at integration. *Journal of Psychotherapy Integration, 12,* 373–383.

Webster's new world/Stedman's concise medical dictionary. (1987). New York: Prentice Hall.

Weddington, W. W., & Cavenar, J. O. (1979). Termination initiated by the therapist: A countertransference storm. *American Journal of Psychiatry, 136*(10), 1302–1305.

Weissman, M. M., Verdeli, H., Gameroff, M. J., Bledsoe, S. E., Betts, K., Mufson, L., et al. (2006). National survey of psychotherapy training in psychiatry, psychology, and social work. *Archives of General Psychiatry, 63,* 925–934.

Wetchler, J. L., & Ofte-Atha, G. R. (1993). Empowering families at termination: A structural/strategic orientation. *Journal of Family Psychotherapy, 4*(1), 33–44.

Wiger, D. E., & Huntley, D. K. (2002). *Essentials of interviewing.* New York: Wiley.

Wilkinson, C. B., & Spurlock, J. (1986). The mental health of black Americans: Mental health diagnosis and treatment. In C. B. Wilkinson (Ed.), *Ethnic psychiatry* (pp. 13–59). New York: Plenum.

Willis, G. (1997). The use of psychological laboratory to study sensitive topics. In L. Harrison & A. Hughes (Eds.), *The validity of self-reporting drug use: Improving the accuracy of survey estimates* (pp. 416–438). NIDA Monograph 167. Rockville, MD: National Institute on Drug Abuse.

Wills, T. A. (1990). Social support and interpersonal relationships. In M. S. Clark (Ed.), *Review of Personality and Social Psychology, 12,* 265–289. Newbury Park, CA: Sage.

Wittenberg, R. (2002). *Opportunities in social work careers* (Rev. ed.). New York: McGraw-Hill.

Wood, E. C., & Wood, C. D. (1990). Referral issues in psychotherapy and psychoanalysis. *American Journal of Psychotherapy, 44*(1), 85–94.

World Health Organization. (1992). *International statistical classification of diseases and related health problems* (10th rev.). Geneva: American Psychiatric Publishing.

Yerkes, R. M., & Dodson, J. D. (1908). The relation of strength to stimulus to rapidity of habit formation. *Journal of Comparative and Neurological Psychology, 18,* 459–482.

Index

About the Author

Herschel Knapp, PhD, MSSW, is a psychotherapist and health science researcher in Los Angeles, California. His experience includes helpline work, acute care in hospitals (ER, ICU, CCU, oncology), and longer-term psychotherapy in both in- and outpatient settings with a diverse client population. He has served as a behavioral science representative advocating for quality of life on the Patient Care Committee, Palliative Care Committee, Ethics Committee, and Cancer Committee. He has taught at the university level, provided intern supervision, and presented numerous clinical trainings in hospitals, schools, and the community. He is currently involved in biobehavioral research directed at improving healthcare services to cancer patients and enhancing access to HIV testing. He is a member of the National Association of Social Workers and the American Psychological Association. His contributions to the field have earned him membership in Phi Kappa Phi Academic Honor Society, Phi Alpha National Honor Society for Social Work, and Who's Who Among Students in American Universities and Colleges. He is the author of the textbook *Therapeutic Communication: Developing Professional Skills* (2007).

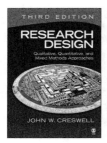    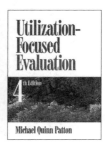